Children with Hearing Difficulties

Alec Webster and David Wood

CASSELL

Cassell Educational Limited
Artillery House
Artillery Row
London SW1P 1RT

First published 1989

British Library Cataloguing in Publication Data
Webster, Alec
    Children with hearing difficulties. — (Special needs
    in ordinary schools)
    1. Deaf children. Education
    I. Title   II. Wood, David, *1944 Dec. 24*–   III. Series
    371.91'2

ISBN 0–304–32201–6

Typeset by Activity Ltd., Salisbury, Wilts.
Printed and bound in Great Britain by Biddles Ltd.,
Guildford and King's Lynn

Contents

Acknowledgements

A book such as this, based as it is on a collaborative research effort which has spanned a decade, owes a debt to many more colleagues than can possibly be acknowledged. Thanks are due to all past and present members of the Deafness Research Group at Nottingham University. They have helped us immeasurably in our main aim: to provide a convincing and coherent approach to the development and education of the hearing-impaired child, based on a firm theoretical and empirical grounding. We owe a special debt to all the children, families, teachers and professionals involved in our studies, and we hope that our account has helped to generate some new ideas about hearing-impaired children and how we might best meet their educational needs. We are also indebted to John Bamford, James Hogg, Peter Mittler, Patricia Scanlon and Valerie Webster for their helpful comments on the manuscript and for their encouragement and support.

Alec Webster
David Wood
Christmas 1988

A 'school for thinking' rather than a school for language or reading would be important for all young children, bright or dull, poor or rich, but for none is it more important than for deaf children.

Hans G. Furth (1973)

Foreword: Towards education for all

AIMS

This series aims to support teachers as they respond to the challenge they face in meeting the needs of all children in their school, particularly those identified as having special educational needs.

Although there have been many useful publications in the field of special educational needs during the last decade, the distinguishing feature of the present series of volumes lies in their concern with specific areas of the curriculum in primary and secondary schools. We have tried to produce a series of conceptually coherent and professionally relevant books, each of which is concerned with ways in which children with varying levels of ability and motivation can be taught together. The books draw on the experience of practising teachers, teacher trainers and researchers and seek to provide practical guidelines on ways in which specific areas of the curriculum can be made more accessible to all children. The volumes provide many examples of curriculum adaptation, classroom activities, teacher–child interactions, as well as the mobilisation of resources inside and outside the school.

The series is organised largely in terms of age and subject groupings, but three 'overview' volumes have been prepared in order to provide an account of some major current issues and developments. Seamus Hegarty's *Meeting Special Needs in Ordinary Schools* gives an introduction to the field of special needs as a whole, whilst Sheila Wolfendale's *Primary Schools and Special Needs* and John Sayer's *Secondary Schools for All?* address issues more specifically concerned with primary and secondary schools respectively. We hope that curriculum specialists will find essential background and contextual material in these overview volumes.

In addition, a section of this series will be concerned with examples of obstacles to learning. All of these specific special needs can be seen on a continuum ranging from mild to severe, or from temporary and transient to long-standing or permanent. These include difficulties in learning or in adjustment and behaviour, as well as problems resulting largely from sensory or physical impairments or from difficulties of communication from whatever cause. We hope that teachers will consult the volumes in this section for guidance on working with children with specific difficulties.

The series aims to make a modest 'distance learning' contribution to meeting the needs of teachers working with the whole range of pupils with special educational needs by offering a set of resource materials relating to specific areas of the primary and secondary curriculum and by suggesting ways in which learning obstacles, whatever their origin, can be identified and addressed.

We hope that these materials will not only be used for private study but be subjected to critical scrutiny by school-based inservice groups sharing common curricular interests and by staff of institutions of higher education concerned with both special needs teaching and specific curriculum areas. The series has been planned to provide a resource for Local Education Authority (LEA) advisers, specialist teachers from all sectors of the education service, educational psychologists, and teacher working parties. We hope that the books will provide a stimulus for dialogue and serve as catalysts for improved practice.

It is our hope that parents will also be encouraged to read about new ideas in teaching children with special needs so that they can be in a better position to work in partnership with teachers on the basis of an informed and critical understanding of current difficulties and developments. The goal of 'Education for All' can only be reached if we succeed in developing a working partnership between teachers, pupils, parents, and the community at large.

ELEMENTS OF A WHOLE-SCHOOL APPROACH

Meeting special educational needs in ordinary schools is much more than a process of opening school doors to admit children previously placed in special schools. It involves a radical re-examination of what all schools have to offer all children. Our efforts will be judged in the long term by our success with children who are already in ordinary schools but whose needs are not being met, for whatever reason.

The additional challenge of achieving full educational as well as social integration for children now in special schools needs to be seen in the wider context of a major reappraisal of what ordinary schools have to offer the pupils already in them. The debate about integration of handicapped and disabled children in ordinary schools should not be allowed to overshadow the movement for curriculum reform in the schools themselves. If successful, this could promote the fuller integration of the children already in the schools.

If this is the aim of current policy, as it is of this series of unit texts, we have to begin by examining ways in which schools and school policies can themselves be a major element in children's difficulties.

Can schools cause special needs?

Traditionally, we have looked for causes of learning difficulty in the child. Children have been subjected to tests and investigations by doctors, psychologists and teachers with the aim of pinpointing the nature of the problem and in the hope that this might lead to specific programmes of teaching and intervention. We less frequently ask ourselves whether what and how we teach and the way in which we organise and manage our schools could themselves be a major cause of children's difficulties.

The shift of emphasis towards a whole-school policy is sometimes described in terms of a move away from the deficit or medical model of special education towards a more environmental or ecological model. Clearly, we are concerned here with an interaction between the two. No one would deny that the origins of some learning difficulties do lie in the child. But even where a clear cause can be established — for example, a child with severe brain damage, or one with a serious sensory or motor disorder — it would be simplistic to attribute all the child's learning difficulties to the basic impairment alone.

The ecological model starts from the position that the growth and development of children can be understood only in relation to the nature of their interactions with the various environments which impinge on them and with which they are constantly interacting. These environments include the home and each individual member of the immediate and extended family. Equally important are other children in the neighbourhood and at school, as well as people with whom the child comes into casual or closer contact. We also need to consider the local and wider community and its various institutions — not least, the powerful influence of television, which for some children represents more hours of information intake than is provided by teachers during eleven years of compulsory education. The ecological model thus describes a gradually widening series of concentric circles, each of which provides a powerful series of influences and possibilities for interaction — and therefore learning.

Schools and schooling are only one of many environmental influences affecting the development and learning of children. A great deal has been learned from other environments before the child enters school and much more will be learned after the child leaves full-time education. Schools represent a relatively powerful series of environments, not all concerned with formal learning. During the hours spent in school, it is hard to estimate the extent to which the number and nature of the interactions experienced by any one child are directly concerned with formal teaching and learning. Social interactions with other children also need to be considered.

Questions concerned with access to the curriculum lie at the heart of any whole-school policy. What factors limit the access of certain children to the curriculum? What modifications are necessary to ensure fuller curriculum access? Are there areas of the curriculum from which some children are excluded? Is this because they are thought 'unlikely to be able to benefit'? And even if they are physically present, are there particular lessons or activities which are inaccessible because textbooks or worksheets demand a level of literacy and comprehension which effectively prevent access? Are there tasks in which children partly or wholly fail to understand the language which the teacher is using? Are some teaching styles inappropriate for individual children?

Is it possible that some learning difficulties arise from the ways in which schools are organised and managed? For example, what messages are we conveying when we separate some children from others? How does the language we use to describe certain children reflect our own values and assumptions? How do schools transmit value judgements about children who succeed and those who do not? In the days when there was talk of comprehensive schools being 'grammar schools for all', what hope was there for children who were experiencing significant learning difficulties? And even today, what messages are we transmitting to children and their peers when we exclude them from participation in some school activities? How many children with special needs will be entered for the new General Certificate of Secondary Education (GCSE) examinations? How many have taken or will take part in Technical and Vocational Education Initiative (TVEI) schemes?

The argument here is not that all children should have access to all aspects of the curriculum. Rather it is a plea for the individualisation of learning opportunities for all children. This requires a broad curriculum with a rich choice of learning opportunities designed to suit the very wide range of individual needs.

Curriculum reform

The last decade has seen an increasingly interventionist approach by Her Majesty's Inspectors of Education (HMI), by officials of the Department of Education and Science (DES) and by individual Secretaries of State. The 'Great Debate', allegedly beginning in 1976, led to a flood of curriculum guidelines from the centre. The garden is secret no longer. Whilst Britain is far from the centrally imposed curriculum found in some other countries, government is increasingly insisting that schools must reflect certain key areas of experience for all pupils, and in particular those concerned with the world of work (*sic*), with science and technology, and with economic awareness. These priorities are also reflected in the prescriptions for teacher education laid down with an increasing degree of firmness from the centre.

There are indications that a major reappraisal of curriculum content and access is already under way and seems to be well supported by teachers. Perhaps the best known and most recent examples can be found in the series of Inner London Education Authority (ILEA) reports concerned with secondary, primary and special education, known as the Hargreaves, Thomas and Fish Reports (ILEA, 1984, 1985a, 1985b). In particular, the Hargreaves Report envisaged a radical reform of the secondary curriculum, based to some extent on his book *Challenge for the Comprehensive School* (Hargreaves, 1982). This envisages a major shift of emphasis from the 'cognitive–academic' curriculum of many secondary schools towards one emphasising more personal involvement by pupils in selecting their own patterns of study from a wider range of choice. If the proposals in these reports were to be even partially implemented, pupils with special needs would stand to benefit from such a wholesale review of the curriculum of the school as a whole.

Pupils with special needs also stand to benefit from other developments in mainstream education. These include new approaches to records of achievement, particularly 'profiling' and a greater emphasis on criterion-referenced assessment. Some caution has already been expressed about the extent to which the new GCSE examinations will reach less able children previously excluded from the Certificate of Secondary Education. Similar caution is justified in relation to the TVEI and the Certificate of Pre-Vocational Education (CPVE). And what about the new training initiatives for school leavers and the 14–19 age group in general? Certainly, the pronouncements of the Manpower Services Commission (MSC) emphasise a policy of provision for all, and have made specific arrangements for young people with special needs, including those with disabilities. In the last analysis, society and its institutions will be judged by their success in preparing the majority of young people to make an effective and valued contribution to the community as a whole.

A CLIMATE OF CHANGE

Despite the very real and sometimes overwhelming difficulties faced by schools and teachers as a result of underfunding and professional unrest, there are encouraging signs of change and reform which, if successful, could have a significant impact not only on children with special needs but on all children. Some of these are briefly mentioned below.

The campaign for equal opportunities

First, we are more aware of the need to confront issues concerned with civil rights and equal opportunities. All professionals concerned with human services are being asked to examine their own attitudes and practices and to question the extent to which these might unwittingly or even deliberately discriminate unfairly against some sections of the population.

We are more conscious than ever of the need to take positive steps to promote the full access of girls and women not only to full educational opportunities but also to the whole range of community resources and services, including employment, leisure, housing, social security and the right to property. We have a similar concern for members of ethnic and religious groups who have been and still are victims of discrimination and restricted opportunities for participation in society and its institutions. It is no accident that the title of the Swann Report on children from ethnic minorities was *Education for All* (Committee of Inquiry, 1985). This too is the theme of the present series and the underlying aim of the movement to meet the whole range of special needs in ordinary schools.

The equal opportunities movement has not itself always fully accepted people with disabilities and special needs. At national level, there is no legislation specifically concerned with discrimination against people with disabilities, though this does exist in some other countries. The Equal Opportunities Commission does not concern itself with disability issues. On the other hand, an increasing number of local authorities and large corporations claim to be 'Equal Opportunities Employers', specifically mentioning disability alongside gender, ethnicity and sexual orientation. Furthermore, the 1986 Disabled Persons Act, arising from a private member's Bill and now on the statute book, seeks to carry forward for adults some of the more positive features of the 1981 Education Act — for example, it provides for the rights of all people with disabilities to take part or be represented in discussion and decision-making concerning services provided for them.

These developments, however, have been largely concerned with children or adults with disabilities, rather than with children already in ordinary schools. Powerful voluntary organisations such as MENCAP (the Royal Society for Mentally Handicapped Children and Adults) and the Spastics Society have helped to raise political and public awareness of the needs of children with disabilities and have fought hard and on the whole successfully to secure better services for them and for their families. Similarly, organisations of adults with disabilities, such as the British Council of Organisations for Disabled People, are pressing hard for better quality, integrated education, given their own personal experiences of segregated provision.

Special needs and social disadvantage

Even these developments have largely bypassed two of the largest groups now in special schools: those with moderate learning difficulties and those with emotional and behavioural difficulties. There are no powerful pressure groups to speak for them, for the same reason that no pressure groups speak for the needs of children with special needs already in ordinary schools. Many of these children come from families which do not readily form themselves into associations and pressure groups. Many of their parents are unemployed, on low incomes or dependent on social security; many live in overcrowded conditions in poor quality housing or have long-standing health problems. Some members of these families have themselves experienced school failure and rejection as children.

Problems of poverty and disadvantage are common in families of children with special needs already in ordinary schools. Low achievement and social disadvantage are clearly associated, though it is important not to assume that there is a simple relation between them. Although most children from socially disadvantaged backgrounds have not been identified as low achieving, there is still a high correlation between social-class membership and educational achievement, with middle-class children distancing themselves increasingly in educational achievements and perhaps also socially from children from working-class backgrounds — another form of segregation within what purports to be the mainstream.

The probability of socially disadvantaged children being identified as having special needs is very much greater than in other children. An early estimate suggested that it was more than seven times as high, when social disadvantage was defined by the presence of all three of the following indices: overcrowding (more than 1.5 persons per room), low income (supplementary benefit or free school meals) and adverse family circumstances (coming from a single-parent home or a home with more than five children) (Wedge and Prosser, 1973). Since this study was published, the number of families coming into these categories has greatly increased as a result of deteriorating economic conditions and changing social circumstances.

In this wider sense, the problem of special needs is largely a problem of social disadvantage and poverty. Children with special needs are therefore doubly vulnerable to underestimation of their abilities: first, because of their family and social backgrounds, and second, because of their low achievements. A recent large-scale study of special needs provision in junior schools suggests that while teachers' attitudes to low-achieving children are broadly positive, they are pessimistic about the ability of such children to derive much benefit from increased special needs provision (Croll and Moses, 1985).

Partnership with parents

The Croll and Moses survey of junior school practice confirms that teachers still tend to attribute many children's difficulties to adverse home circumstances. How many times have we heard comments along the lines of 'What can you expect from a child from that kind of family?' Is this not a form of stereotyping at least as damaging as racist and sexist attitudes?

Partnership with parents of socially disadvantaged children thus presents a very different challenge from that portrayed in the many reports of successful practice in some special schools. Nevertheless, the challenge can be and is being met. Paul Widlake's recent books (1984, 1985) give the lie to the oft-expressed view that some parents are 'not interested in their child's education'. Widlake documents project after project in which teachers and parents have worked well together. Many of these projects have involved teachers visiting homes rather than parents attending school meetings. There is also now ample research to show that children whose parents listen to them reading at home tend to read better and to enjoy reading more than other children (Topping and Wolfendale, 1985; see also Sheila Wolfendale's *Primary Schools and Special Needs*, in the present series).

Support in the classroom

If teachers in ordinary schools are to identify and meet the whole range of special needs, including those of children currently in special schools, they are entitled to support. Above all, this must come from the headteacher and from the senior staff of the school; from any special needs specialists or teams already in the school; from members of the new advisory and support services, as well as from educational psychologists, social workers and any health professionals who may be involved.

This support can take many forms. In the past, support meant removing the child for considerable periods of time into the care of remedial teachers either within the school or coming from outside. Withdrawal now tends to be discouraged, partly because it is thought to be another form of segregation within the ordinary school, and therefore in danger of isolating and stigmatising children, and partly because it deprives children of access to lessons and activities available to other children. In a major survey of special needs provision in middle and secondary schools, Clunies-Ross and Wimhurst (1983) showed that children with special needs were most often withdrawn from science and modern languages in order to find the time to give them extra help with literacy.

Many schools and LEAs are exploring ways in which both teachers and children can be supported without withdrawing children from ordinary classes. For example, special needs teachers increasingly are working alongside their colleagues in ordinary classrooms, not just with a small group of children with special needs but also with all children. Others are working as consultants to their colleagues in discussing the level of difficulty demanded of children following a particular course or specific lesson. An account of recent developments in consultancy is given in Hanko (1985), with particular reference to children with difficulties of behaviour or adjustment.

Although traditional remedial education is undergoing radical reform, major problems remain. Implementation of new approaches is uneven both between and within LEAs. Many schools still have a remedial department or are visited by peripatetic remedial teachers who withdraw children for extra tuition in reading with little time for consultation with school staff. With-drawal is still the preferred mode of providing extra help in primary schools, as suggested in surveys of current practice (Clunies-Ross and Wimhurst, 1983; Hodgson, Clunies-Ross and Hegarty, 1984; Croll and Moses, 1985).

Nevertheless, an increasing number of schools now see with-drawal as only one of a widening range of options, only to be used where the child's individually assessed needs suggest that this is indeed the most appropriate form of provision. Other alternatives are now being considered. The overall aim of most of these involves the development of a working partnership between the ordinary class teacher and members of teams with particular responsibility for meeting special needs. This partnership can take a variety of forms, depending on particular circumstances and individual preferences. Much depends on the sheer credibility of special needs teachers, their perceived capacity to offer support and advice and, where necessary, direct, practical help.

We can think of the presence of the specialist teacher as being on a continuum of visibility. A 'high-profile' specialist may sit alongside a pupil with special needs, providing direct assistance and support in participating in activities being followed by the rest of the class. A 'low-profile' specialist may join with a colleague in what is in effect a team-teaching situation, perhaps spending a little more time with individuals or groups with special needs. An even lower profile is provided by teachers who may not set foot in the classroom at all but who may spend considerable periods of time in discussion with colleagues on ways in which the curriculum can be made more accessible to all children in the class, including the least able. Such discussions may involve an examination of textbooks and other reading assignments for readability, conceptual difficulty and relevance of content, as well as issues concerned with the presentation of the material, language modes and complexity used to explain what is required, and the use of different approaches to teacher–pupil dialogue.

IMPLICATIONS FOR TEACHER TRAINING

Issues of training are raised by the authors of the three overview works in this series but permeate all the volumes concerned with specific areas of the curriculum or specific areas of special needs.

The scale and complexity of changes taking place in the field of special needs and the necessary transformation of the teacher-training curriculum imply an agenda for teacher training that is nothing less than retraining and supporting every teacher in the country in working with pupils with special needs.

Although teacher training represented one of the three major priorities identified by the Warnock Committee, the resources devoted to this priority have been meagre, despite a strong commitment to training from teachers, LEAs, staff of higher education, HMI and the DES itself. Nevertheless, some positive developments can be noted (for more detailed accounts of developments in teacher education see Sayer and Jones, 1985 and Robson, Sebba, Mittler and Davies, 1988).

Initial training

At the initial training level, we now find an insistence that all teachers in training must be exposed to a compulsory component concerned with meeting special needs in the ordinary school. The Council for the Accreditation of Teacher Education (CATE) and HMI seem set to enforce these criteria; institutions that do not meet them will not be accredited for teacher training.

Although this policy is welcome from a special needs perspective, many questions remain. Where will the staff to teach these courses come from? What happened to the Warnock recommendations for each teacher-training institution to have a small team of staff specifically concerned with this area? Even when a team exists, they can succeed in 'permeating' a special needs element into initial teacher training only to the extent that they influence all their fellow specialist tutors to widen their teaching perspectives to include children with special needs.

Special needs departments in higher education face similar problems to those confronting special needs teams in secondary schools. They need to gain access to and influence the work of the whole institution. They also need to avoid the situation where the very existence of an active special needs department results in colleagues regarding special needs as someone else's responsibility, not theirs.

Despite these problems, the outlook in the long term is favourable. More and more teachers in training are at least receiving an introduction to special needs; are being encouraged to seek out information on special needs policy and practice in the schools in which they are doing their teaching practice, and are being introduced to a variety of approaches to meeting their needs. Teaching materials are being prepared specifically for initial teacher-training students. Teacher trainers have also been greatly encouraged by the obvious interest and commitment of students to children with special needs; optional and elective courses on this subject have always been over-subscribed.

Inservice courses for designated teachers

Since 1983, the government has funded a series of one-term full-time courses in polytechnics and universities to provide intensive training for designated teachers with specific responsibility for pupils with special needs in ordinary schools (see *Meeting Special Needs in Ordinary Schools* by Seamus Hegarty in this series for information on research on evaluation of their effectiveness). These courses are innovative in a number of respects. They bring LEA and higher-education staff together in a productive working partnership. The seconded teacher, headteacher, LEA adviser and higher-education tutor enter into a commitment to train and support the teachers in becoming change agents in their own schools. Students spend two days a week in their own schools initiating and implementing change. All teachers with designated responsibilities for pupils with special needs have the right to be considered for these one-term courses, which are now a national priority area for which central funding is available. However, not all teachers can gain access to these courses as the institutions are geographically very unevenly distributed.

Other inservice courses

The future of inservice education for teachers (INSET) in education in general and special needs in particular is in a state of transition. Since April 1987, the government has abolished the central pooling arrangements which previously funded courses and has replaced these by a system in which LEAs are required to identify their training requirements and to submit these to the DES for funding. LEAs are being asked to negotiate training needs with each school as part of a policy of staff development and appraisal. Special needs is one of nineteen national priority areas that will receive 70 per cent funding from the DES, as is training for further education (FE) staff with special needs responsibilities.

These new arrangements, known as Grant Related Inservice Training (GRIST), will change the face of inservice training for all teachers but time is needed to assess their impact on training opportunities and teacher effectiveness (see Mittler, 1986, for an interim account of the implications of the proposed changes). In the meantime, there is serious concern about the future of secondments for courses longer than one term. Additional staffing will also be needed in higher education to respond to the wider range of demand.

An increasing number of 'teaching packages' have become available for teachers working with pupils with special needs. Some (though not all) of these are well designed and evaluated. Most of them are school-based and can be used by small groups of teachers working under the supervision of a trained tutor.

The best known of these is the Special Needs Action Programme (SNAP) originally developed for Coventry primary schools (Muncey and Ainscow, 1982) but now being adapted for secondary schools. This is based on a form of pyramid training in which co-ordinators from each school are trained to train colleagues in their own school or sometimes in a consortium of local schools. Evaluation by a National Foundation for Educational Research (NFER) research team suggests that SNAP is potentially an effective approach to school-based inservice training, providing that strong management support is guaranteed by the headteacher and by senior LEA staff (see Hegarty, *Meeting Special Needs in Ordinary Schools*, this series, for a brief summary).

Does training work?

Many readers of this series of books are likely to have recent experience of training courses. How many of them led to changes in classroom practice? How often have teachers been frustrated by their inability to introduce and implement change in their schools on returning from a course? How many heads actively support their staff in becoming change agents? How many teachers returning from advanced one-year courses have experienced 'the re-entry phenomenon'? At worst, this is quite simply being ignored: neither the LEA adviser, nor the head nor any one else asks about special interests and skills developed on the course and how these could be most effectively put to good use in the school. Instead, the returning member of staff is put through various re-initiation rituals ('Enjoyed your holiday?'), or is given responsibilities bearing no relation to interests developed on the course. Not infrequently, colleagues with less experience and fewer qualifications are promoted over their heads during their absence.

At a time of major initiatives in training, it may seem churlish to raise questions about the effectiveness of staff training. It is necessary to do so because training resources are limited and because the morale and motivation of the teaching force depend on satisfaction with what is offered — indeed, on opportunities to negotiate what is available with course providers. Blind faith in training for training's sake soon leads to disillusionment and frustration.

For the last three years, a team of researchers at Manchester University and Huddersfield Polytechnic have been involved in a DES funded project which aimed to assess the impact of a range of inservice courses on teachers working with pupils with special educational needs (see Robson, Sebba, Mittler and Davies, 1988, for a full account and Sebba and Robson, 1987, for a briefer interim report). A variety of courses was evaluated; some were held for one evening a week for a term; others were one-week full time; some were award-bearing, others were not. The former included the North-West regional diploma in special needs, the first example of a course developed in total partnership between a university and a polytechnic which allows students to take modules from either institution and also gives credit recognition to specific Open University and LEA courses. The research also evaluated the effectiveness of an already published and disseminated course on behavioural methods of teaching — the EDY course (Farrell, 1985).

Whether or not the readers of these books are or will be experiencing a training course, or whether their training consists only of the reading of one or more of the books in this series, it may be useful to conclude by highlighting a number of challenges facing teachers and teacher trainers in the coming decades.

1. We are all out of date in relation to the challenges that we face in our work.

2. Training in isolation achieves very little. Training must be seen as part of a wider programme of change and development of the institution as a whole.
3. Each LEA, each school and each agency needs to develop a strategic approach to staff development, involving detailed identification of training and development needs with the staff as a whole and with each individual member of staff.
4. There must be a commitment by management to enable the staff member to try to implement ideas and methods learned on the course.
5. This implies a corresponding commitment by the training institutions to prepare the student to become an agent of change.
6. There is more to training than attending courses. Much can be learned simply by visiting other schools, seeing teachers and other professionals at work in different settings and exchanging ideas and experiences. Many valuable training experiences can be arranged within a single school or agency, or by a group of teachers from different schools meeting regularly to carry out an agreed task.
7. There is now no shortage of books, periodicals, videos and audio-visual aids concerned with the field of special needs. Every school should therefore have a small staff library which can be used as a resource by staff and parents. We hope that the present series of unit texts will make a useful contribution to such a library.

The publishers and I would like to thank the many people — too numerous to mention — who have helped to create this series. In particular we would like to thank the Associate Editors, James Hogg, Peter Pumfrey, Tessa Roberts and Colin Robson, for their active advice and guidance; the Honorary Advisory Board, Neville Bennett, Marion Blythman, George Cooke, John Fish, Ken Jones, Sylvia Phillips, Klaus Wedell and Phillip Williams, for their comments and suggestions; and the teachers, teacher trainers and special needs advisers who took part in our information surveys.

SOME IMPLICATIONS OF THE EDUCATION REFORM ACT: AN EDITORIAL POSTSCRIPT

Full access to the curriculum is the central theme of this series of books and the fundamental challenge posed by the 1988 Education Reform Act. What are the implications of this Act for children with special educational needs? Will it help or hinder access to the national curriculum? How will they fare under the proposed assessment arrangements? What degree of priority will be given to these children by the new governing bodies, by headteachers, by LEAs and by the community? Will the voice of parents be heard when priority decisions are being taken on how the schools' resources will be used? What are the implications of local management, financial delegation and open enrolment? Is there a risk that children in ordinary schools will be denied access to the national curriculum? Will there be increased pressure to provide them with the 'protection of a statement' and to press for them to be sent to special schools? Will ordinary schools welcome children whose needs call for additional resources and for a fully accessible curriculum? Will they be welcome in grant maintained schools? What is the future of the strong links which have been established between special and ordinary schools during the last few years and which are enabling an increasing number of special school pupils to be timetabled to spend periods in a neighbouring ordinary school? Will the Act make it harder for children in special schools to be integrated into ordinary schools?

These and many other questions have been asked with growing urgency ever since the publication of the first consultation paper on the national curriculum. There was concern and anger that the government appeared to have overlooked children with special educational needs both in its consultation document and in the early versions of the Bill and because it appeared to be ignoring the strong representations on this subject which were being made during the consultation process. The early Bill contained only one special needs clause concerned with exclusion from the national curriculum, accompanied by reiterated official references to the need to be able to exempt children from a second language when they had not yet mastered English. There seemed to be little recognition of the risks to the principles and practice of the 1981 Education Act, to the needs of the 18 per cent of children in ordinary schools and to the dangers of inappropriate exclusion. For many months it was not clear whether grant maintained schools would be subject to the 1981 Act. At a general level, there was concern over the reduced powers of LEAs, given their key role in consultation with parents and their overview of planning and monitoring of special needs provision over the authority as a whole. This last concern was most acutely reflected in relation to the abolition of the ILEA which had not only developed good authority-wide provision but has published far-reaching plans for improved integrated provision in ordinary and special schools. Where are these reports today?

The extent to which these anxieties are justified will depend in part on the way in which the legislation is interpreted in the schools and LEAs, and on the kind of guidance issued from the centre. In this latter respect, there are grounds for optimism. Although it was only when the Bill was in its final parliamentary stages that there was evidence that special needs issues were beginning to be considered, there is increasing evidence that these special needs concerns are receiving a much higher degree of priority. New members with special needs interests were added to the National Curriculum Council and the Schools Examination and Assessment Council. Clear statements of policy and principle from ministers, from the DES and from HMI are establishing the rights of all children to the national curriculum. Exceptions, exclusions, disapplications and modifications can only be made in individual cases for children with statements, with the full participation of parents and professionals and subject to appeal. There will be no blanket exemptions for groups of children, far less for types of school. Each modification will have to be fully justified by reference to the needs of the individual child, and against the background of a policy which is designed to ensure the fullest possible access to the curriculum. Exemptions for children not on statements can only be temporary. In all cases, schools have to indicate what kind of alternative provision is to be made. Modifications can be made in respect of single attainment targets, programmes of study or assessment arrangements. For example, it seems that children may be on programmes of study leading to attainment targets but might need a modified approach to assessment — e.g. oral instead of written, computer-aided rather than oral, etc. All these issues will need to be debated in relation to individual children rather than to 'categories' of pupils.

The national curriculum documents in science, maths and English as well as interim reports on design and technology and Welsh are all firmly committed to the principle of the fullest possible access for all children. The Report of the Task Group on Assessment and Testing (TGAT) went a long way towards meeting special needs concerns with its suggestion that attainment targets should be reported in terms of ten levels and that they should be formative, criterion-referenced and in profile form. These ten levels, which are linked to programmes of study, are designed to ensure progression and continuity and to avoid children being seen to 'fail the tests'. Children will be able to be seen to progress from one level to another for any of the attainment targets, even though they may be several years behind the attainments of other children of the same age. Finally, the specifications and terms of reference given to the development agencies charged with producing Standard Assessment Tasks (SATs) — initially for Key Stage 1 at the age of about seven — clearly specify that SATs must be suitable or adaptable for pupils with special educational needs.

Although the emphasis so far has been largely on children in ordinary schools, the challenge of implementing the national curriculum in all special schools will also need to be addressed. It is clear that special schools are without exception subject to the national curriculum and to the assessment arrangements but a great deal of work needs to be done to develop programmes of study and assessment arrangements which are suitable and age-appropriate for the whole range of pupils with special needs in special schools but without departing in principle from the framework provided by the national curriculum.

At the beginning of 1989, special needs provision is clearly at a highly critical stage. A pessimistic forecast would be that children with special needs, whether in ordinary or special schools, could be marginalised, isolated and excluded from developments in mainstream education. They might be less welcome because priorities may lie with children whose needs are easier and cheaper to meet and who will not adversely affect the school's public performance indicators. Such progress as has been made towards integration of special-school pupils could be halted or reversed and an increasing number of children already in ordinary schools could become educationally and socially segregated in their own schools or inappropriately sent to special schools. The ethos of schools could become divisive and damaging to vulnerable children.

Because these remain real and potentially disastrous possibilities, it is essential to develop determined advocacy at all levels to ensure that the national curriculum and the new legislation are exploited to the full in the interests of all children, particularly those with special educational needs. Such advocacy will need to be well informed as well as determined and will be most effective if it is based on a partnership between professionals, parents and the pupils themselves.

Professor Peter Mittler
University of Manchester
February 1989

REFERENCES

Clunies-Ross, L. and Wimhurst, S. (1983) *The Right Balance: Provision for Slow Learners in Secondary Schools*. Windsor: NFER/Nelson.

Committee of Inquiry (1985) *Education for All*. London: HMSO (The Swann Report).

Croll, P. and Moses, D. (1985) *One in Five: The Assessment and Incidence of Special Educational Needs*. London: Routledge & Kegan Paul.

Farrell, P. (ed.) (1985) *EDY: Its Impact on Staff Training in Mental Handicap*. Manchester: Manchester University Press.

Hanko, G. (1985) *Special Needs in Ordinary Classrooms: An Approach to Teacher Support and Pupil Care in Primary and Secondary Schools*. Oxford: Blackwell.

Hargreaves, D. (1982) *Challenge for the Comprehensive School*. London: Routledge & Kegan Paul.

Hodgson, A., Clunies-Ross, L. and Hegarty, S. (1984) *Learning Together*. Windsor: NFER/Nelson.

Inner London Education Authority (1984) *Improving Secondary Education*. London: ILEA (The Hargreaves Report).

Inner London Education Authority (1985a) *Improving Primary Schools*. London: ILEA (The Thomas Report).

Inner London Education Authority (1985b) *Equal Opportunities for All?* London: ILEA (The Fish Report).

Mittler, P. (1986) The new look in inservice training. *British Journal of Special Education*, **13**, 50–51.

Muncey, J. and Ainscow, M. (1982) Launching SNAP in Coventry. *Special Education: Forward Trends*, **10**, 3–5.

Robson, C., Sebba, J., Mittler, P. and Davies, G. (1988) *Inservice Training and Special Needs: Running Short School-Focused Courses*. Manchester: Manchester University Press.

Sayer, J. and Jones, N. (eds) (1985) *Teacher Training and Special Educational Needs*. Beckenham: Croom Helm.

Sebba, J. and Robson, C. (1987) The development of short, school-focused INSET courses in special educational needs. *Research Papers in Education* **2**, 1–29.

Topping, K. and Wolfendale, S. (eds) (1985) *Parental Involvement in Children's Reading*. Beckenham: Croom Helm.

Wedge, P. and Prosser, H. (1973) *Born to Fail?* London: National Children's Bureau.

Widlake, P. (1984) *How to Reach the Hard to Teach*. Milton Keynes: Open University Press.

Widlake, P. (1985) *Reducing Educational Disadvantage*. London: Routledge & Kegan Paul.

Introduction: Deafness and special needs

This book is about the impact of deafness on the development and education of young children. No one who has personal knowledge of a hearing-impaired child, in the family, through friends, or by way of professional involvement in a school setting, can be unaware of the potential obstacles to learning which may arise for such children. At one end of the scale there is growing appreciation that even very mild and short-lived hearing losses, occurring alongside common childhood illnesses such as colds or flu, can have a deleterious effect on the child's acquisition of speech, language and literacy, especially if the hearing loss remains undetected and untreated. At the other end of the spectrum, the effects of profound and permanent damage to the hearing can be devastating, even when early diagnosis is made, powerful hearing-aids provided and professional help given. Aspects of early bonding, social interaction, speech and language, behavioural and emotional development and academic and intellectual achievement are likely to be implicated.

Our notion of what constitutes an educationally significant hearing loss is, of necessity, very broad and flexible. Hearing loss of any degree interacts in an unpredictable and largely uncharted way with all those other factors which serve to differentiate individuals one from another, such as personality, motivation, specific strengths and weaknesses and the unique social and economic circumstances of the family, together with the experience of different teachers and schools. These points are often neglected and can lead to a great deal of misunderstanding and confusion, when children are lumped together simply on the basis of their deafness for the sake of making provision, the setting up and interpretation of research, or the handing on of advice to others. So this is a book about adults and children as they live, play and learn together, highlighting the richness and diversity of individual experiences. Our major concern lies with the quality of interpersonal encounters, in terms of the social, linguistic and intellectual challenges presented to the child: a tapestry of interactive experience in which deafness weaves yet more threads.

We have written, particularly, with the needs of non-specialist teachers in ordinary schools in mind. Despite the high incidence of mild hearing losses amongst schoolchildren and a long-established tradition of integrating more severely hearing-impaired children into mainstream schools, it is still the case that detailed knowledge of the needs of these children rests with the expert few. Whilst we shall be arguing the case for a greater co-ordination of effort amongst the professionals involved with a hearing-impaired child and the family, there still remains an ongoing and demanding responsibility to raise the general level of awareness in schools of deafness and its implications. Having said that, we have drawn on a fund of recent research which spans both hearing and hearing-impaired children. By the same token, a wide range of people involved in the care and education of children should find the book useful, such as parents, Educational Psychologists and Speech Therapists, together with special educators, such as advisory support staff and teachers of the hearing-impaired.

SCOPE OF THE BOOK

A number of books have appeared recently concerned with various issues in the field of deafness. Clinical aspects of deafness — the anatomy of the ear, how different forms of deafness arise and how the underlying problems can be identified and treated — are covered in the book by Ballantyne and Martin (1984). Some of these medical aspects are important for educationalists to understand. In Chapter 3 of the present book a brief overview of basic clinical facts is given, so that, for example, the distinctions which are drawn between hearing losses of sensori-neural and conductive origin are clear. The detailed review by Bamford and Saunders (1985) is a useful and up-to-date source book covering the implications of varying degrees of hearing loss for sound perception, speech and language growth, and later school achievement. Again, the present book takes into account recent research in auditory perception, although its focus is much more to do with the impact of deafness on social-interactive, as opposed to audiological, processes.

For those who wish to have a more technical coverage of the practical management of audiological aspects, Tucker and Nolan (1984) give very thorough descriptions of the different hearing-aid systems and their operation, as part of a 'whole-child' approach to the fostering of listening and speaking. Several guides to good practice are also available, covering broader issues such as the range of educational provision available and the different communication systems in use (Reed, 1984). The book by Webster and Ellwood (1985), written for classteachers, gives a good distillation of practical strategies in non-technical language, based on tried and tested approaches to hearing-impaired children who are placed in ordinary schools. Finally, for detailed reviews of the literature on the development of deaf children, readers are referred to the impartial reviews by Quigley and Kretschmer (1982), Quigley and Paul (1984) and Webster (1986a). These evaluative studies highlight the major research issues in deaf education, without taking sides with any particular method or philosophy.

What does the present book contribute? We have not intended to provide further clinical or audiological information than is necessary to broach the issues dealt with; nor have we wanted to provide further summaries of research, although this does supply much of the context for the present work. Instead we have endeavoured to put together a coherent approach to the development and education of the hearing-impaired, based directly on empirical evidence. The studies which lie at the core of our approach were undertaken by members of the Deafness Research Group at Nottingham University. This group, comprising teachers, psychologists and academics, in partnership with children, parents and schools, set out to address a number of important questions. The fruits of a research programme which has evolved over the last ten years form the backdrop to this present volume.

In the first place, the Nottingham group began their work aware of a large gap between the growing knowledge and insights emerging from studies of hearing children and our understanding of the linguistic and intellectual development of the hearing-impaired. Findings on the nature of child language acquisition and the rôle of adults in fostering communication point to the importance of everyday interaction in mundane social contexts. Without wishing to diminish the special obstacles associated with deafness, it was hoped that these new ideas would enrich our understanding of deaf children and the challenges facing parents and teachers entrusted with their care and education. Wherever possible it is important that we try to identify ways of appraising and surmounting obstacles. But the most useful approach is to start from our knowledge of typical growth and development in childhood, since this gives clear reference points.

Secondly, to be of any real practical value, research must reflect the concerns of practitioners and give rise to strategies. A great deal of research in the field of deafness has simply fuelled old arguments about which method of communication produces better results (for example, sign language versus oral teaching methods) and where deaf children should be educated (for example, mainstream versus special school). The Deafness Research Group has steered away from polemics and towards the fine grain of the processes of learning and teaching. In other words, 'teachers should …' kinds of argument have been replaced by 'how do …?' and 'how can …?' considerations.

A final point is that, by focusing on the processes which define the social and communicative contexts of deaf individuals and their adult caretakers, methods emerge which can be used to probe other learning situations. Hopefully, all those who read this book, particularly teachers, will be in a better position to think critically about their own interventions.

To summarise, then, the distinctive contribution of the present book is that it has a basis in research, not blind faith, hearsay or argument. Furthermore, the research orientation has given rise to a wide range of usable strategies which should enable children and adults to become more effective learning partners. Importantly, a basic ingredient of the current work is the accurate appraisal and evaluation of the process of learning. Teachers, in particular, exert a large measure of control over the environment in which learning takes place. Many other variables, such as the child's ability to learn or the amount of support enlisted from home, may be outside the teacher's control. So the most significant factors which the teacher can work to improve are those which provide the framework for learning.

The questions we shall be addressing include: How does deafness interfere with very early infant–adult exchanges, such as turn-taking, and how can these be re-established? What characterises natural language encounters between children and their partners and how can these be fostered? When children begin to take part in school, which factors in the listening environment need careful attention, such as acoustic conditions and the management of hearing-aids? Is the curriculum appropriately designed and what modifications are required to enable children to have more meaningful access to a wider range of subject areas? Where are difficulties likely to arise in the curriculum and are there strategies to be adopted which help overcome them?

Inevitably, questions relating to the child's functional grasp of language, literacy, numeracy and social skills arise throughout the text. But the focus is on what, if anything, needs to be done differently for the hearing-impaired child. We take as read that it is the teacher's professional responsibility to work together with parents and other colleagues to plan realistic objectives with each child, and to assess the outcomes of the learning experience at the end of the day.

HOW MANY CHILDREN HAVE A HEARING LOSS?

A distinction is usually drawn between deafness which arises from the faulty transmission of sound across the conductive mechanisms of the middle ear, often in association with an infection, or the accumulation of fluid in the middle ear, and deafness which results from damage to the nerves in the cochlea or auditory pathways. As we shall see later, however, it is not uncommon for hearing losses caused by nerve damage (usually referred to as sensori-neural deafness) to be exacerbated by a conductive loss as well. Generally speaking, the effects of a conductive loss are much less severe than those of a sensori-neural loss, although there may still be significant implications for early child development. In this book we shall be referring to any difficulty which affects the passing of sound into the ear and across the middle-ear canal as a conductive hearing problem, and more specific details concerning physical aspects, such as aetiology, together with identification, diagnosis and treatment, can be found in Chapter 3.

Fortunately, many conductive problems are mild, transitory and amenable to treatment of a medical or surgical kind, which should restore hearing. Even so, there is a wealth of evidence that conductive hearing difficulties are associated with developmental delays in speech and language, and are also linked to impaired school functioning and achievement. We shall be dealing with these issues at some length, since care has to be taken when interpreting the evidence. How far conductive hearing loss *causes*, as opposed to being simply *associated with*, developmental delay is difficult to determine. Whatever the precise implications may be, it is important that adults are vigilant to the possibility of a child suffering from a middle-ear condition, so that appropriate treatment and management can be organised.

It is a surprise to many people to learn that approximately one child in five experiences conductive hearing difficulties at any one point in time (Murphy, 1976). A large number of studies have been carried out, both in the United Kingdom and elsewhere, in order to estimate the number of children with middle-ear disorders at different ages, and to determine what appear to be high-risk groups. Researchers tend to vary the criteria they use in deciding whether a child has a middle-ear disorder or not. (Some report active infections, others report fluid in the ear.) There are also variations in the nature of the samples taken, so that some studies select children at random while others focus on children attending the family doctor or hospital clinic. (The former are much less likely to contain children with middle-ear symptoms than those whose parents were actively seeking medical help.) So the figures given can be taken only as a guide. However, the available data suggest that middle-ear disease occurs most commonly amongst primary school-aged children and is rare over the age of ten years (Zinkus, Gottlieb and Schapiro, 1978).

Looking more closely at the peak ages when mild hearing difficulties tend to arise, about 30 per cent of children under two years are thought to have middle-ear problems (Reichman and Healey, 1983). By the age of three years more than two-thirds of children have had one episode of middle-ear disease, whilst a third have had more than three episodes (Teele, Klein and Rosner, 1984). In one survey of London nurseries, evidence of unsuspected middle-ear disease was found in 35 per cent of children (Shah, 1981). Figures for primary school children suggest that up to 95 per cent suffer middle-ear disease at some time in the first ten years, but 75 per cent of these resolve without any lasting implications (Fiellau-Nikolajsen, 1983). The children thought to be most vulnerable are those whose conductive hearing problems onset during early infancy, and persistently recur (Paradise, 1981). The worrying aspect of all these figures is that children tend to suffer hearing problems at ages which are critical for normal development, whilst a large proportion of middle-ear difficulties appear to go undetected and untreated.

There is some evidence that the prevalence of middle-ear disease in childhood is related to social and economic factors. Examining children at seven years old, the National Child Development Study (Davie, Butler and Goldstein, 1972) reported that one child in twelve had signs of past or present middle-ear disease, with children from social class V more than twice as likely to have purulent, discharging ears as social class I. This is an area of considerable controversy and we shall be treading carefully around these issues in later chapters, particularly in relation to regional variations in identification rates and patterns of treatment. (For further discussion see Webster, Bamford, Thyer and Ayles, in press.)

There are groups of children with known handicapping conditions who are very susceptible to conductive hearing loss. Two such groups are those with cleft palate and those with Down's syndrome. Conductive hearing loss occurs in perhaps 90 per cent of children with cleft palate (Northern and Downs, 1978). The reason for this is that a deficiency in the musculature of the palate may give rise to poor functioning of the Eustachian tube and subsequent middle-ear dysfunction, resulting in a hearing loss. Children with Down's syndrome often have small outer ears and narrow ear canals which are prone to wax blockage. These children are also very vulnerable to infections, and a figure of 78 per cent having a significant hearing loss associated with middle-ear disease is quoted by Bond (1984) for Down's children. It is realistic to consider any child with a congenital abnormality of the ears, nose or throat, or who is prone to repeated throat and chest infections, to be at risk of a conductive hearing impairment.

Since middle-ear deafness has been implicated by many researchers in a range of developmental and learning difficulties, attempts have been made to look for evidence of conductive hearing loss in children categorised as being poor learners or underachievers. A prevalence of conductive hearing loss in about 20 to 25 per cent of children in these groups is reported, compared with about 10 per cent with affected hearing in control groups of ordinary schoolchildren (Masters and Marsh, 1978; Freeman and Parkins, 1979). In a number of studies, children referred for extra help in reading have been examined for middle-ear deafness. As many as 46 per cent of children referred because of learning problems turn out to have histories of conductive hearing loss (Gottlieb, Zinkus and Thompson, 1980).

In subsequent chapters we shall be examining the nature of the relationship between conductive hearing loss and poor school performance. It may well be true that factors which predispose children to conductive deafness also contribute towards poor school achievement, such as parenting styles and home environment. As we have said, how far conductive deafness actually causes, as opposed to simply being associated with, school difficulties, for example in reading, is open to dispute. In the book we shall be drawing out the major implications of mild hearing difficulties for the learning process, together with the kind of practical strategies which may help overcome the difficulties which can arise.

The prevalence of sensori-neural hearing loss in children is far less than that of conductive deafness. This is fortunate because the only available 'treatment' for sensori-neural deafness is the provision of hearing-aids, parent guidance and supportive educational help. The impact of the more severe forms of deafness on a wide range of processes, such as adult–child relationships, social and emotional adjustment and linguistic and intellectual development, can be substantial, if not devastating. Largely because of the severity and permanence of sensori-neural losses, the numbers of children affected have been more systematically recorded by local education authorities, at least until 1983 when the 1981 Education Act was implemented, from which point the classification of schools and pupils under categories of handicap have been abolished.

Figures collected by the Department of Education and Science from LEAs for children with severe and more moderate sensori-neural impairments, awaiting or receiving some form of special education, are given in Webster and Ellwood (1985). Approximately five children in every 10,000 will be discovered to have a moderate sensori-neural loss, with a slightly lower figure of four per 10,000 for more moderate losses. It should be noted that these figures do not take into account children who are fully integrated into normal classrooms, or children who have other handicapping conditions as well as deafness.

Over the decade from 1974 to 1983, a gradual fall-off in the numbers of children with sensori-neural impairments requiring special educational help is recorded by the DES. The major reasons for this trend are medical. Immunisation programmes for German measles (rubella); therapeutic abortions for pregnant women exposed to rubella; advances in the care of mothers and babies, during and after birth — all these factors should be reflected in a diminishing number of congenitally hearing-impaired children. However, this may well be offset by the developing capability of paediatrics to save premature babies with very low birth weight, who have a high risk of hearing-impairment.

Data have recently been published by Newton (1985) on a survey in Greater Manchester of all children with moderate or severe sensori-neural hearing losses. Children were included in the study if they had a bilateral loss averaging 25 decibels (hearing level) or more, in the better ear. Out of 136,720 live births in the four-year period from 1977 to 1980, 111 children (60 boys, 51 girls) were subsequently identified as having a sensori-neural loss, which gives a prevalence rate of 0.8 per 1000. Newton suggests that a figure of 1 per 1000 is a more accurate estimate and would take into account the later diagnosis of small, high-frequency losses, for example, as figures become more complete over time. In Table 1.1 the aetiology of the hearing losses found in the Greater Manchester survey are given. Noticeable are the high percentages of deafness associated with hereditary factors or maternal rubella. Of the 111 children in

Table 1.1 *Aetiology of hearing loss in the Greater Manchester survey (Newton, 1985)*

Causal factor	Number of children (n = 111)	Percentage
Congenital rubella	12	10.81
Cytomegalovirus	3	2.70
Perinatal	15	13.51
Postnatal	5	4.51
Genetic	33	29.73
Unknown	43	38.74

the study, 50 had an additional conductive hearing loss lasting more than three months, with 22 undergoing surgical treatment of their condition during the survey period.

A recent survey of 8-year-old children with permanent hearing losses carried out in the European Community (Martin, 1982) showed that rubella was the commonest cause, accounting for 17 per cent of the sample. Hereditary factors accounted for 10 per cent, whilst the most frequent cause of hearing loss acquired during childhood was meningitis, which accounted for 6 per cent. In a very large proportion of cases (42 per cent) the precise cause of a hearing loss was not known.

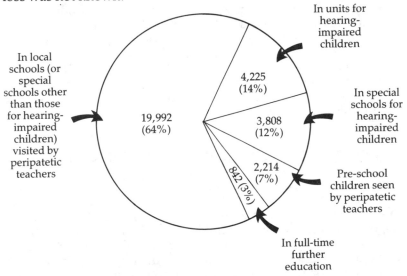

Figure 1.1 *Distribution of 31,081 hearing-impaired children in relation to educational provision (NDCS, 1987)*

Finally, we include in Figure 1.1 some statistics published by the National Deaf Children's Society (1987), which show how an estimated 31,081 children with significant hearing impairments (including conductive hearing losses) are distributed in terms of educational provision in England, Wales and Scotland. By far the greatest majority of children who are known to the specialist services for the hearing-impaired and visited by teachers of the deaf are placed in units attached to mainstream schools or local schools without any special facilities. In other words, the major responsibility for the day-to-day educational needs of hearing-impaired children, albeit the less severely handicapped, is shouldered by non-specialist teaching staff with varying levels of additional specialist support.

This survey of a range of evidence relating to the prevalence of hearing-impairments in schoolchildren indicates that, for milder transient hearing losses of a conductive nature, approximately one child in five may be affected at some point in time, although the precise implications may vary from child to child. About one in 1000 children may have a permanent sensori-neural loss requiring specialist support, and the majority of these children will be placed in mainstream school contexts, at least for some of their educational experience. If there is an overall trend for sensori-neural losses to occur less often, as some statistics indicate, they will be harder to find, and our screening and detection procedures will need to be as efficient and failsafe as possible. Prior to the introduction of measures to combat rubella, an epidemic of German measles meant a certain increase in the numbers of severely hearing-impaired children. That rubella still accounts for deafness in a large number of children is the reason why people must not dismiss lightly the rôle of immunisation. There will never be a time when we can afford to be complacent about the prevention and identification of hearing loss in children.

SPECIAL NEEDS OF THE HEARING-IMPAIRED CHILD

What kind of obstacles to learning may deafness present? We give here a number of case studies, taken from our own contacts with children, their families and schools, to illustrate the diversity of responses which are made by children and their adult caretakers, in different learning contexts. When professionals talk about the needs of children there is a common, but mistaken, tendency to simplify the complex of factors which impinge upon children, their families and schools.

Robert: a child with mild fluctuating conductive hearing loss

Robert had been doing badly in school for some time. His teachers thought that he might be lazy or dull. He tended to daydream and needed much more help and explanation than was usual. Concentration was poor, whilst Robert was often slow to respond and always asked for instructions to be repeated or otherwise forgot what he had to do. On one occasion the classteacher read the story of *Charlie and the Chocolate Factory* and the children were asked to draw a picture of one of the characters. Robert had little clue how to start his drawing and the teacher asked him if he had been listening to the descriptions in the story. 'I thought I'd listened' was Robert's reply. Some days Robert did appear much more 'with it' than others. It was apparent in some practical activities, such as assembling a motorised construction kit, that he could learn quickly. His difficulties were noticeably greater in listening and language work, and he was a poor reader.

At the age of eight, Robert was diagnosed as suffering from 'glue ear'. The resulting intermittent, although mild, conductive hearing loss had interfered with Robert's development of mature speech sounds, limited his vocabulary and sentence structure, and led to difficulties in discriminating sounds, for example in the 'phonic' work his class attempted during reading lessons. Once the condition was recognised, Robert's parents and teachers were alerted to the difficulties accompanying 'glue ear', and coping strategies for the school setting were developed. These included home–school liaison whenever it was suspected that Robert's hearing was dropping, so that medical help could be sought. In the classroom, careful seating was arranged to lessen noise and distraction while maximising visual cues in order to indicate who was talking, when topic changes occurred and what the subject matter was. It was also found helpful for Robert to work in small groups for part of each day on tasks designed to improve speech discrimination and develop listening skills in a variety of settings.

Kim: a child with moderate sensori-neural loss

Kim had a sensori-neural hearing-impairment of unknown cause, diagnosed at two years. The loss was considered to be moderate, between about 50 and 80 decibels, which meant that she could hear the sounds of conversation fairly clearly when she wore hearing-aids and when the listening environment was quiet. She found it difficult talking with a group of friends on the bus going to school and in the youth club or disco, and in other situations where there was a lot of noise interference and where there was uncertainty about who was going to talk next. Kim spoke intelligibly and unfamiliar people were able to understand her speech at the first meeting. She had a well-developed 'everyday' vocabulary, including a broad selection of 'in' words and slang. At eleven years of age Kim attended a large mainstream comprehensive school. She had previously been educated in a special school for deaf children which entailed living away from home during the week. This meant she missed contact with her two brothers and a sister, close in age, with whom she got on very well.

Following the change of school at secondary transfer, Kim lost much of the confidence and vivacity that had convinced her parents and teachers that she would manage successfully in the larger, more challenging environment. Although Kim had coped relatively easily with the majority of the lessons at her new school, being attentive and a good reader, it emerged that she was far from comfortable socially. This was despite the help she received from her family and from a visiting specialist teacher of the hearing-impaired who gave additional tutoring in English and science. In the mainstream class situation Kim was faced with the choice of devoting her attention either to the teacher and lesson or to the 'underground' of the classroom activities between her peers in order to be 'part of the gang'. It became very important to Kim, in her new school situation, not to be seen to be different from the rest. Given the opportunity to 'open up' in an English assignment, Kim revealed that she always felt other girls were laughing at her, but that she often failed to 'get the joke'. She began to feel very embarrassed about wearing her hearing-aids. It was apparent that the change to secondary school had been more difficult for Kim than had been envisaged. Kim's attention to her studies began to decline, and she became involved in sly and petty criminal activities, at one point being caught shoplifting make-up with a core group of 'likely lads and lasses' who were frequently in trouble at school for truancy, bullying and not completing set work.

Kim's apparent obligation to be at least as 'bad' as anyone else, perhaps a reflection of her immature understanding, resulted in much of the goodwill of mainstream teaching staff being lost. Some very thorough and careful negotiations were required, involving parents, teachers, support staff and Kim herself, to restore a more positive approach. Changes were made in how Kim spent her free time in and out of school; more consistent ways of recording teacher expectations were devised, such as daily 'job sheets' and a weekly diary, which were taken home. The learning context was also modified to include more co-operative working in small groups, where pupils had some choice in the task or order of tasks chosen, and where either all or none of the pupils' attention was required to be on the teacher.

Harvinder: a child with severe sensori-neural loss

Harvinder's severe sensori-neural hearing loss was not diagnosed until he was over three years old and about to start part-time nursery. The usual developmental checks had been missed on some occasions, and on others translators had not been available to ease communication with his mother, whose first language was Punjabi. It was during the review of an older sibling with learning difficulties that parental, and subsequently professional, concern over Harvinder's progress was raised. Fortunately, the local school had additional resources for the teaching of hearing-impaired children, and Harvinder, together with his normally hearing twin brother, began attending the nursery class there full time.

It became apparent not only that Harvinder faced difficulties normally associated with a severe hearing loss, but that he had underlying learning difficulties as well. This meant that in many basic skill areas, such as learning to tie shoelaces, recognising pictures of everyday objects, organising his own dinner tray at lunchtime and using scissors to cut round a magazine picture, Harvinder required tasks to be broken down into very small teaching steps in order to cope with them. There was also a problem of communication between the child and his mother in the home. Harvinder was communicating with his peers and teachers in a language which he could not share with the adults in his family. The full impact of this emerged as his mother became unable to manage the dangerous things he did at home, such as turning the gas taps on.

Contact was made with the family through a Punjabi-speaking teacher. It was a decision, taken jointly, that Harvinder's mother would attend both English and signing classes at the school. Children at the school were encouraged to communicate using voice as well as a sign language. Harvinder's mother began to assist in lessons where hearing-impaired children were taught, be incorporated into the usual 'to and fro' of child–teacher interaction in the infant class, and also have the opportunity to feed back success (or otherwise) of the management strategies tried at home.

Alison: a profoundly hearing-impaired child

Alison's parents were primed to expect some degree of hearing loss in their baby as rubella had been suspected in the early stages of pregnancy. At only a few months of age, their fears were confirmed and Alison was diagnosed as being profoundly deaf. With little or no measurable hearing sensitivity, it might be anticipated that a child would have, at best, only limited or distorted perception of speech sounds, even wearing hearing-aids, and that this might pose insuperable problems for the child's own mastery of the language system. Alison's example shows that other factors, apart from degree of hearing loss, are important in determining the levels of linguistic and social competence which a child may reach. These must include the child's natural aptitude for speech and language and the nature of the communication experiences available in the range of learning opportunities presented.

The attitude of Alison's family to her deafness was, in their own words, 'sink or swim', as her father was in the Forces and a chequered path of moves and changes of school lay ahead. From the outset Alison's parents decided her only hope was to treat her as the other children in the family, to make no concessions to her disability and to expose her to as full a range of social situations as possible.

From babyhood she was fitted with powerful and appropriate hearing-aids, and accepted them totally. She mixed easily with other children, acquired a wide vocabulary and developed intelligible speech. She survived many changes of school and teaching style, and spent the final years of her secondary education following examination courses in a wide range of subjects, planning to continue her studies at the local college of further education.

In the last school Alison attended, a unit for hearing-impaired children was available, but Alison was on roll in the main school and fully integrated for all lessons, with no additional help. In her examination years she opted to drop one academic subject in order to concentrate on maths and science. Additional tutoring was arranged amongst teaching staff and peers, so that Alison could re-explore some of the specialised vocabulary, abstract concepts and more difficult textbook material in these subject areas. Despite her sophisticated control of speech and language, there were occasional misinterpretations which needed ironing out. Alison took the opportunity to learn sign language through classes organised in school, in order to communicate better with the other hearing-impaired pupils at the school.

Leanne: a child with both conductive and profound sensori-neural deafness

Leanne was born ten weeks premature and was consequently on the 'at-risk' register of the community physician. By the time of Leanne's first birthday, her mother was convinced that the child was hearing-impaired because she rarely turned when called and was never startled by loud noises, such as the clatter of a dropped pan lid behind her on a hard kitchen floor. On her mother mentioning her concerns at the hospital, Leanne was prescribed antibiotics for the treatment of a middle-ear infection discovered on examination. The Ear, Nose and Throat Consultant advised that Leanne would hear better when the infection cleared.

Regular trips to the doctor for further courses of antibiotics did nothing to relieve parental anxieties over Leanne's hearing. At 24 months Leanne had no response to sounds in the environment, her voice was heard only as an unvarying loud scream to call for attention or to protest, she was still in nappies day and night, and she was 'uncontrollably naughty'. The Health Visitor called at the home to carry out a hearing test, but Leanne passed the visual distraction test (by this time she was adept at following the slightest visual cue). Her mother was told that Leanne was bright but lazy, and would soon catch up with her peers.

By Leanne's third birthday, her mother was too embarrassed by the child's behaviour to take her out except to a few understanding relatives. Leanne did not attend toddler or play group, and a nursery place was not sought. Leanne's mother raised the difficulties again at her next hospital visit, and this time a more objective hearing test revealed a 'significant' hearing loss. Leanne was fitted with hearing-aids, but her recurrent ear infections made the moulds uncomfortable, and for long periods the aids were abandoned. Following diagnosis, the education department was informed of Leanne's difficulties, and the first home visit from a peripatetic teacher of the hearing-impaired occurred when the child was 3½.

On entry to nursery school (aged four), Leanne was still in nappies, lacked any sophisticated communication skills, was terrified of other children and showed anxiety at separating from her mother. She attached herself to a particular teacher who used sign language as part of a repertoire of communication approaches and gently introduced her to tasks leading towards partnership with other children and adults, such as sharing, turn-taking and listening whilst others are talking. After two terms Leanne was toilet-trained and had the beginnings of conversational interaction. The skills which were acquired included agreeing and sharing a topic of conversation, looking appropriately between teacher and object, vocalising in pauses, 'questioning' with gesture and rising tone of voice, and initiating conversations appropriately with others. Subsequently, Leanne attended nursery full time, played co-operatively with other children and travelled to school by taxi without crying for her mother.

Michael: a child with sensori-neural deafness and additional handicaps

Michael's spasticity was noted at birth. He was thought to have additional learning difficulties when speech and language were slow to develop. It was his mother who insisted that he was deaf, and this was subsequently proved to be the case. Advice was available from a Speech Therapist and from a visiting specialist teacher of the hearing-impaired. The nursery which Michael attended also had the help of a physiotherapist. One of the problems which the family encountered was the contrasting and sometimes conflicting advice from the different professionals involved. After two years Michael showed few noticeable gains in the skills mastered. He was incontinent and barely mobile, and required help to feed, dress and wash himself. His mother felt the family were not providing the right kind of nurture for him, and there was a great deal of strain and tension in the home.

Eventually, Michael was recommended for a place in a school for hearing-impaired children which specialised in helping children with additional learning obstacles to overcome. He was taught in a milieu of 'total communication' where speech, a signing system, a method of spelling out words on the fingers and optimal use of a child's residual hearing and hearing-aids were all encouraged. The school was able to provide the necessary physiotherapy and to reduce the pressure on him to communicate by voice alone (complicated by his spasticity of the tongue). The integration of his social, emotional and physical needs into a complete educational package enabled Michael to learn acceptable patterns of social behaviour and to generalise his learning from one situation to another.

These notes, drawn from current case-work, illustrate the complex and unpredictable nature of children's special needs, as the physical facts of deafness interact with an intricate web of psychological, social and family variables. They span a continuum of needs from the transitory and mild to the longstanding and profound. We have been particularly careful not to imply that all hearing-impaired children, *ipso facto*, have developmental difficulties. Neither have we wanted to give the impression that, when any learning, social or emotional difficulties arise, they are necessarily a result of the hearing-impairment itself. It should also be noted that no claims are made on behalf of one method of communication as opposed to another. For both parents and professionals, the important issues which are raised concern who should be consulted when decisions are taken; which options are available for educational provision; what teaching objectives should be set for a child and how can these be evaluated?

THE ORAL VERSUS MANUAL DEBATE

We should make it clear from the outset that we have no wish to enter the debate about which method of communication is likely to benefit the hearing-impaired child more than any other. For those coming new to the educational world of the hearing-impaired, it is important to know that there are very strong views held on this issue by specialist teachers, which are often hotly defended. All those involved with the care and education of hearing-impaired children should be aware of the controversy, but it is our hope that the argument can be kept in the perspective it deserves. For reasons which should become obvious, the oral–manual debate is not central to our own discussion and will not be explored further in the book. However, teachers may meet children in ordinary class settings whose families use sign language at home, or who generate their own signs in school, and questions may be raised about how the teacher should respond.

One argument about the special needs of more severely hearing-impaired children is that many of the potential problems could be avoided if a child's hearing loss is diagnosed early enough and good hearing-aids provided, together with a 'normal' range of family and school experiences. To support this 'oral' position, professionals can usually point to a number of successful, although very deaf, children who became good lip-readers and developed intelligible speech, attended the local school and became fluent readers, later going on to high academic achievements amongst hearing peers. The majority of deaf children, more than 90 per cent according to Meadow (1980), have hearing parents. The oral-only approach is often the preferred parental choice, with the long-term hope that a deaf child will be able to speak normally and be part of hearing society. Not all severely hearing-impaired children are so successful, however. Some children find speech, even with lip-reading and powerful hearing-aids, a very difficult mode of communication.

Another argument about the needs of hearing-impaired children concerns the role of sign language in fostering development. Proponents of signing methods suggest that exposure to sign can lead to much richer and earlier patterns of language interaction, less frustration and isolation, and better progress in school. The benefits of signing for some children, so the argument runs, accrue from the visual salience of signs for those who depend largely on vision for gaining information about the world when hearing is damaged.

There are a lot of misunderstandings about signing systems and it is important that terms are very carefully defined. *British Sign Language*, for example, refers to the natural communication system which deaf people in the United Kingdom use amongst themselves. It used to be thought that sign languages lacked organisation and were not capable of supporting abstract thought. It is now accepted that BSL is a language in its own right, governed by grammatical rules which are different from, but no less complex than, the syntax of spoken languages (Brennan, 1981). The minority of deaf children who are brought up in deaf families whose first language is sign are often thought to encounter fewer social and emotional problems, and to make better academic progress (Meadow, 1980). A strong case is often argued for the 'mother-tongue' teaching of deaf children from deaf families, in the same way that mother-tongue teaching might be recommended for bilingual hearing children whose home language is different from that of the host culture. In both situations, fluency in the first language is felt to enable second language learning and can be used as a medium for instruction.

There are a number of other signing systems which non-specialists may encounter, for example where signing is used with more severely hearing-impaired children who attend units in mainstream schools. A variant of BSL is *Signed English*. This embodies natural signs from the deaf community which are used in spoken English word order, with additional signs and finger spelling to indicate such features as tenses and plural endings, so that a complete visual representation can be given alongside speech. *Sign Supporting English* implies that only some of the spoken English features are illustrated with signs, in order to give additional clues to aid understanding. *Makaton* is a much-simplified version of some of the British signs, most often used with children who are very slow to learn. In the *Paget Gorman* system signs are again used to approximate to English word order, but the vocabulary is an invented one, with many of the signs being ideographic: animal names, for example, share a basic hand shape which visually resembles an animal. *Fingerspelling* uses different hand positions to form the 26 letters of the alphabet, which can be used to spell out English words. In contrast, *Cued Speech* uses a system of single hand shapes around the lips to differentiate speech sounds which look alike or are unseen on the lips.

Where schools have adopted a *Total Communication* approach, this usually implies that the language environment includes normal speech, optimal use of the child's residual hearing and hearing-aids, lip-reading, a manual sign language and finger spelling. Not surprisingly, methods such as Total Communication are very exacting in terms of staff commitment and training, and they are frequently associated with residential education.

One view is that children who sign in mainstream school situations will be restricted in their social and linguistic interactions, unless other children and teachers are also taught the system. At present in the United Kingdom very few schools offer sign language classes to hearing students or adults, although this situation is changing. Similarly, the presence of signing interpreters in classrooms where deaf students participate is uncommon in the United Kingdom. Some teachers feel motivated to learn the basics of the sign system used by a child who comes into mainstream groups. Some specialist support services will organise sign classes for teachers in ordinary schools to enable communication with children who sign. Another view is that if children's needs are so special that they require an esoteric means of communication, then these are probably best met in a special school situation where the whole community of children and staff is already familiar with sign.

Advocates of one method of communication as opposed to another frequently support their fervour with promises of better educational adjustment and achievement. However, when comprehensive surveys have been mounted to try and evaluate the effectiveness of one methodology over another, the evidence is at best inconclusive. Summaries of research in Meadow (1980) and Quigley and Kretschmer (1982) show that, if one examines important factors such as the child's functional mastery of the rules of English grammar, then exposure to sign systems or otherwise appears to have neither a negative nor a positive effect on progress. In the very extensive review by Jensema and Trybus (1978), an attempt was made to outline the major factors which do appear to influence children's developmental progress. Whilst the list of significant factors includes degree of hearing loss, intelligence, cause of deafness, ethnic background and family circumstances, it does not include mode of communication.

There is one other strand of evidence which can help shape our thinking on the oral–manual debate, and that is the collective evidence of several centuries of the history of deaf education. There has always been a bitter three-cornered struggle amongst those who advocate the use of the indigenous signs of the deaf, those who press for signs which approximate to English grammar, and those who want the deaf to speak. The commonsense approach to these controversial issues is a pragmatic one, accepting that what works for some children, their families and teachers may not work for others. A good Local Education Authority will seek to provide a flexible variety of educational opportunities which permit a well-tailored response to the individual needs and circumstances of the child and family. (For further discussion of these issues see Lane, 1984 and Webster, 1985.)

If choice of communication mode is limited in its power to account for differences in children's educational achievement, then smaller units of analysis must be outlined. There are, in fact, large variations in practice between individual schools of the same 'type', and between individual teachers of the same children. It is to the fine grain of the teaching process, and the responses of children to that process, that we look for ways of overcoming the learning obstacles which deafness presents. What this means for the ordinary classteacher is that the quality, not the mode, of adult–child interaction and communication is paramount. Strategies for effective interaction with deaf children who have varying communication needs are covered in Chapter 5, together with some of the questions we hope teachers will ask, of whatever strategies they choose to adopt.

THE LEARNING ENVIRONMENT AND RECENT RESEARCH

There are a number of ways in which recent research evidence encourages us to shift attention away from factors such as mode of communication and towards the finer details of how children and adults interact with each other in the learning environment, and how this can be assessed. In other words, a more productive focus of interest is felt to be the strategies which adults adopt, and the active involvement which children are prompted to take, as they live, play and learn together.

Three trends can be said to characterise recent thinking in developmental psychology as a whole, and child language research in particular (see, for example, Donaldson, Grieve and Pratt, 1983). The first of these is the importance of interpersonal contexts for the development of language and thinking. Children are born with the capacity to use symbols in order to code events and to represent ideas about the world: it is this potential for symbolic thinking which makes it possible for children to learn language and to use language as a means to learn more. However, the basic impetus for learning is a social one. The child has a need to discover more about objects and events in the environment, to pass on material wants and to express feelings. But all of this occurs, in the early years at least, through interaction with familiar adults in everyday social contexts. In these early encounters the child is not simply exploring the world since an important aspect is the sustaining and negotiation of social contacts with those who share the environment. In later chapters we shall be looking at the distinctive qualities of the social and linguistic encounters enjoyed by children and adults, especially where a hearing loss intrudes. In our view, the way in which social encounters between adults and children are patterned is very important in determining how strategies for thinking and language are passed on.

A distinctive feature of the way in which children interact with other people in learning language is the child's interpretation of the social context. Children are influenced by the setting in which language is used and are concerned to unearth what a person means. What words themselves signify is only one element of how meaning is conveyed. In trying to reconstruct meaning, children pay a lot of attention to situational clues: what the speaker does as well as says. All sorts of problems may arise for the child when communication is not directed to fairly obvious goals or supported by the social context. There is a risk of that happening when, for example, efforts are made to teach language directly, as a kind of class exercise, remote from the contexts in which language spontaneously arises. (For further discussion of these points see Webster and McConnell, 1987.)

A second recent trend has been to highlight the importance of purpose and meaning in the learning process. Thus, whilst we assume a social context in which a speaker is trying to share meaning with a listener, we must also assume that there is something meaningful to communicate. Adults and children do not talk about nothing: both must have something purposeful to say. In accounting for the child's acquisition of skills, both in thinking and in language, we must consider what it is that the child is attempting to do. Indeed, this is precisely what parents do when they communicate with their children. Initially, it is the home which provides the experiences which matter to the participants (however mundane) and around which communication revolves. There are some important implications from this when we come to consider the devising of an effective learning environment. Children are impelled to use language and to learn in situations which are meaningful to themselves and to their lives.

Furthermore, and this is a particularly important aspect for hearing-impaired children, the child's own awareness of the function and intention of learning is critical. When children are put in the position of passive assimilators in the learning process, they will be increasingly less likely to become responsible for their own learning, to learn how to learn. This line of enquiry we shall be pursuing in relation to the child's classroom experience. Are adults controlling and didactic, or do they involve the children themselves in planning appropriate activities, setting objectives and evaluating achievements? How far are children enabled to initiate their own learning activities, to question and to reflect? Writers such as Donaldson (1978) have suggested that one important key to educational success in young children is the degree to which they are helped to become aware of their own thinking and their own language. In other words, successful children achieve conscious control of some important aspects of their own learning strategies.

The third, and perhaps most important, of the recent trends in developmental psychology is to focus on what children can do, as opposed to what they are incapable of. Observations of babies within hours of their birth have shown that they are far more capable than once was supposed. Studies by researchers such as Bower (1977) and Trevarthen (1979) show that newborn infants can imitate movements made by an adult and discriminate smells, and are selective in their response to sounds. By two weeks of age, babies are able to distinguish the mother's face and voice from those of a stranger. In one fascinating experiment, infants of a few months old were able to select which of two films of mothers' moving faces matched the accompanying taped speech sounds (Kuhl, 1983). It is not so much that we now think babies are far cleverer than we had ever imagined previously, but rather that children from early infancy onwards act on the world and make sense of it, and are not simply passive recipients of information. This, too, has implications for the learning process. How we harness the child's sense of enquiry is a major determinant in our discussions about the educational curriculum for children of all ages.

It is against a background of research evidence such as this that it is now recognised how well equipped infants are in getting to grips with the world and establishing interactions with others. We can cast the child in the rôle of scientist. In acquiring language, for example, it is not enough simply to expose the child to examples of the adult language system. The child has to discover how the system functions by actively testing it out. In this sense, the three trends we have mentioned come together. In familiar and purposeful everyday social contexts, the child actively pieces together the rules of language by becoming aware of its functional power. Whilst children are actively creating a model of the language system for themselves, the rôle of adults is that of language partner rather than teacher, providing well-tailored evidence from which the child can learn.

Most adults seem fairly proficient in the strategies they adopt with young children as they interact with one another. In conversation, for example, adults seem intuitively able to give just the right amount of feedback, by expanding and paraphrasing what the child says. An important principle here is that of contingency. Children learn most effectively when the help which adults offer is contingent upon the child's developing competence. To be contingent, adults must be aware of what the child is trying to do; provide experiences which give just sufficient challenge to the child; allow room for initiative; structure a task so that the child is likely to be successful; offer help when difficulties are faced; and step back when the child demonstrates mastery. It should be noted that the adult's rôle in this process is not as teacher, but as facilitator. Whilst adults provide the stimulus and opportunity for learning to take place, it is the child's task to organise and make sense of the learning experience.

Not surprisingly, it is difficult for some adults to make their responses contingent upon the child in some learning situations. In school, teaching styles vary enormously and one can observe similar variation in the degree of contingency achieved with children from one adult to another. When we come to consider the special learning difficulties which many hearing-impaired children face, the three aspects of interpersonal context, purpose and meaning, together with the active rôle of children in the learning process, are key issues. We have been careful not to locate obstacles to learning within the children themselves. As we have already said, the major variables which adults, particularly teachers, control are the conditions within which learning takes place and the responses which are given contingently upon the child's efforts.

SPECIAL NEEDS AND THE 1981 EDUCATION ACT

The report of the Warnock Committee (DES, 1978a), and the legislation which implemented many of its findings, reflects some very complex changes in both philosophy and practice which challenge all those involved with children with special needs. It is not intended to cover the Warnock Report or the 1981 Education Act in any detail in this book, and those who require further information are referred to the book by Hegarty in the present series (Hegarty, 1987). Nevertheless, the general principles which underlie the 1981 Education Act are in sympathy with the emphasis we have brought to this book, particularly in relation to the approaches we advocate towards individual children, the issues of assessment and ongoing monitoring of children's progress, and the involvement of parents in the educational process. One of the most contentious and least well-understood areas in relation to the education of hearing-impaired children concerns the policy of integration set out in the 1981 Education Act, which we shall be addressing in some detail in the section which follows.

In the period which led up to the 1981 Education Act, special education was defined in relation to categories of disability. Categories such as deaf, partial hearing, ESN(S) and maladjusted were used to label children and then determine the kind of educational provision which was required. Special education, in many people's minds, was synonymous with special schools, units or classes. One of the dangers inherent in this approach is that the nomenclature used colours expectations and attitudes towards children. For example, if it is generally believed that a severe to profound hearing loss precludes children from acquiring normal speech and language, achieving academic success or participating socially with hearing peers, then adult expectations may be lowered, fewer opportunities and challenges offered, and fewer demands made. This would apply to all children who suffer under a label which carries self-fulfilling prophecies with it, no matter how competent or determined the child happens to be.

The deficit model, as it is sometimes called, encourages people to attribute every problem which arises to the child's disability. Instead of examining aspects such as teaching styles and materials, and the appropriateness of the curriculum, schools which adhere to the deficit model may be tempted to expect all children to thrive on the same educational diet. Where children fail, laziness, poor motivation or limited home support may be blamed. Responsibility for change remains with the child, rather than with those who organise the learning environment.

Under the 1981 Education Act, professionals are no longer to use categories of handicap in determining a child's special needs. Special educational needs are instead defined in relation to the goals which adults set for children. For example, commonly held goals for children would include the achievement of independence and an increasing understanding of the world. Whatever obstacle stands in the way of the child in working towards these goals constitutes a special need. In terms of hearing loss, special needs may be spread along a continuum from the mild and transitory at one end to the profound and permanent at the other. Special educational help can also be thought of in terms of a continuum of provision. Some children overcome obstacles to learning with minimal help, others require a heavily structured programme of intervention and resources to enable the child to progress. The importance of this view of special education is that it moves the focus of attention away from categories of handicap and factors within the child's disability towards conditions for learning.

In broad terms, the 1981 Education Act makes a plea for regarding children as individuals. The individual circumstances of a child's home; the child's approach to learning and response to experience; the child's ability to relate to others; confidence in adjusting to new situations and meeting challenges; what is learned speedily or poorly; and the distinctive profile of attainments in different skill areas — all these produce a spectrum of features unique to the child. Educationalists are charged with the task of creating a framework of resources which is flexible enough to adjust to the individual needs and circumstances of the child. The Warnock view of special needs is in accord with our own notions of what constitutes an educationally significant hearing loss, and how that may be ameliorated through intervention. On a far more encompassing scale than hitherto, the 1981 Education Act suggests that many more children may have special needs and of a more diverse character than was previously realised. In recognition of that fact, special education must itself become more sensitive, adaptable and differentiated.

The Warnock view encompasses many children who already attend normal schools, and it is spurious to draw a distinction between children in mainstream education and those in special schools. However a child is helped, whether through additional resources in the normal class setting, withdrawal to special classes or special school placement, must be appraised as part of the continuum of responses to individual children's needs.

INTEGRATION

Integration is not a principle to be pursued, whatever the cost, as an end in itself. In fact, integration is a process and not a target to aim for. Ultimately, it is the quality of a child's experience which is most important, wherever education is provided. Integration subsumes a variety of practices which should be evaluated in relation to what they enable a child to achieve. The real goals that should be pursued are the skills we hope the child can acquire in thinking, language, literacy and numeracy, social competence, and so on. It follows that, whatever educational provision is made for a child, there is an ongoing professional responsibility to appraise how well tailored resources are to the child's profile of needs.

The 1981 Education Act has a great deal to say, amongst other things, about the integration of children with special needs within mainstream teaching environments. This Act placed on Local Education Authorities the general duty to help children who have special needs within the context of an ordinary school. Children cannot be excluded because of the nature or severity of their handicap, and parental views must be taken into account. The ambit of an LEA's responsibilities is limited by three conditions: that integration is compatible with the child receiving the help required; that other children are not compromised in the process; and that resources are being used efficiently. It has sometimes been suggested that the Warnock Report recommended the closure of special schools, with the subsequent integration of these children into the mainstream. This, in fact, is untrue. What Warnock did say was that special schools could establish closer links with the mainstream, perhaps acting as resource centres or providing more specialised, intensive help on a short-term basis. They should be a part of the continuum of provision which an LEA can call upon in its response to children's special needs. If the wider concept of special educational need is accepted, then integration ceases to be an either/or question. It is, as we have said, simply an alternative means of helping children to learn which can both enrich and be enriched by the context of an ordinary school.

There have always been a significant number of children with major hearing losses who have benefited from mainstream school situations. In the 1960s, the Department of Education and Science carried out a survey of some 90 classes for hearing-impaired children in ordinary schools (DES, 1967). About a third of the children in the survey had severe to profound hearing losses, supported in various ways by special units and teachers of the deaf. In the climate of the 1960s, when other groups of children with special needs were receiving some kind of segregated provision, there was perhaps the danger that deaf children were merely 'located' in the mainstream, sharing nothing other than the site. Other children may have enjoyed social integration: playing, eating and sharing assemblies together. Integration should be judged on the amount of real sharing of experiences which takes place, particularly within the classroom. In its fullest sense, integration is functional and implies that children participate in a wholly meaningful way in the learning community of the school.

For a number of reasons, the trend to integrate more severely hearing-impaired children in ordinary schools is likely to be a growing one. Pressure from parents, changes in philosophy, a more stringent economic climate, a concern for earlier diagnosis and intervention, and developments in technology, such as radio hearing-aids, have all widened the possibilities for integration and brought many more non-specialists into contact with children with varying degrees of hearing loss. And yet not everyone is in accord with this trend. Integration as an issue has some very complex ramifications for the deaf community which we shall mention here but not pursue further in the book. (For further discussion see Booth, 1983.)

An integrated educational programme, where no special methods such as sign language are used, is aimed at preparing children for life in a hearing community. However, there are many people handicapped by deafness who also regard themselves as members of a community. For the adult deaf, sign language is seen as the basis of cultural identity and transmission. Although the situation is beginning to change in the United Kingdom, the active acceptance and teaching of sign is largely confined to the special schools for the hearing-impaired, particularly for older children. So the issue of oralism versus manualism is also inextricably linked with the integration versus special school debate.

We hope that non-specialists will be able to keep these issues in perspective and be aware of the strong feelings which they evoke amongst people who are deaf themselves and those who are directly involved professionally. As we have said, in a good Local Education Authority there will be a flexible variety of options available, so that the needs of the child and the wishes of the family can be taken fully into account. In the end, decisions regarding school placement will rest on the child's strength of personality, confidence in relating to others, motivation and ability to learn, and whether the security and protection of small teaching groups or the presence of other hearing-impaired children is desired. An important aspect is the ongoing appraisal of any school placement so that adjustments can be made as appropriate.

The study by Lynas (1986), which examines how deaf and hearing students view themselves, amply illustrates that an integrated education does not miraculously convert deaf into hearing individuals. Whilst deaf children are felt to achieve more academically in ordinary rather than special school settings, they do not always achieve results comparable to hearing peers. Likewise, social acceptance and emotional adjustment are not always easily achieved, but depend directly on the opportunities deaf and hearing children have for co-operating and interacting with each other. Certain conditions have to be met for integration to be well perceived by deaf and hearing students, and by the staff who teach them. In Lynas's study, confidence in working with deaf children and sensitivity to their needs came from resources of time, knowledge, realistic advice and effective support strategies. It is towards meeting some of these inservice demands that this book has been written.

At the time of writing, new government legislation under the Education Reform Act is likely to have a significant impact on both the kind and the degree of integration which children with special needs are able to enjoy, as schools move into a 'market economy'. At this stage there are many uncertainties about how willing schools will be to integrate children, to adapt the curriculum, or to provide supportive teaching, where such approaches may have financial restraints or consequences. We shall discuss aspects of the Education Reform Act again, in Chapter 3.

PARENTS AND PROFESSIONALS

An important principle which we hold is that there is no one perspective on hearing-impairment which should exclude, or is more important than, any other. The parents of a hearing-impaired child are likely to come into contact with a wide range of professionals, such as Audiologists, doctors, Ear, Nose and Throat Consultants, Speech Therapists, Educational Psychologists and teachers of the deaf. Professionals must be careful to share information with each other and with the most significant adults in the child's life: parents and teachers. Parents sometimes have to cope with conflicting ideas and suggestions from the professionals they meet. That possibility will remain so long as the professionals continue to debate amongst themselves about the benefits of one kind of school placement or method of communication as compared with another.

Around the time of initial diagnosis of deafness there can be a curious 'all or nothing' quality about the advice which parents receive. A mother may have noticed that her baby is visually rather than auditorily startled when she approaches the cot, but these early concerns about a child's hearing may be brushed aside by a Health Visitor or family doctor. We shall have more to say about the difficulties in screening young babies and children for hearing loss in Chapter 3. Suffice it to say that there is a growing awareness that parents are often the first to realise that their child's hearing is not normal and they continue to have important and sensitive insights into their child's needs. So the early concerns of a mother or father should be taken seriously and acted upon. Once a hearing loss is confirmed, advice may arrive in a flurry. A child may require audiological assessments, ENT examinations, possibly the fitting of ear moulds and hearing-aids, and the process of counselling the family begins. In some areas a child may be referred to a regional or national centre for advice. If the child's deafness is part of a range of medical conditions, parents can be saturated by hospital visits and suspended in anxiety for many months. Even when the health services are well organised and delivered, this early period is inevitably difficult for a hearing-impaired child and the family. (See, for example, parental accounts in Gregory, 1976.)

Whilst professionals exercise some choice in whether they work with deaf children, parents are usually thrust into having a deaf child and have to find ways of coming to terms with the fact emotionally. The discovery of a handicapping condition such as deafness in an infant often leads to a sequence of emotional reactions. Initial shock and numbness make information difficult to assimilate. Parents may feel guilty, bitter or angry, and this may be vented on the professionals who are trying to help. Sometimes parents go through a period of panic when they feel they cannot accept responsibility for their child. Eventually, most parents accept the situation and are able to work in partnership with professionals to achieve realistic plans and expectations. It has often been said that the parents of a deaf child grieve for the normal child they have lost. It is important, at this early stage, that parents are not left with feelings of inadequacy in their own abilities to help their child.

Perhaps the most far-reaching of the implications of the 1981 Education Act concern the more strategic role parents should be able to play in contributing to the assessment of their child's special needs, together with a more central involvement in processes of decision-making, the setting of appropriate teaching objectives, the highlighting of effective adult strategies and conditions for learning, and the ongoing evaluation and review of progress over time. Professionals are taxed with the responsibility of being accessible to parents, keeping them fully informed and dealing with them openly and honestly. We have already paid some attention to the significance of very early infant–adult encounters in mundane, domestic environments for subsequent development, particularly in language. The child's active efforts to establish social interactions with others, and in so doing to discover the power and function of language and the rules of its system, begin in the home context. Any intervention should supplement and sustain the family's essential involvement in the child's learning.

We shall be looking in some detail at the rôles, particular contributions and sequence of involvement of different professional agencies in later chapters. It can pose problems for professionals who operate from quite separate systems, such as health and education, to arrive at close working relationships between themselves and with the family. In some areas a core team is identified in order to establish effective lines of communication between the separate agencies involved, to clarify boundaries of expertise, determine key contacts with a family and co-ordinate plans. In the article by Webster, Scanlon and Bown (1985) the setting up and operation of such a team is described, where Medical Officers, teachers of the deaf and psychologists meet regularly with families to provide a cohesive framework of professional advice and support. Tumin (1978), herself the parent of a deaf child, suggests that the three most frequent sources of complaint by parents are inadequate information, unrealistic advice and not listening to what parents themselves have to say. All three are the result of poor communication between professionals *vis-à-vis* the needs of the child and the family, and are focal points for evolving good practice.

Developmental principles

A 'quiet revolution' has taken place in our understanding of normal child development. Bruner and Haste (1987) make this claim in a recent collection of articles which addresses the theme of how children make sense of the world, how they reconstruct a model of the environment, the rules which are followed and the systems which operate, from the experiences they enjoy. At one time, children were considered to be passive assimilators who just needed sufficient exposure to information and experience in order to 'soak up' what they needed to know. More recently, we have begun to accept that children are 'scientists', active in making hypotheses about the world, reflecting on experience and formulating their own proposals about how things work. But in making sense of the situations in which they find themselves, we have usually thought of children as lone operators, working independently at their problem-solving. Piaget's method, for example, was to provide the child with novel materials or situations, and then observe and question what the child did with them as evidence of emerging understanding.

The 'revolution' in our thinking to which Bruner and Haste refer concerns the rôle which adults take in shaping and scaffolding their interactions with children in order to foster development. In other words, children are not lone voyagers in discovering and piecing together the evidence from their social and intellectual encounters. The roots of this theoretical stance are to be found in writers such as Vygotsky (1962), who emphasised the importance of everyday social interactions between adults and children in the formation of intelligence and competence, particularly in language. In this chapter, the focus of attention is given to the context of adult–child encounters, the strategies which adults adopt and the active engagement which children take up, in the mundane processes of living, playing and learning together. No apology is made for beginning with an account of ordinary hearing children, their families and schools, since it is felt that clear bench-marks, based on our understanding of normal development, can only enrich and inform our approach to hearing-impaired children.

We begin with some contrasting theoretical perspectives. It is important to be aware that people's views about the nature of children's learning and development change markedly over periods of historical time, with some themes falling out of favour whilst other ideas are absorbed, reshaped and re-expressed in contemporary accounts. The important point is that how we depict childhood, the images we hold of children as learners, has a profound influence on how we set about the teaching process. When we come to consider aspects of schools as communities where adults and children are engaged in the teaching–learning process, or when we focus more specifically on areas of the curriculum, such as approaches to literacy, then our theoretical stance has a direct impact on what we consider to be 'ideal' conditions for learning.

What follows, briefly, in this chapter, concerns early infancy, how babies can be seen to act on the environment and the patterning of exchanges with adults prior to the emergence of speech. The structure, content and functions of language are considered, highlighting features which appear to facilitate development in the home context. The transition from home to school is a turning point in the nature and purpose of adult responsiveness, as children encounter formal instruction, designed to cultivate new kinds of thinking and the acquisition of tools for pursuing activities such as science and mathematics. Finally, we shall be looking at the linguistic and cognitive skills which children bring to literacy and numeracy, and the demands and developments, in turn, to which these activities give rise.

All of these issues form the backdrop to our study of the impact of deafness on the processes of linguistic, cultural and educational transmission in Chapter 4. In Chapter 1 we mentioned a growing awareness of the gulf between, on the one hand, knowledge and insights emerging from studies of normal development and, on the other hand, our application of ideas from child development theory in the field of hearing-impairment. It is this gap which we hope to narrow. In contrast to many approaches to deafness where the emphasis lies narrowly with auditory deficits, or loss of access to speech sounds, in our view broad features of adult–child interactions in social and linguistic contexts, together with shared encounters in thinking and understanding, are threatened by childhood deafness.

THEORETICAL PERSPECTIVES: THE CONTRIBUTION OF PIAGET

So great has been the influence of Piaget on contemporary views of child development that there will be very few teachers who are unfamiliar, at least in part, with his work. Piaget's theories have had a powerful effect on what goes on in primary classrooms, yet he never made the claim that his work should be applied to teaching. Piaget's main interest lay in epistemology: how we know what we know; how this knowledge is constituted; and how knowledge develops, or is constructed, over time. Piaget's method was to confront children with an ingenious situation or set of materials, observe their responses, and then question them closely on how they arrived at their answers. The method was aimed at elucidating the nature of the child's thinking at different points in development. The 'tests' which Piaget and his co-workers devised appear relatively simple, whilst his approach to discussion and questioning of children was largely unstructured. The theorising to which his observations gave rise are, however, complex and extensive. It is, in fact, the nature of logic which Piaget was attempting to chart, and not, as is frequently assumed, the course of child development. Appreciation of this distinction, together with an awareness of his methodology, are important factors to bear in mind when consideration is given to the recent challenges which have been made to Piaget's findings.

At the heart of Piagetian theory is the view that learning and development arise out of the child's own action and problem-solving. By acting on the world and discovering the consequences of action, the child comes to know and understand it. In play and exploration children get to know the world in terms of the effects of their actions upon it. As new insights are uncovered through this self-directed activity, ways may be sought subsequently to express them linguistically. But what sets the pace in the child's thinking is the child's interaction with the physical world of objects and events. Language merely encapsulates and expresses what the child has already experienced physically. The significance of this perspective has often been translated by teachers into the practical argument that children should learn by direct, 'hands-on' experience. 'Discovery' methods imply that children should first do, then discuss, draw or write.

Piaget observed and documented the development of his own three children as they grew from infancy through childhood, providing rich, theoretical interpretations of seemingly common-place aspects of their activities. When, for example, infants are observed repeatedly dropping objects to the ground and waiting for a parent to retrieve them, Piaget argues that we are witnessing the beginnings of the baby's mental life through the development of *anticipation*. Such simple, repetitive games mark the foundations of thought as infants begin to imagine and anticipate the effects of their own actions on the world. Eventually, the consequences of actions can be imagined internally by the child, without actually having to carry them out. This learned co-ordination between actions and their outcomes Piaget highlights as the 'bedrock' of children's thinking, and it is this process which lies behind his famous phrase that 'thought is internalised action'.

An emphasis on the central importance of the child's own actions as the foundation of thought and understanding is found throughout Piaget's writings on development. Consider, to take a more 'educational' example, the child's construction of the concept of number. Most 5- or 6-year-olds are unable to appreciate the fact that the number of objects in a set (say the number of sweets in a bag) will always remain the same (providing, of course, that no sweets are eaten, lost, taken away or added). The child at this stage is 'perceptually' dominated. This feature of children's thinking is easily demonstrated. For example, if the bag of sweets is spread out over a wide area, the child is likely to judge that they are more numerous than when scooped together. The child's concept of amount or number is determined by the *appearance* of the set, not the 'real' number.

Even if children can recite lists of numbers, it does not follow that they can understand the *concepts* underlying the counting process. Teaching children practices like how to count before they have developed the number concept leads to mere 'rote' learning, not understanding. More generally, attempts to teach children procedures or verbal 'tricks', like reciting numbers, cannot foster development. If we assume that such tactics are important in fostering understanding, we shall fall prey to what Piaget called 'magical thinking'. Children will come, in time, to understand number by their own actions on sets of objects. They will discover that it is in the nature of things that you cannot change the number of objects in a given set simply by moving them around. Then they will really understand what number words really mean: that they refer to an abstract concept. We, as parents and teachers, may then claim credit for having 'taught' them number concepts by asking them to recite number labels. Such claims, according to Piaget, are wrong. More generally still, any attempt to teach, question, drill or demonstrate things to children before they are ready to learn can only engender frustration, bemusement and, perhaps, a sense of incompetence.

What part does social experience play in children's development? Piaget does suggest that through talking with others, particularly other children, points of view may be reconsidered if conflicts arise. But it is the child's interaction with the physical world which provides the timing and motivation for change, and any social facilitation of development only works when the child is ready to move forward. So, for Piaget, processes of social interaction have a low-key effect and are not implicated in fostering development.

At the core of Piaget's theory is the proposition that children's thinking is different in kind from that of more mature individuals. However, all children develop through the same sequence of stages before achieving mature, rational thought. Each stage is built on the one which precedes it, whilst the structure of children's thinking at each stage has distinctive features, not shared by children at other stages or by adults. At any one stage, then, the child has a particular logic for exploring the world, which changes as events and experiences are encountered that challenge the logic constructed. Each stage yields a different way of understanding from the one it grows out of and replaces, by a series of intellectual revolutions. It follows that the impact of teaching on what the child learns varies as a function of the child's developmental stage. It may be possible, using the example already given, to teach a 5-year-old to recite the numbers from one to five by rote methods. But a true concept of numbers, that some properties of sets remain invariant despite changes in appearance, will depend on the child's own self-directed physical actions.

How does the child's own activity lead to changes in understanding? Piaget describes the strategies which children use to explore as 'schemata'. Grasping and mouthing an object, like a bottle, are examples of the latter. Piaget also describes two main ways through which experience is organised. Firstly, new features can be taken in by, or assimilated to, an existing schema. For example, if a bottle can be grasped and mouthed, any new container, such as a beaker, can be assimilated successfully to the schema, in order to drink. The second process is that of accommodation. Here the basic strategies, concepts or schemata must be changed in order to cope with new situations. For example, if the beaker is now placed out of reach, the child must crawl towards it before grasping, mouthing and sucking. Experience is always approached with the child's existing repertoire of schemata. Through assimilation and accommodation, the child's schemata gradually become more sophisticated. Some accommodations require dramatic shifts in the structure of the child's understanding of the world, particularly those which herald a change in stage.

In the first two years or so (the sensori-motor stage) the child's concepts are dominated by physical explorations such as reaching, pulling, grasping and mouthing. Initially, children do not distinguish between their own bodies and outside objects or events. The baby may repeat an action such as hitting a mobile over the cot in order to set it in motion, but the action and its consequence are part of a continuous flow: an undifferentiated schema, where the child's hand movements are not, for the child, a separate or distinct part of the whole experience of interacting with the mobile. In time, thanks to experiences in playing with their bodies and the body's potential for movement, infants begin to discover the physical limits or contours of their own bodies and thus start to distinguish 'self' from 'objects' (including other people). Here, too, action remains all important. The infant begins to realise that a given perceptual impression (what adults, for example, might call the sight of a bottle) can be grasped, moved, put into the mouth and, under certain conditions, sucked to yield specific tastes and internal feelings.

Thus objects, like bottles of liquid, become *known* to the child in terms of what they can do to them and to what effect. As the baby starts to anticipate the tastes and feelings which follow on from specific actions on particular perceptual impressions, thought about objects and recognition of objects begins. Infants may then begin to discover the fact that similar effects on the world can be realised by different actions. Thus a bottle may be gained by grasping and sucking or, if it fails to come to hand when reached towards, by looking at a parent and making a sound. The point at which infants can begin to imagine different ways of achieving the same ends without actually performing them is the onset of practical intelligence, as internalised mental actions start to represent physical actions. Towards the end of the period, the infant is able to represent the world in other symbols. When the child uses bricks to play cars, the pretend objects are assimilated into existing ideas about the world, with the important shift that one thing can now symbolise another in the child's imagination.

In the second, preconceptual, stage, from around two to seven years, the child's thinking is characterised by 'transductive' logic. What Piaget means by this term is best illustrated with an example. When, say, a young child announces that it cannot yet be night-time because the curtains are not drawn, the child shows some evidence of reasoning, but it is a form of reasoning governed by past associations between events which form a regular sequence. From an adult's perspective, children's thinking at this stage often seems idiosyncratic and rather capricious, as they centre on 'irrelevant' aspects of situations to make sense of events in the world. Whereas adults and other children reason deductively and logically, the child in the intuitive stage seems to leap from idea to idea without regard for the demands of logic. Such reasoning is 'transductive'.

Because young children have yet to develop the ability to guide their perception of the world and their thinking about it in line with the dictates of logic, their understanding of concepts which seem 'natural' and transparent to adults is, in fact, 'preconceptual'. Piaget invented a range of ingenious problems which he used to explore and illustrate the nature of such children's thinking. In one, for instance, he asked young children to make judgements about the amount of liquid in two containers. If the containers are identical in shape and size and the liquid in each comes to the same level, 4- and 5-year-olds usually have no hesitation in judging that both contain the same amount. However if, in full view of the child, the content of one is poured into another container with a different shape (for example, longer and narrower) children at this age and stage will probably say that there is more liquid in this new container than there is in the one left untouched. Here, too, as in the night-time example, children base their judgement on one feature of the situation (usually height) but do not, and cannot, take account of the fact that other considerations (such as differences in width) must, logically, be taken into account in reaching a judgement. In Piaget's terms, children in this stage cannot *co-ordinate* more than one focus of attention. Thus they literally cannot see that when the liquid is poured from one container to another it does not involve a change in amount. Attention to relative height reveals a change in appearance which, lacking logic, children believe signals a change in amount.

In the third stage of concrete operations, from around seven to eleven years, schemata such as addition, subtraction and multiplication are gained. The child is aware that certain properties of objects, such as weight, volume or quantity, stay the same even when visible changes take place, as in the water jar experiment. To do this the child has to step back from the perceptual evidence, and weigh all the relevant aspects together with the relationships between them. The child's thinking is no longer intuitive, based on single points of comparison. Inductive logic also characterises this stage: the child can abstract features of objects to form generalisations of classes (such as: dogs and cats are both animals).

In the last period of cognitive development (formal operations) from age twelve years on, the structure of the child's intelligence develops towards increasing levels of abstraction, released from the concrete 'here and now'. Eventually, the adolescent is able to reason about hypothetical events with no material evidence. For Piaget, the natural culmination of intellectual growth is the achievement of formal, logical thinking which enables the internal setting up of hypotheses and propositions about the world. In many people's minds, formal thinking is associated with the kind of intellectual demands made by secondary schooling in the later stages, in disciplines where a high level of conceptual understanding is required.

Piaget's work has not been accepted uncritically. For example, a number of researchers have rerun some of the classical experiments with slight modifications to examine the conditions under which children are able to display the level of their intellectual development. Piaget illustrated the concept of egocentrism using a 'three mountains' demonstration in which a three-dimensional model is shown to the child. A number of pictures are given to the child which depict how the mountain scene appears from different observation points. When children below six years were shown pictures of the model from different angles and asked which picture represents what another person, or doll, might see from a separate vantage point, the children usually selected the picture which represented their own point of view. Piaget interprets this as 'egocentrism': the child cannot stand back from the situation to construct or imagine another point of view. Donaldson (1978), however, describes several situations in which children as young as three years are able to see other points of view and are not egocentric in their thinking. Instead of the three mountains task, children were given a task involving a doll hiding from a policeman. This task also requires judgements to be made on what can be seen from different vantage points. The motives of the dolls and the policeman were quickly grasped by 3-year-olds in this experiment, who were able to make the kind of objective judgements of which Piaget felt young children incapable.

The essential modification which Donaldson made is that the new task is much more dramatically relevant to the child. When tasks are given to children in which the actions to be performed or imagined involve familiar, meaningful activities (like 'hiding') the child may respond appropriately. Similarly, in a rerun of a conservation experiment, one of the original beakers used had a cracked, razor-sharp rim. The child's attention was drawn to this and it was explained that using such a beaker would be dangerous. The liquid was then transferred to another (differently shaped) container. Asked to compare quantities after pouring, children were more likely to be successful than when no reason for the experimenter's actions was given (Light, Buckingham and Roberts, 1979).

Many other points have been made about Piaget's methods of observation and questioning. Children may simply misunderstand instructions, or misread what it is that the experimenter covertly requires of the child. Most of these criticisms are directed at Piaget's underestimation of the social conditions in which these experiments took place. Whilst such criticisms may be important to our view of child development, they do not really have much bearing on Piaget's primary concern: the nature of logic. More recently, however, critical attention has been drawn to the significance of formal logic in relation to schooling, literacy and adult problem-solving (Wood, 1988).

Perhaps the greatest contribution which Piaget has made to our understanding of child development is his emphasis on children as active enquirers, constructing their own models of the world through physical experiment and exploration, architects of their own understanding. These seminal views find their place in our own designs for the ideal learning environment.

SOVIET PSYCHOLOGY AND CHILD DEVELOPMENT

Other accounts of development, such as those provided by Soviet psychologists (Luria, 1961; Vygotsky, 1962), differ in some important respects from Piagetian theory. Unlike Piaget, Vygotsky ascribes great importance to the rôle of teaching in the development of the young. Indeed, he defines intelligence as the capacity to learn from instruction. Adults frequently help children to accomplish things which they are unable to achieve alone. When children encounter the activities involved in using their culture's symbols, in terms of its languages, books, media and visual arts, they are introduced to value systems and social constructions which become a part of their thinking. It is through social relationships, Luria suggests, that 'age-old human experience is passed onto the child' (Luria, 1961, page 1). A child's potential for learning is often realised in social and intellectual encounters with the more mature. In Vygotsky's terms, interactions between children and more knowledgeable peers, siblings, parents, relatives and teachers are the main vehicle for transmitting cultural practices and knowledge.

Vygotsky refers to the gap between what children can do alone and what might be achieved with the help of others more skilled than themselves as the 'zone of proximal development'. Whilst Piaget saw learning 'readiness' in terms of the child's current level of thinking, with the teacher contributing appropriate materials and activities to aid the child's discovery, Vygotsky discusses 'readiness' in relation to what could be achieved with appropriate teaching. In other words, co-operatively achieved success is at the heart of learning and development.

Soviet psychologists also differ radically from Piaget in their view of the contribution which language makes to thinking and learning. Piaget argues that language has no influential effect on the child's thinking, at least in the stages before formal operations, since mental operations derive from physical action, not talk. The Soviet position is that language both facilitates and regulates thinking activity. Vygotsky says that thought and speech develop along separate lines in the first two years of life. Initially, the child's speech is external and serves a social function. Later on, speech begins to serve an internal function in providing the tools for thinking. Words become the inner code for representing the world, the basic structures of understanding.

Both Piaget and the Soviet psychologists emphasise the importance of direct physical experience as children grasp, lift, handle and push objects around. However, the Soviet view is that language does not simply reflect concepts already formed non-verbally. Rather, language begins to organise and modify thinking and behaviour. Through talking with others the child is exposed to the range of functions of language, what can be 'done' with words, and to the actions and activities to which they refer. How does all this come about? Well, the Soviet psychologists argue that mature thinking involves a degree of self-regulation. It involves planning, making suggestions to, reminding and evaluating oneself. Through social interaction with the more mature, children are exposed to examples of how others tackle problems and manage their thinking. Such self-regulatory practices are gradually internalised by the child. By co-operating in the performance of everyday tasks, children discover ways of planning, organising and regulating their own practical and cognitive activities. What children learn in terms of skills, values, attitudes and rôles will be common features shared by others in their social environment. Later on, when children enter school, they will be introduced to ways of thinking which may be relatively unfamiliar. To the extent that these involve aspects of attention control, literacy and numeracy, schools offer children special forms of such 'self-regulation'.

The important contribution that Vygotsky and his colleagues have made to our own thinking concerns the rôles of adults and teachers in structuring and fostering development. Through social encounters children experience the power and function of language, and have access to a wide range of shared cultural values and meanings. For the Soviet psychologists the processes which underlie thinking are not exclusive inventions of the child, but are reconstructed in the course of co-operative interactions with the more mature. An emphasis on the social functions of language, together with an approach to the school curriculum which emphasises the child's own planning and self-regulation of thinking, lies at the heart of our own philosophy.

BRUNER'S THEORIES OF EDUCATION

Finally, we give here a brief summary of the views of a seminal contemporary psychologist, J. S. Bruner. He shares with Piaget and the Soviet theorists an emphasis on the importance of physical action and problem-solving. Like Piaget, Bruner believes that abstract thinking should grow out of practical experience. When children are taught how to manipulate abstract procedures, such as solving mathematical equations, without understanding the concepts which lie behind them, empty knowledge — procedures without meaning — are the result. Such learning cannot be generalised successfully, or used to solve real-life problems, and is likely to be quickly forgotten. However, Bruner was interested not so much in an overall structure of logic as in the problem-solving strategies brought by children and adults to specific situations. Bruner suggests that individuals do not utilise a single method or logic in thinking and reasoning. Instead, they adopt one of a number of strategies which differ in scope, power and efficiency. Bruner's approach to learning is a useful one, for example in accounting for some of the differences between good and poor readers, and we shall be considering aspects of children's reading strategies in detail later in the book. For Bruner (1984), reading is firmly set within a nexus of language learning activities where children test out their own hypotheses about print, just as they do about spoken language. This has important implications for how reading is introduced to children: whether teaching builds on what children already know about spoken language, in a personalised and meaningful way, tied to relevant experience; or whether reading is broken down into small sub-steps, such as letter-shapes and sounds, taught through repetition, as a linear, decoding activity.

Effective learning, in Bruner's terms, is about the child coming to know 'how', not simply 'that'. Knowing 'how' is constituted in the child's acquisition of skills, plans and procedures. Bruner shares with Vygotsky the belief that learning (including learning to read) is a collaborative process, and the nature of the adult–child partnership is crucial. In Chapter 1 the notion of adult contingency was mentioned. Adults respond contingently when they pace the amount of help given to children on the basis of the child's moment-to-moment understanding, and stand back when the child has grasped enough of the task at hand to allow room for initiative. Responsive adults structure tasks for and with children, so that the purpose of an activity is clear and success is experienced as demands are made, without losing sight of what the long-range goal may be. The adult 'scaffolds' the learning situation by focusing the child's attention on the relevant aspects of the task, making suggestions, reminding the child and giving prompts when the child veers off course, weighing the significance of any findings with the child and giving insights into how the adult might manage the problem, whilst also providing praise and reassurance to maintain interest and confirm achievements (Wood, Bruner and Ross, 1976).

Bruner emphasises that, whilst we may have accepted the idea of the child as 'active scientist', constructing hypotheses about the world and interacting with the physical environment, we still tend to think of children working alone at their problem-solving. Departing from Piaget, Bruner argues that making sense of the world is a social process which is always situated within a cultural and historical context. Furthermore, it is through language that children interact with adults, and language which, at one and the same time, aids the child's entry into culture. It does so by providing a medium for interpreting and evaluating events. Value-laden views uttered by a 4-year-old, such as 'I'm only a girl' or 'The much you don't like things, the gooder they are for you' (such as cabbage), are examples of cultural attitudes recreated and handed on.

A word about methodology is appropriate. In keeping with the older view of the child as an independent little researcher, making sense of the world, Piaget's method was to provide the child with new materials or controlled situations, as a basis for observation and questioning. Bruner's new emphasis, in contrast, leads to observations of the child in a normally complex situation, such as at home or in school, and studying the child's ordinary efforts to cope with it. Bruner suggests that it is only by taking into account the social intentions of conversation partners in their mundane settings that we can interpret how meanings are negotiated, whilst also gaining access to the developmental process: how adults are intuitively expert at engaging children as language novices and fostering their abilities.

To illustrate this shift in method, an example is taken from Bruner and Haste (1987). A 2-year-old, Sophie, is sat on her father's knee while he is being interviewed. She tries to attract his attention by talking to him and pulling at him, and eventually announces 'Want to do a poo'. The interviewer suggest she might be taken upstairs, but the father replies that Sophie is expressing boredom, rather than biological need, and the child is placated with a set of Russian dolls and told to wait until she gets home. Here, despite what the participants say, the real script of the situation is: 'Daddy is busy, Sophie is bored, child tries to distract adult'. In fact, what the child says is not taken literally and can only be understood by referring to the script. In Bruner's terms this demonstrates how competent small children are in understanding the social context, and at reading intentions and motives (no less competent than the father, who responds by making explicit the child's covert motives).

Sophie and her father adjust what they say and do in ways which incorporate individual needs, interpretation of the social context and strategies for manipulating others. One can understand the child's behaviour only by observing how she tries to cope with this everyday, but contextually rich encounter. From the father's responses, the child is also indirectly learning something about socially appropriate behaviour. Bruner's highlighting of language interaction as the 'scaffold' which enables the child to express and understand the nature of events and underlying intentions is central to much of current thinking. We shall be returning at a number of points in this book to the framework of interaction within which adults and children negotiate their linguistic and social meanings.

Bruner has also written a great deal about the rôles of schools and teachers (Bruner, 1971). Effective teaching exposes children to ways of thinking which are inherent in the subject matter. In early linguistic interactions the child is engaged as a language partner almost from the outset, taking turns and filling slots in conversation, well before the emergence of speech. In beginning reading, children are helped by facilitative adults to behave as readers from the outset, as meaning is uncovered in stories shared, and the function and purpose of reading is apparent. By the same token, when children are introduced to subjects such as science, history or mathematics, Bruner would argue that children must learn the intentions and strategies which motivate the discipline and those who practise it. That is, rather than simply learning rote facts and information *contained within* the subject, children acquire the procedures, skills and sense of purpose which *underlie* the subject. At all levels, effective learning and teaching means that children are asked to behave as conversation partners, readers, historians, geographers or whichever, from the start.

Schools change children. Learning in classrooms, according to Bruner, involves social practices, linguistic skills and intellectual demands that are seldom if ever encountered in other learning contexts. Schools are a relatively recent invention and some non-technical and non-literate societies still manage to survive, and their children to develop, without them. In such societies, children learn their adult rôles and acquire cultural skills through observation, play and gradual mastery in the same contexts that those skills are practised by the mature. Learning in school is much more 'decontextualised', in that children are often asked to think and learn about events that lie outside the classroom and to develop and perfect skills that may only eventually be applied in the workplace. The change from the contextualised learning of non-schooled cultures to learning in classrooms, Bruner goes on to say, creates new demands on the functions of language and leads to new ways of thinking. We will explore this general idea later in a discussion of the development of reading and writing.

Whilst, if Bruner is right, schools engender new ways of learning and thinking, they may not provide optimum environments for types or styles of adult–child interaction which lie at the heart of the development of language and communication. This argument, and its implications for the education of deaf and hearing-impaired children, will be of concern to us anon.

We have spent some time on the three images of development offered by Piaget, the Soviet psychologists and Bruner in order to make explicit the theoretical foundations which underpin our thinking. All three value highly the notion that children are active in their problem-solving, architects of their own 'knowing'. But there are distinct differences in their views on the rôles which language, communication and schools play in the developmental process. It is from Bruner and Vygotsky, for example, that we have taken an emphasis on learning as a collaborative partnership between children and adults, through which children gradually acquire expertise and reconstruct cultural values and attitudes. From all three, influences are acknowledged which have had a profound effect on how we construe the nature of children's development, and how, in turn, we might set about designing optimal conditions for learning.

FROM COMMUNICATION TO LANGUAGE

Whatever view one takes about the rôle of communication in development, that view has to be consistent with what we know about the course of language acquisition in children. Thanks to two decades of vigorous research into language acquisition, we know a great deal. Here, we review some of the major findings which have emerged from this work, before moving on to consider its implications for the education of hearing-impaired children.

The most obvious starting point for thinking about the emergence of language in children is the appearance of their first recognisable words. However, the child's first words actually represent the culmination of a process of communication which begins at birth. Observations of newborn babies, for example, show that they arrive in the world already sensitive to very specific types of experience and with an inborn capacity to organise those experiences. Neonates are not, as was once widely supposed, born as 'blank slates' or passive, unformed beings. The use of video-tape and the invention of sensitive experimental methods for studying infant behaviour have demonstrated, to the contrary, that they are selective, active and self-organising in the earliest days and weeks of life. For example, a touch on the neonate's cheek will usually elicit a rooting, sucking response. Babies also respond selectively to sounds and will turn to locate a sound source. Gentle, low-frequency, repetitive sounds tend to soothe, whilst loud, percussive noises tend to startle. Offered a choice between the mother's breastpad and that of another breastfeeding woman, infants will usually turn to their mother's. Neonates show marked preferences for looking at human faces, whilst the combination of a human face and speech is almost irresistibly attractive.

By two weeks of age, babies are able to distinguish the mother's face and voice from those of a stranger. In the experiment reported by Kuhl (1983), infants of two months were more likely to look at films of their mother's moving faces which matched up with the accompanying taped speech sounds. Other studies have shown that, given appropriate circumstances, babies will strive to control their own environment in order to sustain events that interest them. One of the problems in trying to study the capacities of the very young is that their bodies are so weak in the first few months of life that they cannot, for instance, raise their arms. The muscles are so underdeveloped that they are unable to fight gravity. However, even the youngest baby can suck! When provided with a nipple containing a small switch which can be used to control lights or to bring a film into focus, they soon discover how to turn lights on or to maintain an attractive picture in focus by adjusting their own sucking behaviour. Thus the apparent incompetence of babies stems, at least in part, from the weakness of their bodies, not from an inability to sense or control their environment.

These and many other studies (Bower, 1977) have led students of infant behaviour to reject the view that infants are helpless, psychologically unformed and unable to learn. Rather, we now recognise that babies are oriented from the moment of birth to test out the environment, to explore and manipulate, to recognise regularities, to achieve goals and make sense of things, but above all else to interact with their caregivers and maintain social contact. The studies by Trevarthen (1979), in highlighting this apparent sociability of the human infant at such an early age, lead to the suggestion that some form of in-built, biological mechanism for survival is involved. Split-screen film of mothers sitting opposite their babies of three months of age show that the infant's social interactions are already highly structured. The infant's gestures and movements, such as frowning or tongue-movements, alternate with similar responses from the mother, in a relationship of mutual attention which has been described as 'protoconversation'.

From the outset, then, babies display an urge to act on and learn more about the environment, through social interaction and communication with others. Mothers collaborate by deliberately stimulating the infant through singing, handling and cuddling. During feeding there may be periods of intense sucking, alternated with pauses when the mother may talk to or 'jiggle' the child. She may follow the flow of the baby's attention and put into words what she thinks the child is feeling or experiencing: 'You've had enough now, haven't you?', 'Who's a tired boy?', 'Let's change that nasty nappy'. The baby's laughing, cooing, crying and gurgling is often reciprocated by the mother taking a turn to respond. Many early interactions have this on/off, first you/then me pattern, as both infant and mother learn to read signals in each other's behaviour.

In all these situations, the child's activity is suffused with adult commentary, which overlays and offers an interpretation of ongoing experiences whilst also engaging the child. Almost all that the infant offers in terms of facial expressions, movements and sounds is likely to be interpreted as 'meaningful' by the adults, and their meaning put into words. Because the adult's reactions are tied contingently to the child's, what might be spontaneous responses from the child are taken up, made sense of in relation to the surrounding context, and attributed with meaning. Infants are thus construed as conversational partners, as if they already had intentions to communicate. When babies come to produce an action with the clear expectation that the adult will respond in a predictable way, they may show signs of alarm and anxiety if the adult does not respond as expected. By being treated as though they had intentions, infants come to expect that things will happen as a result of their own actions. These early exchanges can be considered as foundations for later conversation skills, as the conventions of giving a message and eliciting a response are met, rehearsed and perfected.

Early infant environments have some other features which enable the sharing of meaning between adult and baby, and set adult speech within predictable 'formats' or routines. The infant's world often presents repetitive cycles of bathing, dressing, feeding and changing, interspersed with play. In short, the infant's experiences are externally structured and regulated by caretakers. Within such familiar formats, infants come to discover connections between tones of voice, utterances, persons and events. One of the authors' children, aged fifteen months, upon hearing 'night-night' would begin thumb-sucking in anticipation of being laid in the cot. The mere sight of the changing mat was enough to bring screams of protest at the anticipated nappy-change to come! The familiarity of these routines, and the adult speech and behaviours which accompany them, enable infants to discover regularities, patterns and acts of communication in their encounters with others.

In this period of childhood, infants also spend a long time doing a very limited number of things. Another of the authors' children, at about twelve months of age, would sit opening and closing cupboards for hours on end, later extending this to doors, drawers, tins with lids, boxes, and so forth. Other children bang or throw everything in reach, or try out a range of actions on the same object. Bruner refers to this as 'systematicity' (1983, page 28), whereby the child tries out routines, systematically dealing with objects, making a lot out of a little, seeking or imposing order and rules on environmental events. In early play, as in later language activities, children seem geared to generate and to combine a small set of elements, in order to create a larger set of possibilities.

THE TRIANGLE OF REFERENCE

By six months the infant's predisposition towards other humans and the willingness of adults to respond have established the basis for communication. An important development from this is enjoyed in turn-taking games when joint attention is distributed over a patterned sequence of events. Games such as 'Clap hands', 'This little piggy went to market' and 'I can see you' encourage the child to listen to the sounds and rhythms of speech and, at a critical point, the child is expected to respond in return. Alternate exchanges, when first the adult then the child responds, are prototypes for later dialogues in which a fundamental part is knowing when to talk and when to listen.

An important step is taken when the outside world is brought into the mutual attention of the adult and child (see Figure 2.1). An object or event in the environment attracts the child's interest. The infant's visual exploration is 'mirrored' by the adult, who looks where the baby looks and talks about the presumed object of the infant's attentions. More remarkably, by the second half of the first year the baby begins to follow the adult's line of gaze. Such shared attention to common objects and events increases the probability that adult and child will be looking at the same things and, when the adult names things or interprets an event, the shared visual experience of the world is tied to the patterns of language used to refer to it. To put this another way, the adult helps to bring the infant's experience into conjunction with language, emphasising the relationship between speech sounds and events.

In the first year, a strong 'No!' from adult to child in a situation, for example where a child is eating soil in the garden, conveys meaning through intonation or mood, well before words are recognised. Infants begin to recognise questions ('What's that?') and statements ('That's a ... ') through intonation contours, and are able to fill gaps or pauses left by the adult, if only by a grunt or 'da'. Game formats at this stage, such as 'Bye-bye', 'Peek-a-boo' or 'Ride a cock horse', help the child to recognise tones, words and phrases in repetitive contexts, about the time that object-labelling begins. It can be said

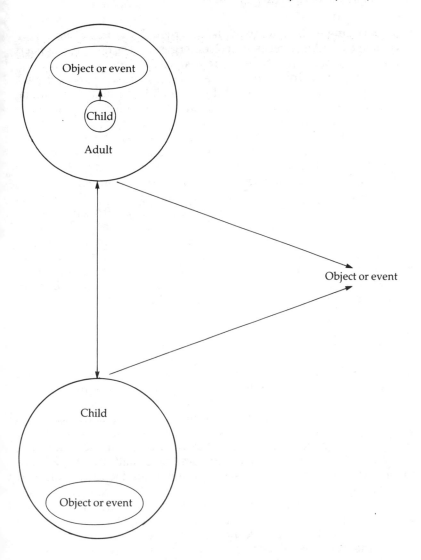

The infant attends to some object or event in the situation. The adult entertains a theory or interpretation of what the infant is attending to and, perhaps, a sense of what the infant is feeling (e.g. fear on seeing a dog; joy on catching sight of a loved one). This theory influences both what the adult says and the tone of voice in which it is said.

Figure 2.1 *Triangle of reference*

that a 'triangle of reference' is completed by the child at an increasingly verbal level as speech emerges, and as the adult expects more precise meanings to be expressed by the child.

To summarise, the period of language acquisition begins well before the first words, when adults and children interact in familiar formats, which serve as a kind of microcosm for later language dialogue. Whilst adults seem set to provide the right conditions for learning, children come into the world with a number of resources which orient them towards humans, means–end exploration and language. A first principle is that infants are active and goal-directed in seeking out patterns and regularities in the environment. Second, infants are inherently social and are geared to respond to human faces and behaviour. This leads to a third principle, that both infant and adult are capable of reading intentions in each other's behaviour and respond to many features of a context, not just sounds or words. Finally, even small babies are capable of abstracting rules and making predictions, as the experiments with neonates reported earlier demonstrate. None of these principles engenders language *per se*, but they do make language possible.

STAGE I: FIRST SOUNDS AND WORDS

Children's entry into language rests on a number of preceding accomplishments. The child must develop a sensitivity to the distinctive sound contrasts of the particular language being used. At the same time, the patterning of grammatical constraints has to be discovered, so that children gradually come to 'know' and use the rules which govern how words are formed, and how they are organised in phrase, clause and sentence patterns to form a meaningful sequence. Sounds and grammar are inextricably linked with the child's growing awareness of how the world works and how the child can gain purchase on the world: in other words, how to realise intentions and get things done through language. Within the early months of pre-verbal development, children come to realise the existence of a code, a relationship between sounds and meanings. But how far can language acquisition be thought of as cracking that linguistic code?

In fact, children learning language are doing far more than mastering a code. Children do not simply imitate the sounds of speech that they hear around them. Entry into language is really a process of co-operating and negotiating with the more mature members of the speech community. What is negotiated are ways of using language to make intentions clear and to understand the meanings of others. This view of language acquisition as a process of active rediscovery or reinvention of language through the vigorous efforts of the child has some important implications. Firstly, whilst adults may provide opportunities for linguistic interaction and adopt a range of strategies which enable the child to make sense of the system, the adult's rôle in this process is one of facilitator, not teacher. Second, linguistic communication cannot be studied separately from the contexts in which it arises and in which it is used. Communication is usually tied to a meaningful and purposeful situation which has real significance for the participants, however mundane. Finally, the answer to the question 'How do children learn language?' is to be found in the way in which the child's language partners pattern their encounters so that the child has a 'privileged access' to the shared system (Bruner, 1983, page 11).

The linguist Halliday (1975) recorded the utterances of his son, Nigel, from nine to eighteen months of age, in order to discover the range of functions which language serves. Halliday was careful not to base his analysis on the child's first sounds or the early structure of the child's grammar. Rather, he developed a theory about the underlying purposes or systems of meaning in language, and from this fashioned an account of the growth of verbal communication. He looks beyond the form of language itself (i.e. sound patterns and word order) to the context of interaction within which language is used. Halliday has given us a useful account of the intentions children realise through language, the kinds of things they get to do with their first words or sounds. According to Halliday, there are seven distinct functions which children use as a means to an end, with the initial power of language focused in the social action it serves.

(1) Instrumental

This is the 'I want' function, used to express material needs such as hunger or thirst, which enables the child to obtain goods and services, or a coveted toy.

(2) Regulatory

In this function, children use language to control the behaviour of others, in just the same way that others try to control them. It is the 'Do as I tell you' function, and includes meanings such as 'Let's go home now', 'Play with me' and 'Do that again'.

(3) Interactional

Children use language in this function to interact socially with those around them. This could be glossed as the 'me and you' function, including meanings such as 'Hello', 'I'm missing you' and 'I'm happy to see you'.

(4) Personal

Here language is used to express personal feelings, interest and pleasure in things, together with reactions of boredom, withdrawal or disgust. Halliday calls this the 'Here I come' function: 'I'm fed up in the car', 'I like cuddling Daddy', 'That's too hot'.

(5) Heuristic

The heuristic, or learning, function is used by the child to explore the environment and find things out. This is the 'Tell me why?' function, which later develops into a wide range of questioning forms, such as 'Where?', 'What?' and 'Who?'. In the early stages, this is the means by which the child makes demands for labels, but it is also the means by which children later categorise and discover the world.

(6) Imaginative

This is the means by which children create worlds of their own, the 'Let's pretend' function of language. Gradually, this will evolve into pretend play, story and make-believe. Through this function, the young child is able to express meanings such as 'What if?', 'I wish ... ' and 'I might be ... '.

(7) Informative

The final function of language is also the last to emerge in infancy, although it is dominant in adults' use of language and in adults' image of language use. This is the 'Let me tell you something' function, and includes meanings such as 'There's a strange animal in the garden' and 'Mummy's got one too'.

Halliday's account is useful for a number of reasons. He reinforces the point that children learn how to mean, how to communicate their needs, intentions, likes and dislikes, well before they are able to produce the sounds and words of the adult system. The wide range of functions to which language is put serve mainly social, interactive, manipulative and expressive purposes. Children use the informative function least of all to begin with: an important issue when we come to consider a programme of intervention for children with language learning difficulties at home or in school.

In the following example, adapted from Halliday (1975, page 90), Nigel, as a 1-year-old, has been listing some of the things he saw the day before:

Mother: Oh you saw some flags?
Nigel *(holding out palm)*: Geeya.
Mother: And you had some gravel.
Nigel *(touching palm, lips rounded, very quiet)*: Ooh!
Father: And you hurt your hand with the gravel?
Mother: No, that was with the stick, the one with prickles on.
Nigel: Bla.
Mother: And there was blood on it, yes.

Nigel is engaged by his parents in this dialogue as a genuine language partner, with something important to say. Conversation is handed back to the child when slots are left for him to fill. The adults interpret his utterances, however immature or incomplete they may seem, and make them explicit, reading his intentions and putting them into words. A helpful factor here is that the family know a great deal about the infant's social world and are able to make this kind of generous interpretation of what the child is trying to say from knowing the child's day-to-day experience.

As Halliday shows, infants are capable of expressing intentions, demands and feelings through non-verbal communication and the rhythm and intonation of their voices, well before they master the vocabulary or grammar of their native tongue. More important is the stress such a view lays on the importance of interaction between infants and adults in laying the foundations for the acquisition of speech itself. Looked at in this way, the development of understanding and use of spoken language cannot be divorced from a broader study of *communication*. To be sure, as the child gains increasing command of the native tongue, reliance on non-verbal and pre-verbal communication becomes less marked, as does the rôle of the more mature in making sense of what it is the child is trying to mean.

With the growing mastery of speech and the structures of language comes greater responsibility for making oneself understood without reliance on shared experience, common formats or non-verbal communication. Though acts of speech, in our view, are never completely divorced from non-verbal communication (until, perhaps, we come to consider written communication), the role of grammar in the achievement of mutual understanding clearly becomes more central as children grow to master their native tongue. Research into the growth of such mastery is now well established, and the major stages that children pass through *en route* to mature language have been identified. However, before we turn to a consideration of these, it should be borne in mind, when models of development are presented, that this is one aspect of human behaviour where the sum is always greater than its constituent parts.

Linguists have recently delineated series of stages in language growth, with each stage characterised by particular features. Whilst we do make references to such stages, it should also be remembered that there can be tremendous differences between children, as well as variations within the individual, in the rate at which skills and strategies are acquired. What seems to hold true is that most ordinary children pass through similar stages of language growth as they move towards the adult system. Some children do this more or less quickly than others, with many overlaps between stages. For further discussion and details of stage analyses see Webster and McConnell (1987).

What features characterise the first stages of sound or phonological development? A very wide range of sounds can be produced by the human vocal apparatus, although only a small set of sound contrasts are used in the adult system. In English there are 40 or so distinctive sound contrasts, or phonemes, which make up the phonology of the language. (As an example of a phoneme, 'him' is discriminated from 'hid' by the contrast between 'm' and 'd' at the end of the word.) To begin with, infants express their feelings or states of being with cooing, crying, gurgling, laughing and vocalising. This is sometimes considered to be a practice phase when infants can also develop finer control of tongue, lip and speech muscles. It has been noticed that the early vocalisations of hearing-impaired infants up to the age of about six months are similar to those of normally hearing children. This suggests that this early stage does not depend on children being able to hear the speech of those around them. Infants from different cultural backgrounds also show little influence of the home language at this stage.

In learning to refer and to mean there is an obvious payoff for the child in working out how to produce and interpret the sounds of the more mature system. So, fairly quickly, the child is influenced by the speech sounds heard, and vocalisation becomes much more purposeful and speechlike, with sounds like consonants, vowels, their combination and repetition appearing. This is usually referred to as 'babble'. Sounds not used in the speech environment eventually drop out of the child's babble, whilst features such as rhythm, tone of voice and intonation take on the characteristics of the specific language being used by others. In the case of the hearing-impaired child, by the end of the first year a deaf child's vocalisations would be fewer, flatter and less rhythmical, with much less variation in tone than those of the hearing child.

From about nine months onwards, infants begin to use sounds consistently which can be interpreted as first words. One of the authors' children used 'bo-bo' to refer to her feeding bottle, and with a range of gestures, pointing and intonation 'bo-bo' could mean 'I'm thirsty', 'Where's my bottle?' or 'This is too hot'. Most children control consonant sounds such as 'b', 'm', 'p', or 'w', produced at the front of the mouth, before back consonants, such as 'k' or 'g'. So, too, children often simplify the pronunciation of words with many sounds, such as 'apa' for 'apples', 'beki' for 'breakfast' and 'cho-cho' for 'chocolate'. In these early stages almost all children reduce the sounds in clusters of consonants that begin words to a single consonant, such as 'dink' for 'drink' and 'poon' for 'spoon'. It is also usual for children to babble sounds in the pre-word stage which later disappear as the child learns how to use speech sounds more systematically. An observation sometimes made of deaf children is that they appear to 'stop talking', having babbled. But it can also be observed in hearing children that fluency falters as the babbling stage moves into the organisation of more speechlike utterances. One child, who produced a perfect 'turtle' at fifteen months to refer to a toy in his bath, later began to say 'kurka' in line with the way he said other words at this time (de Villiers and de Villiers, 1979).

The first words usually appear, as we have said, by nine to twelve months, although some 8-month-olds are already using words, whilst some 18-month-olds have yet to produce a recognisable one. We have mentioned that the 'here and now' of the environment is brought into the mutual attention of the adult and child to form a reference triangle (Figure 2.1). So it is not surprising to learn that, when studies have been made of children's early vocabularies, the first words acquired, from an adult perspective, appear to refer to food ('biccy', 'dink'), toys ('teddy', 'brm-brm') and animals ('doggy', 'horsey'). In Nelson's (1973) study, by the time children had vocabularies of 50 words, at approximately two years, words were used for vehicles, clothing, body parts and people. One of the problems in appraising the early vocabularies of children is that the same word may be used in different contexts to convey a range of meanings, so number of words *per se* is a poor indicator of a child's meaning potential at this stage. By the same token, not a great deal can be said with any certainty about the grammar of these early utterances.

We end this section on the child's entry into verbal language with an example recorded by one of the authors, near to a child's first birthday, which illustrates some of the major facets of this first stage.

Child: Gone.
Adult: Yes, it's gone.
Child: Nana.
Adult: You dropped the banana, didn't you?
Child: Bye-bye.
Adult: Say 'bye-bye' to the banana. We're not playing *that* game, so
we put it in the fridge.

This is a mundane, familiar setting. The child's intentions are interpreted and articulated by the adult, who picks up the child's utterances and hands them back in a more explicit form, which, at one and the same time, provides a better language model and a lesson in table manners. The child is already treated as a language partner with something significant to add to the scenario, but it is what the participants do in relation to the context which enables meanings to be read, and the child to comprehend and convey more than she can say. The child has already achieved 'autonomy' (a term we shall be using with reference to the early stages of deaf children's linguistic development) because she offers more than she is asked, and is able to add something new.

STAGE II: TWO WORDS TOGETHER

By the time a child has acquired about 50 words, between the ages of approximately 18 and 24 months, single utterances begin to be combined to make sentence patterns with two elements of structure. Some examples of Stage II sentences are 'Daddy car', 'That book', 'Dolly sleep' and 'Shoe off'. Children use their ability to generate and combine, demonstrated in the 'systematicity' of their earlier play, by applying a well-used word such as 'want', 'all-gone' or 'more' to a range of others: 'More gravy', 'More book', 'No more'. Question words (serving Halliday's heuristic function) are developed at this stage, by children attaching 'where' or 'what' to the beginning of an utterance, with a rising intonation: 'Where Daddy?', 'What that?'. Negative forms may also be combined with other words to produce sentences: 'Not fall', 'No milk'.

As word combinations begin to be used, sound contrasts are also built up and refined. The child learns the distinctions which account for the difference between words such as 'tip', 'tap', 'lap', 'lip' and so on. At this stage, much of the child's meaning-making will include pointing and looking responses, grasping and open-handed reaching, and tugging at the hands and clothes of an adult, in relation to objects in the environment.

STAGE III: THREE-ELEMENT SENTENCES

Between the ages of approximately 24 and 30 months, children begin to use sentences containing three main elements: 'Mummy get book', 'Put teddy chair', 'Me not little'. Function words like prepositions (in, to, of), pronouns (I, they, he) and demonstratives and determiners (my, this, the) enable children to interrelate words and express more elaborate meanings. Plural noun forms are discovered which may give rise to the overgeneralisation of rules: 'boys', 'cats', 'mouses', 'foots', 'tooths', 'breads'. Errors of this kind are a clear source of evidence that the child is systematically unearthing regularities in the language system, and not simply imitating adults. As meaning is negotiated with language partners, adults provide the evidence from which children are able to formulate hypotheses and check them out.

It is around the third stage that children begin to acquire the various auxiliaries and suffixes which mark tense. This is a big step forward in terms of meaning-making because it enables children to make increasingly intelligible references, and to refer to past and future events. They can talk about not only what is currently taking place, but also things which have happened and their plans for the future. In English, the different past tenses may take some time to sort out. Some of the irregular tense forms, like 'ran', 'broke', 'gave' and 'ate', might be discovered before the child appreciates past tense rules. Appropriate past tense endings for regular words are then produced which suggest that the child has begun to look for systematic rules in modifying words, such as 'live'–'lived', 'kick'–'kicked'. Errors may then be made on irregular verbs, even though these were used correctly beforehand, such as 'runned', 'breaked', 'gived' and 'eated'. Whilst the child is busy sorting out which verbs follow the rules and which do not, there may be a preference to mark tense with an adverbial, rather than a word ending: 'Yesterday go shopping'. Some double tense markings, such as 'He did sticked out his tongue', and omission of auxiliaries, such as 'Mummy been to work', are commonplace.

The sequence of acquisition of suffixes like '-ing' and '-ed' gives us some evidence that children often hear and can understand speech which is in advance of their own expressive speech. Why do children acquire '-ed' past tense markers after the present progressive, '-ing'? Is it because the past is less close to the child's immediate experience and thus harder to remember? Or is it because adults generally talk to children about things which are in progress, rather than things which have been and gone? The answer is more straightforward than explanations of relative difficulty or frequency of exposure will allow. Children use '-ing' before '-ed' because it has more acoustic stress in speech and is therefore more audible. Studies of children acquiring other languages, such as Turkish, lend weight to this conclusion (Gleitman and Wanner, 1982). Some aspects of language development, then, depend on biological phenomena (such as where stress is found) and have little to do with adult instruction, informal or otherwise.

In fact, there is some evidence which suggests that receptive and expressive language may develop interactively, with productive language ahead of receptive for some of the time. For example, at about 2½ years one of the authors' children used a number of words and phrases which she had heard and subsequently reworked but clearly did not understand, such as 'gift vulture' (gift voucher), 'spit and span' (spick and span) and 'food is fittening' (fattening).

STAGE IV: SENTENCE OF FOUR ELEMENTS

From about 2½ to 3 years children discover and master most types of simple sentence structure: 'Robin going on a swing in a minute', 'You didn't put the clothes away very goodly', 'Can you jam me a piece of bread?' Many of the rules for changing words as they are combined to express different meanings are learned, together with more mature negative forms ('didn't', 'nobody', 'don't') and inversion of the subject and verb to form a question: 'Where are you going?' Tag questions, such as 'didn't you?', are still to come, whilst there are many inconsistencies, over- and under-generalisations in the way words are modified as they are used together. This is testimony to the creative, problem-solving approach of the young child, where pressure to mean resounds in sentences such as 'It's funner being a child than a baby, isn't it?'

STAGE V: COMPLEX SENTENCES

By the age of about three years, children begin to use complex sentence structures. At Stage V children are able to link two or more ideas together. The earliest process to appear is the co-ordination of separate clauses by conjunctions such as 'and', 'but', 'that', 'so' and 'if'. Later, clauses may be subordinated using the conjunctions 'because' or 'when', as in 'Robin's sleeping 'cos he's tired'. In the following example, taken from Wiles (1981, page 65), a child describes the first days of school using 'and', which is the first of the linking devices to appear, in order to produce an extended sequence:

Adult: What did you do at school today?
Child: I done apparatus and I done reading.

Adult: Oh, you did apparatus and reading, did you?
Child: And I done writing, and I done painting.

Despite the mother's provision of a more correct grammatical model ('did' instead of 'done'), an insistence on adopting a more mature form is likely to fail when the child has not yet achieved control of a particular structure. One of the authors' children, given a more specific imitation request at four years of age, produced a response which again indicates how structures outside the child's current control are assimilated into existing levels of mastery:

Child: I've drinken most of mine already.
Adult: You mean you've drunk most of it?
Child: Yes, I've drunken most of it.

So, whilst the range of expression available to the child widens considerably, there are many aspects of grammar, such as irregular verbs, tense forms and agreement amongst words used together, which still have to be sorted out, through trial and error. By now, however, children can use their creative resources for most of the linguistic functions: expressing feelings, asking and answering questions, instructing, suggesting, interacting, stating intentions and commenting on those of others, offering information and imagining, together with contradicting, interrupting, changing the subject matter, teasing, lying and cheating! Children will also have discovered numerous ways besides tense of going beyond the here and now, such as time markers: 'after lunch', 'tomorrow morning', 'when Mummy comes home'; whilst distinctions, such as 'We always have fish on Fridays', are made.

Many of the grammatical developments up to this stage have added to the length of the sentence. There now appear processes which make for greater economy of expression, such as embedding. The child learns to embed one sentence within another by using a preposition or adverb to join clauses: 'The flowers which we planted yesterday have all drooped'. Other cohesive processes appear, such as pronouns, which relate a present clause back to a preceding one: 'Kitty caught a rabbit and he got it stuck in the catflap'. This has often been described as the most exciting and inventive period of language growth as children discover devices and processes which enable them to produce extended and interrelated sentences. Their range of expression then has an unlimited prospect.

BEYOND STAGE V

Whilst the child is still a long way from mastering the adult system, by the age of 3½ to 4 years much of the creative power of grammar has usually been realised. Stable patterns of word order and a wide range of sentence types give the impression of proficiency, although there may be many 'local' grammatical errors which still have to be ironed out, such as in noun inflections, pronouns and determiners. Some school-age children are still producing mistakes such as 'they hurt himself', 'her doing it' and 'interestingest'. Children begin to express a complex range of attitudes and intentions as structures such as 'ought', 'must', 'if' and 'should' are acquired, whilst unusual variations, such as 'neither did I' are sorted out. Complex verb phrases, such as 'she might have been able to' are developed at this stage, together with a more adult range of sentence connecting devices, such as 'actually' and 'however'. It is around this time, too, that the child's pronunciation system is brought into line with the adult sound system. Even so, the school-age child may occasionally have problems pronouncing the complex sequence of sounds in words like 'probably', 'twelfth', 'escalator' and 'photographer'.

There are a number of experimental studies in which linguists have used play materials and puppets to investigate children's understanding of ambiguous structures which may have two or more different interpretations but 'identical' grammar: 'Ask Mummy what to do/Tell Mummy what to do', 'Bring your bag home/Take your bag home'. Five-year-olds given a blindfolded doll and asked the question 'Is the doll easy to see?' tend to answer 'No, it can't', whereas 7-year-olds respond more like adults. Seven-year-olds asked to play-act with puppets and toys the meaning of sentences such as 'Lizzie hit her brother' demonstrate their unawareness of shifts in meaning when the passive voice is used. 'Lizzie was hit by her brother' may be acted out in just the same way as the previous sentence, betraying the assumption that many children often make, quite rightly, that the first noun in a sentence is usually the agent and not the object of the action. An important point to note, here, is that errors in children's use of words, such as 'ask/tell', are much more evident in a contrived research or clinic setting, stripped of situational clues. Such *in vitro* studies, taken together with evidence from research conducted *in vivo*, may help us both to understand the reliance of grammatical development on communication and to gain a clearer picture of a child's relative reliance on contextual and specifically verbal clues to intended meaning.

How do children come to understand distinctions between words such as 'this'/'that', 'here'/'there', 'come'/'go' and 'before'/'after'? There are a great many words with no fixed meaning which serve a variety of functions and levels. Words like 'it', 'on', 'what', 'who' and 'that' are used for different purposes, depending on the sentence and the situation. For example, in the sentence 'Jenny is eating the cake that her Daddy bought', 'that' indicates or points to the object of the preceding clause, 'cake'. Pronouns like 'I' and 'you' require an appreciation of relationships: 'I' refers to the speaker, 'you' to the listener; and, whilst children are addressed by 'you', they must not call themselves that. 'These' and 'those' point to things which are 'here' or 'there' respectively. The important point is that children have to think about, and work at, what others are trying to convey, and putting their own ideas into words. They have a great many specifically linguistic puzzles to solve. But in ordinary conversational interaction (as opposed to contrived experiments), it is the context which supports the use and interpretation of what words and structures mean.

Beyond Stage V takes us to the point at which children become explicitly aware of the language system they use. On the one hand, children can be said to have an implicit awareness of language, in the sense that they can use it without being able to say how it is put together. Explicit awareness, on the other hand, can be described as an ability to stand back from language and think about how it works, to treat language as 'a problem space in its own right' (Karmiloff-Smith, 1978). In other words, children continue to experiment with language for its own sake. Knowing that there are different layers of meaning in words and sentence patterns is the fount of most humour in puns and jokes. At five, one of the authors' children displayed just this kind of explicit awareness when she said, having stumbled, 'I have two left feet, a right one and a wrong one!'. How far this awareness of the language they use helps children as they approach reading and other school-related tasks, we shall be taking up later.

LANGUAGE AND THINKING AT HOME

We have tried to give an outline of the development which children move through from early pre-verbal stages to the point at which the generative power of language is realised, without losing sight of the inherently social and interactive nature of the process. As we suggested at the beginning of this chapter, the change in our understanding of child development centres upon the rôle which adults take in helping children piece together the evidence from their social, linguistic and intellectual experience. One consequence of this shift concerns methodology. Rather than studying children exclusively in contrived experimental situations (*in vitro*), researchers have also gone to the ordinary setting of the family (*in vivo*) in order to make observations. In so doing we gain access to the strategies which adults intuitively use in order to engage children and foster their abilities, in the familiar home context. In the following section we shall be outlining some significant contrasts between home and school, and the implications for development.

In the very early stages, we have noted, infants have a predilection to respond and attend to humans, to detect regularity and pattern, and to make sense of situations. The complex interplay between what people say and what they actually mean is evidenced when babies are teased, such as pretending to eat a child's dinner or that bedtime is near. A 1-year-old is aware when our facial expressions and body signals convey fun, out of synchrony with what we might say in mock seriousness. An enabling factor here is the predictable reoccurrence of situations, people and events in the routine world of the infant. As Halliday (1975) suggests, the infant has a wide range of communicative intentions and comprehends a great deal about the environment, well before recognisable words are used. What adults negotiate with children are the specific linguistic conventions for communicating.

Recordings of adult speech to children reveal some special properties which ensure a mutual understanding and maximise the probability that what is said is within reach of the child's mind and ear: a 'privileged access' to the shared linguistic system. Three major processes can be outlined. One serves to hold attention, the second simplifies the linguistic structures used, whilst the third clarifies the meaning content. Some of these features have also been observed as older children interact with the less mature and in talk between lovers and to plants, pets and poker dice! A summary is provided in Table 2.1, taken from Webster and McConnell (1987), whilst a comprehensive study of adult–child talk is provided in the book by Snow and Ferguson (1977).

In the first process the child's attention is captured and held, whilst a feeling of affection is also conveyed. A higher pitch, or special 'nursery' tone of voice, is used for talking to children, which may signal that a child, rather than another adult, is being addressed. When recordings of adults talking to children of different ages are compared, the adults' pitch is highest to the youngest children. Adults often whisper to children or speak directly into their ears, a clear signal for the child to listen. Intonation patterns may be exaggerated. A frequent attention-claiming device is to preface an utterance with an exclamation, such as 'Goodness gracious, it's bathtime already', or to use the child's name at the beginning of a sentence, such as 'Jenny, put your shoes on'. Special vocabulary or 'pet' names also provide clues that the adult is addressing a particular child: 'Is Robby-bobby-boo ready for his num-nums?' Some ways of capturing children's attention use non-verbal means, such as kneeling to the child's eye-level, touching the child, gesturing and pointing.

A second process is that of simplifying: choosing the right way to say something which ensures the child understands. Adults may achieve this by using shorter sentences and less complex grammar, avoiding structures such as co-ordinated or embedded clauses. Vocabulary may be shortened or given a special kind of emphasis, such as 'tummy', 'night-night' and 'din-din'. Some word endings, like plurals and determiners, appear less often, with other features, such as pronouns, dispensed with altogether: 'Mummy's going to change baby's nappy'. Another way of helping the child share meaning is to limit the range of vocabulary used initially, so that poodles, Dobermans and Afghans are all 'doggies'.

The issue of language 'complexity' is not entirely straightforward. It does seem clear that children need *some* exposure to more complex sentences in order to limit the range of hypotheses they can form about language structure. Designers of computer 'language learning' programs, for example, have found that a computer exposed only to large amounts of simple language (e.g. 'Tom hit Joe') fails to discover the grammar because a large number of rules could account for such constructions. Presented with more complex examples, the number of possible rules which govern how sentences are constructed is narrowed down (Gleitman and Wanner, 1982). This has important implications, which we shall address later in the book, in relation to the conversational interactions enjoyed by teachers and hearing-impaired children in the classroom, and to the range of opportunities provided for children to explore linguistic usage and function.

The third process in adult–child talk is that of clarifying. Adults speak more clearly, with a slower enunciation and leaving pauses between sentences, giving time for children to respond. Talk usually revolves around children's immediate 'here and now' world: what is likely to be filling their senses. Commentaries are given on the child's play, objects are labelled, explanations given, links made with other objects and events. Attending to the child's gestures, facial expressions and looking behaviour, adult's interpret any vocal utterances that the child may offer. By the same token, the child has a good idea of what is being talked about as the adult's language makes reference to familiar situations with familiar objects present. Accordingly, present tense is used more often than past or future. To begin with, more content words, such as nouns, are used than function words, such as 'it', 'that' or 'of'. Sentence frames may be repeated in order to introduce new words, or focus on key vocabulary: 'Where's the dolly?', 'That's a nice dolly', 'Give dolly a drink'.

Adults are rarely conscious of the devices they use to share meaning with children and to tie relevant, everyday events to appropriate language. The focus of interest is on reaching understanding, not the form of language *per se*. Language is so implicit in the social interaction it serves as to be transparent to the participants, 'like water to the fish'. It could be said that language emerges as a by-product, secondary to the experiences it is suffused with. In the past linguists have argued that, in order to achieve language acquisition in childhood, infants must have some in-built facility or 'Language Acquisition Device', sometimes referred to as LAD. They are born with the neurological equipment which enables them to perceive and analyse the structure of speech through mere exposure to the adult system. This argument, we now know, is inadequate in a number of important respects. Whilst accepting the contribution that children make in actively testing out their own 'theories' of how language works, the needs of the language novice seem especially well met in the adjustments which adults make, however unwittingly. So much so that theorists such as Bruner (1983) pay just as much heed to the 'Language Acquisition Support Service', or LASS, which children receive.

A recent source of data on how children interact with their parents at home, how they collaborate in conversation and the strategies used to

Table 2.1 *Features of adult speech to infants (Webster and McConnell, 1987, page 50)*

Attention-getting	Speaking in a high pitch or nursery tone
	Whispering in child's ear
	Exaggerating intonation and rhythm
	Making use of child's name to start a sentence
	Prefacing speech with exclamation
	Special vocabulary or nicknames for child
	Touching, eye-level contact, gesturing and pointing
Simplifying	Using short sentences
	Using simple structures, avoiding complex sentences
	Omitting word endings
	Avoiding pronouns
	Selecting simple vocabulary
Clarifying	Speaking slowly and clearly
	Pausing between sentences
	Employing 'here and now' topics of conversation in familiar environments
	Providing commentary on child's play
	Using present tense
	Using more content words, fewer function words
	Repeating key words
	Providing sentence frames for new vocabulary

negotiate meaning, has been provided by the Bristol child language studies (Wells, 1981; 1985; 1987). A total of 128 pre-school children were selected from a random sample of more than 1000 resident in Bristol. In selecting the children, equal numbers of boys and girls were chosen, representing a range of socio-economic backgrounds and seasons of birth. (However, children of one-parent or 'unwaged' families were not included.) Half the children were fifteen months old and half were 3½ years old when the study commenced. Observations were made in every family at three-month intervals. Using a radio-microphone attached to a child's clothing, all that was said by the child or in the child's presence was picked up by the microphone and transmitted to a receiver, where the speech signals were recorded and later transcribed and analysed.

Wells emphasises the intimate relations between the topics of conversations with children and the fabric of day-to-day life. In family after family, conversations centred on mundane, recurrent events like meals, dressing and undressing, toileting, safety and personal property. More extended conversations explored topics such as what could be seen from the window, how things work and what might happen in a television programme. There was a marked degree of consistency across samples, in the devices and strategies used in dialogue, as well as the order in which linguistic features appear, in line with the stage theory outlined earlier. Wells also reports a general absence of deliberate instruction, apart from a few polite expressions, such as 'please' and 'thank you', and some vocabulary teaching with 2-year-olds at the labelling stage. Not surprisingly, in view of what we have said about the 'transparency' of language structure to those who use it, parents rarely teach or correct grammar.

Wells also dismisses imitation as the basis of learning. For example, whilst children learn to answer questions well before they ask them, far more questions are heard by them than answers. Similarly, whilst children request permission well before they grant permission to others, in the speech addressed to them they are granted permission far more frequently than they are asked for it. These findings seem little more than confirmations of common sense. But what they make clear is that children are not learning to talk in order to *copy* the speech of their parents. Rather, they reconstruct the rules which appear to underlie the language used around them in order to *reciprocate*, and to participate in family life.

Which adult strategies are most effective? Sheer amount of conversation is important, in that children's rate of progress in the Bristol study was clearly related to quantity of dialogue experienced. However, the more salient factors of adult–child interaction are highlighted in this example from the Bristol data (Wells, 1987, page 46):

Child: Ot, Mummy?
Adult: Hot? Yes, that's the radiator.
Child: Been — burn?
Adult: Burn?
Child: Yeh.
Adult: Yes, you know it'll burn don't you?
Child: Oh! Ooh!
Adult: Take your hand off it.

It is the child who introduces the topic, which is then 'agreed' by the adult who confirms the appropriateness of the child's comment, 'Hot? Yes ... ', and adds useful vocabulary and information. The two participants alternate in taking turns to speak, with the child accepted as an equal partner with something important to say, however limited the means. What is said in each turn relates in part to what was said by the previous speaker.

Notice how the adult in her utterances often includes elements of the child's preceding offering. Although there is still considerable debate amongst students of child language about the rôle played by such 'fine-tuning' of adult speech to children, there are several lines of evidence which show that children's rates of language development are influenced by such features of adult language. What is not yet clear is whether the important influence lies in the adult's readiness to pick up the child's topic of talk or in the complexity of the grammar of their speech. One view is that by expanding and paraphrasing what children say, adults provide more mature 'models' of language which help the child to discover new features of language structure. Another view is that adult sensitivity to what the child is trying to talk about is the important factor.

Whilst such arguments continue, the important point for practical purposes is that adult responsiveness to children's attempts to converse does play an important part in facilitating the acquisition of language. The most useful lessons to be drawn from such observations, to our mind, are encapsulated in the following recommendations from one of the leading child language researchers, Roger Brown, who writes:

> Believe that your child can understand more than he or she can say, and seek, above all, to communicate. To understand and be understood. To keep your minds fixed on the same target. In doing that, you will, without thinking about it, make 100 or maybe 1000 alterations in your speech and action. Do not try to practice them as such. There is no set of rules of how to talk to a child that can even approach what you unconsciously know. If you concentrate on communicating, everything else will follow (1977, page 26).

But Brown is speaking of interactions between individual children and their parents. Encouraging purposeful conversation with groups of children in classrooms, even where children suffer no disabilities, is an altogether more formidable task, as we shall see.

Earlier we mentioned the triangle of shared reference (Figure 2.1). The moves of the language game fit around this triangle: what the speaker intends to say, how the message relates to the context and how the listener interprets the message. Notice, too, in the example from Wells, how the adult checks the proffered interpretation of the child's meaning, 'Burn?', allowing room for renegotiation if this is not what the child intended to convey. The dialogue is sustained around a topic of direct mutual concern, showing how, with adult help, a sequence of ideas can be jointly put together, which the child would be unable to achieve alone. Looking beyond the child's words to the intentions they realise, the adult's finely tuned responses enable the dialogue to reach a meaningful conclusion for both parties.

The Bristol studies give many other examples of what Bruner and the Soviet psychologists describe as 'cooperatively achieved success'. At home the sharing of everyday household chores, such as doing the laundry, baking, dusting, changing the beds, painting, making jelly, gardening and raking the ashes, provide the stimulus for questions, as the child seeks to learn more. In the following example (Wells, 1987, page 59), a 4-year-old is watching her mother shovel wood ash from the grate into a bucket:

Child: What are you doing that for?
Adult: I'm gathering it up and putting it outside so that Daddy can put it on the garden.
Child: Why does he have to put it in the garden?
Adult: To make the compost right.
Child: Does that make the grass grow?
Adult: Yes.
Child: Why does it?
Adult: You know how I tell you that you need to eat different things like eggs and cabbage and rice pudding to make you grow into a big girl.
Child: Yes.
Adult: Well, plants need different food, too. And ash is one of the things that's good for them.

It is the child who instigates this discussion around a shared, 'hands-on' experience, and the adult takes the opportunity to clarify the activity in terms the child understands. The child is not only exposed to adult ways of managing and reasoning, but is also given covert messages about sex-rôles, cultural expectations and valued behaviour.

In the Bristol study, parents and children enjoyed a wide variety of shared activity, including watching television, pretend games and fantasy play, drawing and writing. Wells suggests that conversation provides a medium for acting in the world and for reflecting on it with others more knowledgeable: talking in order to learn. Two final points from this work are important to mention here. First, whilst there were wide variations in the amount and quality of conversation recorded across the families sampled in the study, the differences were not significantly associated with socio-economic class. Second, of all the things which parents do with children, the factor most associated with later academic achievements in school was how frequently stories were read with the child at home (Wells, 1987).

Many of the Bristol findings are supported by the work of Tizard and Hughes (1984), in which radio-microphone recordings were made of 4-year-olds at home and in nursery school. One striking finding was the sheer amount of talk between children and their mothers. On average the children in this study held 27 conversations an hour. If the 'turns' are counted, when first one person contributes then another, on average each conversation lasted sixteen turns. Half of these conversations were started by the children. At home there were few distinctions between working-class or middle-class families in the amount, frequency or nature of conversations: in all family contexts a richness of talk, interaction and intellectual challenge is depicted, an endless 'asking and answering' of questions (page 73). Talk arose out of the child's play, where the adult would supply commentary, new possibilities, information and ideas, which extended and developed the child's thinking.

The range of talk covered topics such as family relationships, time, science, history, geography, plants, animals, size, colour and number of objects. In the course of simply living and chatting together, on average 150 turns an hour imparted information. However, it was more often than not the child who asked for information, motivated by a context in which the child desired to find out more. On few occasions did the adults use language to direct or manage. Fewer than 28 turns per hour were concerned with control ('Don't spill it'). Adults were observed playing 'hunt the thimble', cards and tickling games with their children. They drew pictures together, wrote shopping lists and changed babies, planned holidays, talked about sex-rôles and argued irritably with one another. Typically, interactions were sustained over long periods. Parents have the time, even when primarily engaged in a chore such as ironing, to respond to the child's questions. Every activity, including reading stories, seemed to be punctuated by the child asking for clarification or more information. Importantly, since the adult and child know each other intimately, talk centred around things of significance to the participants, and was free ranging, referring to events and activities out of the immediate context.

The following example, taken from Tizard and Hughes (1984, page 124), illustrates what these authors call 'passages of intellectual search':

Child: Is our roof a sloping roof?
Adult: Mmm. We've got two sloping roofs, and they sort of meet in the middle.
Child: Why have we?
Adult: Oh, it's just the way our house is built. Most people have sloping roofs so that the rain can run off them. Otherwise, if you have a flat roof, the rain would sit in the middle of the roof and make a big puddle, and then it would start coming through.
Child: Our school has a flat roof, you know?
Adult: Yes it does actually, doesn't it?
Child: And the rain sits there and goes through?

Episodes like this, where adults and children puzzle over inconsistencies and ask further questions to resolve them are taken as compelling evidence of the pre-school child's logical power, in pursuit of relatively abstract knowledge. But what happens to such children as they transfer from the culture of the home to the learning context of the school?

LANGUAGE AND THINKING IN SCHOOL

By the time most children attend school they are already competent communicators. Through their own active enquiries and with the help of supporting adults, they have made sense of some aspects of their world. For many children, however, the transition from home to school marks a turning point in the nature and purpose of learning, reflected, for example, in a different kind of adult responsiveness from that experienced at home. Home and school present contrasting opportunities for learning. Some of these contrasts are obvious. In school, children spend a lot of time in groups, whether working alone or at shared tasks. At home, adult–child interactions may be more intimate. This is likely to affect the range and depth of interaction enjoyed by children. Adults who converse with children in school and who share little of the child's experiences out of the classroom may find common ground harder to come by. On the other hand, children make demands on peers and can co-operate to learn with other children, thus bringing them into contact with a wider set of values and experiences, especially in multicultural communities.

More subtle contrasts are to be found in the aims and objectives which teachers set themselves in school, compared with adults at home. Characteristic of home contexts is that adults rarely consciously instruct children, although the activities they share are usually purposeful: language and learning arise incidentally from the experiences which parents and children enjoy together, more often than not spontaneously. Such learning is sporadic and may not cover a whole range of important issues. One important aspect of schooling is to broaden, in a more systematic and deliberate way, the learning curriculum. Children work at assigned tasks which may have more meaning and relevance to the teacher than is apparent to the child.

Policy documents such as the Bullock Report (DES, 1975) or the Primary School Survey (DES, 1978) set out 'effective records' of what children may achieve in school, including processes such as reporting past and present experiences, perceiving cause and effect, predicting, imagining, explaining, justifying and reflecting upon evidence. (For further discussion of DES policy documents see Webster and McConnell, 1987.) At the time of writing, the Education Reform Act proposes, in a far more prescriptive way than ever before, what 'foundation' and 'core' subjects should be taught in the school curriculum, together with programmes of study in each subject and national attainment targets at different age points. Undoubtedly, these developments will have a significant impact on the kinds of experience and interaction enjoyed by teacher and child, since there may be a government-planned curriculum to follow and target skills to inculcate.

To what extent do teachers present children with experiences which are special? One of Bruner's arguments is that schools make demands which are specific to the culture of the school, and which change children by engendering new ways of thinking and new forms of learning. Schools introduce children to different methods of discovering, analysing and relating information. One function of schooling is to introduce children to ideas beyond the 'here and now', to help children manipulate and analyse concepts, to reflect on the abstract. As children progress through school, language itself is used as a resource for learning. Reading, writing and thinking about language move the child towards 'disembedded' modes of learning, free from the immediate context (Donaldson, 1978). Sustained attention, self-regulation and the ability to take responsibility for one's own learning are valued highly. One of the questions which Bruner and others have asked, given their implicit aims, is whether schools do in fact provide the optimum environment for some kinds of activity such as language-learning, and if not, can they be modified?

Several recent studies have examined in detail the ways in which children and adults interact in more formal school settings. In the study by Wood, McMahon and Cranstoun (1980), conversations were recorded between adults and children in nurseries and playgroups. Despite what many of the teachers who were observed in this research said about their 'educational' intentions, many spent the majority of their time managing children and resources. Their interactions with children reflected a concern to make sure children were in the right place at the right time and with the right equipment. The formidable constraints of working with large groups of demanding pre-schoolers are usually enlisted to account for this kind of teaching style:

Child: This is the biggest car what I made.
Adult: Oh, the biggest car. Go and wash your hands dear.
Child: I'm not going to wash mine.
Adult: OK, don't wash yours then. Janet, have you had your milk dear? No, well go and get it then, before it's all gone. John, I think you'd better go and get a tissue for that nose of yours. There's one in the loo. Off you go.

In this extract (page 12), recorded during a painting activity, the teacher does not take up the opportunity to talk about the child's painting and there is little sustained dialogue with any of the children in the group. Of the adult functions assessed in this study, directive and instructive comments occur much more frequently than, for example, discussing why things happen.

One of the outcomes of this study was an attempt to highlight which of the adult 'moves' in conversation leads to greater involvement of children and more productive interaction. Central to the analysis is the concept of 'control'. High-control moves include the adult asking questions, particularly closed questions which require a limited response, such as 'Yes' or 'No', or 'display' questions which are aimed at testing the child since the adult already has the answer: 'How many fingers am I holding up?' Other high-control moves include asking the child to repeat a better model, correcting and instructing. They are 'high control' in the sense that they limit what the child does in the following turn: they do not lead children on in their thinking or conversation.

In contrast, adult moves which exert low control over dialogue are more often followed by a response from the child. These include listening carefully to what children say, taking cues from that and handing conversation back to the child, allowing time for reply. Remarking on the child's current activity and play, giving the child comments from personal experience and 'phatic' responses or social oil ('Ooh lovely', 'That's nice'), all appear to engage children more effectively as language partners. It will not have escaped notice that many of the strategies used by parents intuitively at home fall into the low-control category. We shall be returning to some of these concepts in Chapters 4 and 5 in relation to hearing-impaired children.

In the Bristol studies referred to earlier (Wells, 1981; 1985; 1987), 32 of the sample of 128 children who had been observed in their family settings were subsequently followed up at school. Comparing children's experience of language use at home and in school, the Bristol group found significant differences in the number of times children talked to adults in school and in the quality and nature of interactions. Apart from speaking much less in school, children get fewer turns, ask fewer questions, make fewer requests and initiate a much smaller proportion of conversations. In school, children use grammatically less complex sentences and express a narrower range of meanings. Teachers initiate a much higher proportion of exchanges than do parents at home, they make more requests and ask more questions, particularly 'display' questions. Unlike parents, they tend not to take up children's utterances in order to extend the child's meaning, and are much more likely to develop the topics which they themselves have introduced.

The overall picture conveyed by the Bristol study is that children are often asked to take a passive, respondent rôle in school, carrying out teachers' requests or answering teachers' questions. Teachers often engender a sense of purposefulness, but provide few opportunities for children to share in the planning of activities or to reflect on what they are doing in the sort of exploratory talk which typifies recordings made at home. For no child was the oral language experience of the classroom richer than that of the home, and social class was not a determining factor. However, there were some family background differences in the number of times children were read to, and in awareness of the value and purpose of literacy. Such differences put some children at a disadvantage when they came to school.

These findings are supported by the Tizard and Hughes (1984) research, which also followed into school children who had been observed at home. Particular children from working-class families were seen as persistent questioners at home, but became very subdued in school. Teachers were felt to make fewer intellectual demands on certain children, involved them much less in discussion and fostered a respondent style of interaction, where the child's rôle was to answer and not ask questions. For all children, there was much less talk between children and adults than at home, with fewer recorded examples of language used to recall past events or to plan. On average, children took part in ten conversations per hour with teachers, compared with 27 per hour with their mothers. The average length of conversation was sixteen turns at home, compared with eight at school. Talk was largely initiated and dominated by teachers, in terms of questioning and taking the conversational initiative from the child.

In the following extract (pages 190–1) a child is rolling out clay when the teacher sits down with her:

Adult: What's that going to be, Joyce?
Child: (No reply)
Adult: How are you making it?
Child: Rolling it.
Adult: You're rolling it, are you? Isn't that lovely? Oh, what's happening to it when you roll it?
Child: Getting bigger.
Adult: Getting bigger. Is it getting fatter?
Child: Yeah.
Adult: Is it, or is it getting longer?
Child: Longer.
Adult: Longer. Are my hands bigger than your hands?
Child: My hands are little.
Adult: Your hands are little, yes.
Child: It's getting bigger …

The first question one can ask is why this conversation is taking place at all. The teacher uses the opportunity to test out what the child does and does not know. There then follow a number of questions designed to develop the child's thinking, to do with shape and size. Tizard and Hughes are unconvinced of the success of the teacher's cognitive demands in this kind of episode. The educational intentions are clear, but the attempt to introduce appropriate vocabulary and elicit a correct response, to hand over information which the teacher already has, results in confusion. The child is not engaged as a learning partner, raising questions for herself and discussing and thinking through the adult's responses, which characterise 'passages of intellectual search' shared at home. For the working-class children in the study, lack of familiarity with this form of adult behaviour is a source of discontinuity between the culture of the home and that of the school.

Two other sources of evidence are mentioned here, which support the general findings of the studies reported in more detail but draw somewhat different conclusions about the rôle of the teacher. In the ORACLE studies of some 60 primary and middle school teachers and their classes, observations of the learning process were made, with a focus on aspects such as the distribution of teacher-attention and the nature of classroom interactions (Galton, Simon and Croll, 1980). The most striking finding of this study was that, whilst teachers spent most of their lesson time interacting with their classes, each individual pupil interacted with the teacher for an estimated 2.3 per cent of the total time observed. Children worked alone for the bulk of the time, even when grouped for an activity, whilst 72 per cent of pupil–pupil interactions were not task related. Teaching is described as 'overwhelmingly factual and managerial' (page 157), with little sense of co-operating to learn. Whilst children spent most of their time on '3Rs', teachers were mainly didactic and did not stimulate their pupils by discovery, self-probing, problem-solving activities: children are talked at, rather than with.

In the second source of evidence on the classroom process, Bennett and colleagues offer some explanations as to why teachers operate in the way that they do (Bennett, Desforges, Cockburn and Wilkinson, 1984). Bennett's study shows how a group of 'able' teachers have difficulties in appraising children's strengths and weaknesses, and in matching the demands of learning tasks to the child's level of competence. Teachers often assigned tasks to children in literacy and numeracy work which took little account of the child's existing knowledge and skills. For example, 50 per cent of number tasks given to low achievers overestimated their attainments, such as setting division sums before the child understood the process involved. Only rarely did tasks involve restructuring (children discovering ideas for themselves), or enrichment (using acquired skills on new problems). Most tasks involved the presentation of new ideas and skills, practice and revision (three-quarters of all language work observed involved practice). Many tasks did not realise the teacher's intentions anyway, such as setting a child the job of copying sentences from the blackboard in order to improve poor writing output.

Bennett lays such problems at the feet of theorists who underestimate the complexity of the teaching process, and who recommend child-centred approaches which fail to take into account the management demands of the classroom. However, the fact that a programme of inservice training did enable teachers to ascertain more realistic starting points and to structure tasks appropriately undermines his argument. Teachers can be helped towards more effective classroom styles, towards an individuation of learning experiences, where creative, problem-solving approaches to learning have their place alongside rote practice and rehearsal.

A COGNITIVELY ORIENTED CURRICULUM

Not everyone agrees with the idea that children must be taught in order to learn. Even when theorists agree about the importance of teaching, different opinions exist about what it involves. Rather than emphasising teaching as a process of transmission, the handing over of information which the teacher has, we have preferred to depict learning as knowing 'how', rather than knowing 'that'. An ideal learning environment thus involves children as active problem-solvers, reconstructing knowledge and skills for themselves, through interactive encounters with the more mature. When children co-operate to learn with peers they are also exposed to points of view and ways of thinking which provide important growing points. This is not to say that children left to their own devices will perform tasks, tackle questions or recall information as successfully as when they are supported and guided by a skilled adult. But the most important issue is that how we construe children as learners has an influence on what we consider to be the most effective rôle for the teacher and how optimum conditions for learning can be devised.

Two important books have recently been published which address the question of what makes for effective schooling. In the first work (Mortimore *et al.*, 1988), a group of 2000 pupils was followed through four years of primary schooling, between the ages of seven and eleven years, in 50 randomly selected schools. A major aim was to establish the factors which explained variations in pupils' attainment and progress in the 3Rs, attitudes to school, self-concepts and behaviour. Twelve key factors were highlighted, including aspects to do with leadership, identifying inservice needs, classroom organisation and the involvement of teachers in planning the curriculum.

Children made better progress in schools where classteachers kept individual pupil records, where work outlines were forecasted, and where parents were regularly involved in progress meetings and helped in the classroom. Too narrow a focus on basic skills had a negative effect, as did an emphasis on punishment, rather than praise, as a motivator. In class, high levels of feedback to individuals and a balance of class, group and individual interactions were most effective. The content of teacher–pupil talk was vitally important: progress was encouraged where teachers used creative, problem-solving methods, but discouraged where teachers directed pupils' work without discussing it or explaining its purpose. Finally, teachers who kept noise and movement down to a minimum, who told stories to children and who listened to children read individually were most effective.

The second study (Rutter, Maughan, Mortimore and Ouston, 1979) compared the progress of more than 2000 pupils in twelve secondary schools, collecting data on attendance, exam results, behaviour in school and delinquency outside. Irrespective of catchment area, good attainments and behaviour were associated with schools where there was a sharing of responsibility for learning and for the environment between pupils and staff. Pupil outcomes were better when teachers set good models of time-keeping and behaviour, and made frequent use of praise and individual feedback, in an atmosphere of firmness and trust. Aspects such as displaying good work, asking pupils to take care of resources and actively engaging pupils in the classroom, together with the joint sharing of activities outside the classroom, all help to create democratic, as opposed to authoritarian, learning conditions.

In Figure 2.2 a model of adult–child interactions is given. This is similar to descriptions of optimum learning environments which have emerged in relation to compensatory teaching programmes (such as 'High/Scope') for disadvantaged children in the USA (see, for example, Hohmann, Banet and Weikart, 1979). Within this model two axes, or continua, describe the typical rôles of adult and child as they interact, in terms of degree of initiative shared. The optimum learning environment is felt to fall within the north-west quadrant. Here, children are helped to make informed choices about their learning activities, rather than simply being directed to get on with a task. This approach gives children a sense of responsibility for planning and making decisions about activities: enabling a child to identify, pursue and complete self-chosen goals. The importance of direct experience is acknowledged, with the adult guiding children's learning, structuring tasks for and with children, whilst maintaining an overview of the key experiences and skills to cover.

Essentially and ideally, children approach new experiences as active enquirers, explorers or experimenters. Adults help the child to mark out problems to tackle, and negotiate resources, materials and possible strategies. Wherever possible, children are asked to think of themselves as sources of information and to be creative in their own questioning. When difficulties arise, the adult helps the child to reflect why one method may work where another has failed. When new skills are acquired, time is spent on broadening their application to other content areas of the curriculum, so that links are made between subject boundaries and the function of learning made apparent. Important, here, is the timing and pacing of adult intervention should the child falter. Elsewhere we have described this as adult contingency: gauging a child's moment-to-moment understanding of a task, providing more help and information where needed, but allowing the child more initiative when the child succeeds. In this way the child is never held back by teaching which is overdirective, nor left alone when in difficulty. Both require an astute awareness of the learner's starting point.

Through co-operating to learn, both with peers and with adults, children discover ways of planning, organising and proceeding with their learning. Having identified, planned and tackled a task, there is an important review stage, again shared with the adult. Children are asked to reflect on how they went about their learning, what they have gained, how they could have proceeded any differently and what to

ADULT
ACTIVE

Cognitively oriented

A helps C make plans

A negotiates tasks with C

A guides C's problem-solving

C encouraged to
explore/experiment/reflect

C tests out own hypotheses with
A's help

Cycle of plan/do/review

C thinks of self as a source of
information

Learning is interactive

Adult-structured

A initiates without negotiating
with C

A hands over information to C

A structures pace, task, sequence of
steps

Rote learning, drilling

C expected to 'soak-up' information

Passive, respondent learning styles

Behavioural, programmed
approach

A exercises control

CHILD
ACTIVE

CHILD
PASSIVE

Child-centred

Unstructured activities in a rich
environment

Free play

C initiates without negotiating
with A

Non-interactive (A may step in to
manage)

C controls choices

Custodial care

Main concerns are for C's safety
and physical needs

A watches over C

Non-interactive styles

ADULT
PASSIVE

Figure 2.2 *Curriculum model of adult–child interactions*

move on to next. At this evaluation stage the teacher is careful to react to the process or strategy that a child has chosen, rather than simply to mark the product, or quantity of output. Where both adult and child are able to negotiate the task, where concepts are discovered and then applied more broadly by the child, where there is a sense of children recreating knowledge and expertise for themselves, and where a sense of awareness of 'how' to go about one's own learning is fostered — then we are approaching an optimum learning environment.

Can such a curriculum be translated into classroom practice? The Bennett and colleagues (1984) study shows that even 'able' teachers find it difficult to appraise children accurately, to structure appropriate tasks and to provide enrichment activities for concepts children have had some part in discovering for themselves. However, when we come to discuss the learning needs of hearing-impaired children and how they might be met in mainstream (Chapters 4 and 5), these issues are at the very heart of good practice. We do not require a special psychology for the hearing-impaired. But we do need to be aware of the special problems that deafness brings and of the effects that these may have on our own abilities as communicators and teachers. All that we have said in this chapter regarding normal developmental milestones, what children bring to learning and the rôles which adults adopt is equally significant for children who are hearing-impaired, perhaps more so. In Chapter 5 we shall demonstrate how resources of time, materials and human beings can be used optimally for the hearing-impaired, in working towards effective learning environments.

3

Hearing and hearing loss

In describing the course of normal development we assume the child has a nurturing social environment and potential for learning, together with healthy body systems, including intact senses. In this chapter, some of the basic facts of hearing and hearing loss are considered, such as the anatomy of the ear and the physical characteristics of the sounds to which the ear, auditory pathways and brain respond. A brief overview is given so that those unfamiliar with the field of hearing-impairment are aware of the clinical parameters by which hearing loss is defined and described. It is important to understand the varying ways in which hearing losses may arise, how these are identified and diagnosed, what treatments are available, and the significance in auditory terms that a hearing loss may carry for the child. Distinctions, for example, between conductive and sensori-neural hearing losses require some technical insights as a basis for approaching the more important issues: the impact which different forms of deafness have on childhood.

A word of caution: hearing-impaired children do not fall easily into homogeneous groups. Whilst it is important to know the answer to questions such as 'How was the child's hearing loss caused?', 'What is the nature and severity of the impairment?', 'Did the loss occur at birth or in infancy, when the child had already begun to speak?', 'When was it identified and how treated?' and 'Has the child derived much benefit from hearing-aids?', in fact the degree and nature of a child's deafness account for only a few of the differences between individuals. Some children with relatively mild hearing losses may have marked educational problems, whilst other children with profound impairments manage remarkably well, given appropriate services, support and teaching help.

Deafness manifests itself in many ways, interacting with an uncharted range of other variables. Some of these 'other' variables may be obvious. Any additional obstacles to learning that the child has to cope with, such as a visual or motor difficulty, will have an impact on the child's development. Similarly, the child's unique personality, family, and cultural and linguistic environment will exert a significant influence. However, there may be other important factors in determining how well a child progresses, which are unrevealed and unexplored.

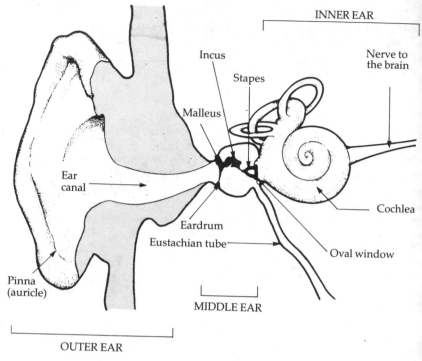

Figure 3.1 *Cross-section of the hearing system*

THE NORMAL HEARING SYSTEM

A diagram of the ear is given in Figure 3.1, which for descriptive purposes is divided into three parts. It is useful to bear in mind these separate sections of the hearing system since a hearing loss will involve one or more parts of the system, and sometimes there may be malfunction involving different parts of the system concurrently. The healthy hearing system depends on the three separate sections working normally.

Every object which produces a sound, such as a door bell, violin string or human vocal cord, does so by causing the air to vibrate in a particular way. The ear is designed to pick up sound vibrations from the air and, ultimately, to pass on this information to the brain, where it can be interpreted and given meaning, and perhaps responded to. The outer ear consists of the pinna or auricle, and the external auditory canal. The outer ear structures which are visible on the sides of our heads are relatively unimportant in man. The auricle in many animals is provided with muscles so that it can be moved into position to detect and localise sounds. In man the auricle works like an inert funnel. Even so, besides the simple function of trapping and feeding sound into and along the ear canal, the auricle does have certain enhancement and perceptual effects which facilitate localisation, given that sound signals are collected at different points in time and space.

The external auditory canal is about 2.5 centimetres long in adults, and is lined with skin which contains hairs and the glands which secrete 'cerumen' or wax. The deepest part of the canal is separated from the middle-ear cavity by the eardrum or tympanic membrane, a fibrous membrane stretched tightly across the auditory canal, and to which one of the ossicles, the malleus, is attached. The middle-ear cavity is an air-filled space, about the size of a fingernail, in the bone of the skull. It houses the three minute bones known as the malleus (hammer), incus (anvil) and stapes (stirrup). Sound vibrations which meet the eardrum at the end of the ear canal in turn cause the thin membrane of the drum to vibrate. The function of the linked chain of tiny bones is to conduct incoming sound vibrations from the eardrum across the middle-ear cavity to the oval window, another membrane-covered opening, which is the avenue into the inner ear. The sound signals are intensified *en route* via the lever action of the ossicles.

The middle ear is lined with mucous membrane like the inside of the mouth, and in health contains only air. The tube which ventilates the middle ear is known as the Eustachian tube. This connects the middle-ear cavity to the back of the nose and throat. In adults the Eustachian tube is 3 or 4 centimetres long, but in children it is shorter, wider and more horizontal. Since the Eustachian tube is the main route by which infections enter the middle ear, its size and shape in young children contributes to the frequency with which infants are affected by middle-ear disease. When we swallow, the tube normally opens up to allow air into the middle-ear cavity. Changes in air pressure may cause discomfort in the middle ear. If we go rapidly up or down in an aeroplane, for example, the atmospheric pressure alters, whilst the pressure of the air in the middle ear remains much the same. Swallowing causes a reflex opening of the Eustachian tube and equalises the air pressure on both outer and inner sides of the eardrum, which is why sweets are sometimes given out at take-off and landing. It is important to be aware of the function of the Eustachian tube because it is very often implicated when a conductive hearing loss arises.

By far the most complicated part of the ear is the inner section. Not all the structures of the inner ear are concerned with hearing. The semicircular canals are involved in balance. The structure concerned with hearing is the cochlea, a spiral tube which resembles the shell of a snail. The function of the cochlea is to convert information transmitted through the oval window into electrical nerve impulses. Up to this point in the process of hearing, the sensory input has been mechanical in nature. Since a vibratory type of energy cannot be transmitted via the nervous system, it has to be converted into another form. This conversion takes place in the inner ear, involving the hair cells within the cochlea. The sound vibrations that have passed from the eardrum, across the chain of ossicles and through the oval window then displace fluids and membranes within the labyrinth of the cochlea, and cause movement in the hair cells. Nerve impulses are triggered in the neurones which innervate the hair cells. The mechanisms by which the nerves of the cochlea analyse the characteristics of sounds which reach them are very complex. It is not yet fully understood how nerve impulses are carried along the auditory pathways and to the brain. Suffice it to say that at this point, when messages received and analysed by the ear are carried to the brain, the individual must then interpret their meaning and decide how to respond.

CONDUCTIVE HEARING-IMPAIRMENT

Any factor or condition which affects the progress of sound into the ear canal or across the middle-ear system is referred to as a conductive hearing problem. Conductive impairments are thus due to mechanical obstructions which can often be treated. Although conductive losses are known to be associated with a range of speech, language and learning difficulties, in general the effects of a conductive impairment on childhood are less severe than the impact of a sensori-neural impairment. When the nerves of a child's hearing are damaged there is no medical treatment which can restore hearing: the hearing mechanisms are permanently harmed. So conductive difficulties differ from sensori-neural difficulties in terms of duration, effect on hearing, amenability to treatment and impact on development. However, it is not uncommon for a conductive hearing loss to exacerbate a hearing loss caused by sensori-neural impairment, which reduces the child's hearing sensitivity further still.

Anything which totally blocks the external ear canal will cause a conductive deafness. Children have been known to put dried peas, marbles, pebbles, beads and other small objects into their ears. Some children are born with malformed outer ears, such as with a small external opening or a solid mass of tissues in the ear canal. Occasionally, bony outgrowths develop from the canal wall, narrowing the opening. Closure or occlusion of the ear canal would have to be more or less complete to cause a significant degree of deafness. So long as the other parts of the hearing system are perfectly normal, surgical removal of foreign bodies, or the creation of an effective outer opening, should restore hearing. However, congenital problems with the external features of the ear are often associated with malformations of other parts of the system.

Some degree of deafness may be caused by scarring or perforations of the eardrum, as a result of disease or perhaps through trauma. The eardrum can be ruptured by penetration of foreign bodies or unskilled attempts to remove them, as well as by sudden compression, such as by a hand slap. A hard plug of wax impinging on the eardrum may also cause a conductive loss. Wax is a normal secretion from the ceruminous glands in the ear canal and is usually soft enough to find its own way out of the ear. Wax can be compacted by poking implements into the ear in an overzealous attempt to remove it. Because it is hygroscopic, that is, it absorbs fluids, a plug of wax may swell up and occlude the canal when water enters the ear after washing or swimming.

By far the most common cause of an acquired conductive impairment in children is otitis media. We have said that the whole of the middle-ear cleft, including the Eustachian tube, is lined with mucous membrane, continuous with the lining of the upper respiratory tract of the nose and throat. Otitis media can arise acutely by the rapid spread of infection into the middle ear via the Eustachian tube. A head cold, when the child has symptoms such as a runny nose, coughs and sneezes, and catarrh, may lead to otitis media; whilst more virulent infections, such as measles or scarlet fever, will cause a more severe inflammation of the middle ear. Tonsils and adenoids, which lie at the base of the Eustachian tube, may also be enlarged. The shorter, wider and more horizontal Eustachian tube in children, together with the susceptibility of young children to infections, contributes to the increased incidence of otitis media in the early years. Inflammations which obstruct the Eustachian tube or affect its opening presage a complex chain of events.

If the Eustachian tube is prevented from aerating the middle-ear, air pressure inside the cavity will fall relative to the atmosphere outside. This has the effect of pushing the eardrum inwards, restricting its movement. Stretched and taut, the tympanic membrane will not be elastic enough to vibrate freely in response to incoming sound waves. If the Eustachian tube dysfunction persists and the middle ear remains unventilated, a watery fluid is produced in the middle-ear cleft. A child may have the symptoms of fullness in the affected ear, or a sensation of bubbling or fluid. This effusion of thin fluid will affect hearing because the free movement of the tiny bones in the sound-conducting mechanisms of the middle ear is impeded. It is the increased stiffness of the system which obstructs the transmission of sound energy to the inner ear. However, hearing loss caused by thin fluid can come and go quickly, which makes it disconcerting for teachers and parents to decide whether a child really does have a hearing loss when the evidence for it seems to fluctuate. Obviously, children are more likely to be affected in winter months, when there are more infections about, than in the summer.

If acute otitis media is left medically untreated, the whole of the middle-ear cleft and the eardrum may become inflamed, producing pus, which is released should the eardrum burst. Some children have repeated infections and middle-ear inflammations which may not have recovered before a new attack takes hold. It was fashionable at one time to ascribe 'glue ear' to incomplete treatment with antibiotics (Ballantyne and Martin, 1984). When a child complains of earache, it would be usual for parents to seek treatment from their GP; within a day or two of taking antibiotics the child feels much better. If the complete course of treatment is not given carefully, the infection subsides but is not really controlled. Thick mucus, or 'glue', remains in the middle ear, causing a conductive hearing loss, but also acting as an ideal culture for future infection. According to the incomplete treatment theory, the tissues of the middle ear undergo a cycle of infection, healing, scarring and further infection. 'Glue ear', then, is to be found most commonly in children who have had frequent attacks of acute otitis media treated with antibiotics. However, another view is that 'glue ear' is probably a chronic form of serous otitis media associated with blockage of the Eustachian tube and middle-ear effusion.

There are many different forms of otitis media in childhood. In some cases children may have fluid in the middle ear without any symptoms such as earache. In many cases, otitis media clears spontaneously over a period of one to three months and does not recur. However, in a number of children the condition is persistent and various complications can ensue, such as adhesion of the ossicles, if the disease is unresolved. The traditional view of otitis media is that Eustachian tube dysfunction is usually responsible for accumulation of fluid in the middle ear. In some children the reason for the persistence of the disease is not really understood. Recently, some researchers have suggested that allergies and other kinds of deficiency in immune mechanisms of the body may play a part in causing middle-ear disease (Smyth and Hall, 1983).

Medical and surgical management of otitis media

It is important to seek medical advice as soon as possible when a child has symptoms of otitis media, such as earache. In many children otitis media arises acutely with a rapid spread of infection into the middle ear, often caused by a common cold or other upper respiratory tract infection. The first course of action may be to prescribe antibiotics in order to arrest the inflammatory process. It has been suggested that parents sometimes fail to complete the prescribed treatment because the child's discomfort, given antibiotics, disappears quickly. Infection recurs some time later because it has remained in a sub-acute form and not really resolved (Ballantyne and Martin, 1984). Many parents do not return to their GPs to check the outcome of treatment, nor are they asked to. We have said that otitis media can take many forms, often resulting in blocking of the Eustachian tube and accumulation of fluid in the middle ear. Thin fluid may evacuate spontaneously when a simple infection is resolved and the Eustachian tube reopens. Thick 'glue', as a result of repeated infections, is more difficult to eradicate but can lead to a marked hearing loss and is associated with a range of developmental consequences.

Conservative medical treatment of otitis media includes the prescription of decongestant drugs to dry out the middle-ear cavity, together with inflation of the Eustachian tube in order to unblock it. Medical opinion varies as to the efficacy of this treatment: side effects, such as drowsiness and behaviour disturbances, may be counter-productive. There is also surgical treatment if other methods fail. Tonsils and adenoids may be enlarged and block the Eustachian tube. An ENT surgeon may wish to remove these in children who suffer repeated colds and infections. Myringotomy may be performed under general anaesthetic, in which a small incision is made in the eardrum and any fluid or 'glue' sucked out. In the chronic condition the inflamed lining of the ear may continue to exude thick mucus whilst the Eustachian tube remains blocked, and so the perforation in the eardrum needs to be kept open. A small plastic tube called a grommet may be inserted in the eardrum in order to create a 'controlled perforation'. The grommet has a dumb-bell constriction near the middle which holds it in place when the eardrum heals. This allows air into the middle ear and serves the same function as the Eustachian tube. The grommet allows the mucosal linings of the middle ear to return to normal, by which time the Eustachian tube has opened and hearing been restored. This treatment has been likened to opening a window in a damp bathroom in order to dry it out.

Middle-ear surgery can make an immediate improvement to the child's hearing sensitivity. However, some doubts have been expressed about the long-term benefits of surgical treatment. In some cases, grommets are rejected spontaneously after a few weeks and it may be necessary to repeat the operation a number of times if 'glue' reforms. On average, grommets stay in the ear about six months. Several alternatives, such as a T-shaped grommet, have been designed to stay in position for as long as possible, and these may be retained for up to two years or more. A minor problem of the grommet is that it should preclude swimming and diving because that would offset the benefits of the operation and could lead to further infection, although opinions vary on this point. More importantly, it should not be assumed that once a child has been treated for otitis media the problem is therefore cured. In fact every middle-ear episode seems to predispose some children to yet another. For that reason, teachers and parents should be vigilant to the signs and symptoms of a hearing loss, highlighted in Table 3.1, even when a child has received treatment.

The extent of 'glue ear' surgery is a current medical controversy. Surveys of the condition show that it tends to occur much more frequently in poor socio-economic conditions and alongside other health risks. Yet the children who are most likely to be identified and surgically treated for 'glue ear' are from more affluent and healthy sectors of society. The number of operations performed also varies markedly from one area of the United Kingdom to another, depending on factors such as pressure from parents and the willingness of surgeons to intervene. It has been suggested that the rapid increase in 'glue ear' surgery is an example of middle-class parents seeking medical solutions to their children's educational problems. (For further discussion see Webster, Bamford, Thyer and Ayles, in press; Webster, 1988a.)

SENSORI-NEURAL HEARING-IMPAIRMENT

Sensori-neural hearing losses are associated with defects in the fine structures of the inner ear or auditory pathways to the brain. There are many ways in which the cochlea and nerves of hearing may be irreversibly harmed. Unfortunately, medical science is unable to offer any treatment which can repair damage to the inner ear or auditory nerve in order to restore hearing: sensori-neural hearing-impairments are permanent. We have grouped some of the major causes of sensori-neural deafness according to the time when the disease process or disturbance of development takes place. For a large number of children the exact cause of sensori-neural deafness may never be known. When a hearing loss is identified, factors affecting the mother's pregnancy, the child's birth or events in early infancy have to be examined in retrospect. More often than not, all that can be given is a *likely* reason for a sensori-neural loss.

Prenatal causes

Sensori-neural hearing-impairment may be inherited, even where there has been no deafness in earlier generations. For example, an individual who carries a particular gene which causes deafness may produce a hearing-impaired child if his or her partner is also a carrier. Such a couple would have a one-in-four chance of having a hearing-impaired child with each pregnancy. This process is known as a recessive genetic tendency. In other families deafness may be inherited directly from either or both parents, if they carry a dominant gene. Some hereditary syndromes involve a group of features. In Usher's syndrome, for example, deafness is associated with a progressive visual difficulty. Inherited weaknesses vary from minor defects in the hair cells to total absence of the cochlea. Genetic counselling is one way of reducing the numbers of children born with hereditary hearing defects.

The discovery in the 1940s that mothers who had suffered from German measles (rubella) in early pregnancy later gave birth to damaged babies was the first evidence that it was possible for infections in a pregnant woman to affect the growing foetus. The first three months of pregnancy is the period when the embryo's delicate organs are forming. Between the fifth and twelfth weeks, for example, all the coils of the foetal cochlea will have formed. In adults a rubella infection may be so mild as to go unnoticed, the only symptom being a slight rash. However, an expectant mother who gets German measles in the first trimester of pregnancy is at risk of having a baby with serious heart defects, visual disabilities and brain damage, together with a hearing-impairment. Because of the potentially serious effects of the rubella virus on the embryo there is a national immunisation programme for girls approaching puberty to reduce the number of affected babies. At the time of writing, the Department of Health has initiated a programme to extend testing for mumps, measles and rubella to pre-school children, both boys and girls. It is important to test all expectant mothers for rubella antibodies to see if they are immune. If a woman contracts rubella during early pregnancy then a therapeutic abortion may be recommended.

Many other viral infections contracted at important stages of pregnancy can cause sensori-neural deafness, such as influenza. Cytomegalovirus infection of a pregnant woman accounts for the birth of a small proportion of deaf children (see Table 1.1). Sometimes, CMV-damaged babies may suffer from additional neurological complications, although hearing-impairment is regarded as the primary consequence of CMV infection of the mother during pregnancy. Certain drugs are also thought to damage the immature cochlea if taken during early pregnancy. The toxic effects of drugs, rubella or other infections arrest the development of nerve cells in the cochlea. The impact of prenatal factors will depend on the stage of maturity reached by the embryo.

Perinatal causes

The perinatal period refers to the time of birth and a short period before and after birth. A difficult labour or a long, complicated birth could result in the baby being short of oxygen. Lack of oxygen (anoxia) and birth injuries caused by the use of instruments are both associated with perinatal handicaps, including deafness. However, hospitals take great care to monitor babies during birth if the labour is not straightforward. Premature babies also have a high risk of hearing-impairment because of their vulnerability to birth injuries and infections, and the immature brain is especially susceptible to anoxia. Any infant born before having spent the normal 40 weeks in the womb may be described as premature, although the term is used medically to denote babies who weigh less than 2.5 kilograms.

Severe jaundice is another condition which can damage the nerve pathway from the cochlea to the brain and cause other neurological complications. Jaundice is caused by an incompatibility between the rhesus blood groups of the mother and child. In about 85 per cent of Europeans the rhesus (Rh) factor is present on the red blood cells, whilst the remaining 15 per cent whose red cells do not possess this factor are termed Rh-negative. If an Rh-negative mother is carrying an Rh-positive baby, the Rh factor passes from the child's blood, through the placenta, into the mother's circulation. Antibodies are formed which cause a destruction of the red blood cells in the foetus, releasing a bile pigment (bilirubin) into the child's bloodstream. The mother's liver disposes of the bilirubin until the time of birth. The child's immature liver is unable to cope with the bilirubin, which causes the yellow staining of the skin, or jaundice. If the child's blood is not replaced within a few hours of birth, the pigment may affect nerve cells in the cochlea and brain. Fortunately, jaundice is another problem which is better understood and better controlled than it used to be, and nowadays fewer children suffer deafness as a consequence of jaundice.

Improved maternal care during the period of the birth is a good reason for hoping that fewer handicapped babies may be born. However, there is a strong possibility that the growing capability of paediatric medicine to save premature babies with very low birth weight will result in more infants surviving in special care units who would otherwise have died. This is a group of children who will have a high risk of hearing-impairment in association with other forms of handicap. Perinatal factors are often associated with high-frequency deafness. The reason for this, according to Ballantyne and Martin (1984), is that the inner ear has developed normally during pregnancy and the parts of the cochlea most vulnerable and exposed to subsequent damage are the nerve cells sensitive to high tones.

Postnatal causes

Probably the commonest postnatal cause of deafness in young children is meningitis. This is an acute inflammation of the covering of the brain and spinal cord, due to micro-organisms such as the meningococcus. Mental handicap, spasticity, as well as a severe hearing loss, may result from meningitis. Deafness occurs early in the disease, often within the first week, and so very prompt treatment is indicated. Some of the drugs used to combat meningitis, such as streptomycin, have a toxic effect on the ear, with deafness resulting from treatment of the primary disease. Great care has to be exercised when potentially harmful drugs are prescribed to combat infections. Drugs which are known to be toxic to the ear would be used only if an infection did not respond to other, less toxic drugs.

Severe sensori-neural deafness may result from almost any of the commonly occurring childhood infections such as mumps, scarlet fever and measles. Mumps in a very few children may give rise to total deafness in one ear, leaving the other ear unaffected. Measles may cause a moderate sensori-neural loss in both ears, with sensitivity reduced for high frequencies more than for low tones. Adventitious deafness due to inflammatory diseases has decreased in incidence because of vaccinations which have helped to eliminate some of the viral diseases responsible, together with greater sophistication in the use of drugs. Rarely, deafness is acquired in childhood through trauma, such as a head injury which fractures the base of the skull, or exposure to high-intensity noise.

However acquired, a critical factor in postnatal deafness is whether the child has any experience of normal socio-linguistic interaction before the hearing loss occurs. Children with well-established speech and language skills may still have serious developmental difficulties in the wake of acquired deafness, but these difficulties are unlikely to be as severe as they may be for the infant who suffers a hearing loss in the very early stages of language growth.

IDENTIFYING A HEARING LOSS

In rare circumstances a child with a severe sensori-neural hearing loss may escape detection for a number of years. Occasionally, children with moderate or high-frequency deafness may come to light at school-entry, for example when an aware teacher suspects a hearing difficulty and takes the appropriate steps to gain further opinion. Often, parents are the first to suspect that their child has a hearing problem, but professionals may not take these concerns seriously and may fob parents off with 'wait and see' advice. Obviously, the sooner a hearing loss is detected, the sooner that the impact of deafness can be reduced at source. This applies to both mild conductive deafness and more severe sensori-neural impairments. If some of the long-term consequences of conductive deafness are to be avoided, vigilance and care over treatment must be taken, together with the implementation of appropriate helpful strategies at home and in school. To the unsuspecting parent or teacher, children with conductive deafness may appear unco-operative, dull or lazy, when in fact there are periods when the child cannot listen effectively. For the child with a severe sensori-neural loss, the prospects of developing a sophisticated range of social, linguistic and educational skills are crucially dependent upon early diagnosis. Hopefully, as diagnostic services improve, more babies and infants will have their deafness detected and hearing-aids provided within the first year of life.

Detection does depend in the first place on suspicion. There are many grounds for suspecting a hearing difficulty. We shall be examining some of the informal signs which should alert adults to the possibility of a child having a hearing-impairment, together with the formal assessments which can be made to identify a loss. A helpful distinction is usually drawn between the processes of identification and diagnosis. The former seeks to determine whether a child's sensitivity for hearing is abnormal; the latter endeavours to explain why.

Children at risk

It is known that sensori-neural deafness is likely to occur in certain circumstances. In advance of a child's birth, deafness may be anticipated because of genetic factors in the family history. One or both parents may carry a dominant genetic tendency, and there may be other hearing-impaired siblings in the family. Similarly, there may have been factors in a mother's pregnancy, such as contact with rubella or other infection, which predispose a child to suffer a hearing-impairment. Rh sensitivity, prematurity, difficulties in the delivery of a baby or anoxia should alert professionals to the possibility of deafness. Paediatricians in special care baby units, for example, should alert the audiological services when any factors potentially harmful for hearing have arisen.

One way of proceeding is to keep a careful record of 'at-risk' babies and to ensure that hearing is monitored from an early period onwards. Vulnerable children include those who may have acquired deafness in early babyhood or infancy, through measles or meningitis. Children with a handicapping condition frequently associated with hearing-impairment, such as cerebral palsy, should also be carefully followed up. We could also include in our list of 'at-risk' children any child with a congenital abnormality, such as cleft palate, where there is particular susceptibility to conductive hearing loss. Children with Down's syndrome also fall into this category. Children with speech and language delay could also be more thoroughly investigated for the possibility of hearing loss. Developmental screening checklists for speech and language difficulties in young children are given in Webster and McConnell (1987).

Early screening

In the United Kingdom, early screening and testing procedures are organised by the community health services to try and pick out children who may have hearing difficulties as soon as possible. Since in no more than approximately half of the instances of sensori-neural deafness can the exact cause be pinpointed, the screening of only 'at-risk' children would still leave many cases undetected. Health Visitors endeavour to screen every baby around the age of seven or eight months, either at home or in a child health clinic. Familiar sounds with a wide frequency bandwidth, such as a rattle or the soft call of the child's name, are given in a controlled way to see whether the infant responds. Further details of this procedure are given later. Suffice it to say that there are many reasons why babies fail or pass the screen apart from hearing, and the method has not gone uncriticised. For that reason, other, more 'objective' methods of screening babies for hearing loss are being developed.

In some areas Health Visitors also ask parents to complete a questionnaire which seeks details of the child and family history but also gives an opportunity for parents to register any concerns they might have. The straightforward question 'Have you ever been worried about your child's hearing?' is a very important and effective screening device in itself. There is a growing recognition that parents have sensitive insights and can make important contributions towards identifying a child's special needs. A father may have noticed that his baby of a few months is always visually startled when approached, despite his having signalled his presence by voice. A mother senses something is amiss when sudden loud sounds, such as an unexpected sneeze, low-flying aircraft or dog barking, fail to produce any reaction in her infant. Early parental concerns shared with the Health Visitor or GP should never be brushed aside. A thorough assessment should always be arranged. Concerns about a child's hearing at this stage would normally be passed on to a community medical officer with special responsibility for audiology. Alternatively, the GP might refer a child directly to a hospital ENT department. In some areas a family may be referred for advice to a regional centre of excellence, such as the Nuffield Hearing and Speech Centre.

Health Visitors routinely visit the families of pre-school children and should be alert to any delays or difficulties in speech and language. Another hearing screen is usually given by a school nurse or audiology technician, just after the child enters school at four or five years of age.

If concern is expressed in school at any time, the school nurse can follow this up and refer on to the appropriate medical officer for further advice if need be. The next step may be for the child to be seen at a hospital ENT department for advice and treatment. An alternative route for the child of school age is via the family doctor direct to the audiology or ENT department of a hospital. In a very few areas parents can ask for an appointment at an audiology department directly. From this brief outline it is obvious that the co-ordination of information and advice amongst the various agencies involved can be difficult to achieve, even where lines of communication are well established. There is always the possibility of a child with a hearing loss slipping through the screening net.

THE TEACHER'S AWARENESS

Whether or not a child has passed a screening test, or has medical records which declare normal hearing, if an adult who knows the child in school feels worried about that child's hearing, then concerns should be shared with parents and further expert advice sought. Every now and then children do miss earlier screening tests or escape detection, and there is always the possibility that a child in school may acquire deafness in one ear or both following a viral infection. Conductive hearing losses appear to peak in numbers around the period of nursery or infant age, but the fluctuating nature of the condition means they may be difficult to detect. Teachers in school are in a good position to observe some of the warning signs of a hearing loss, and it is important for school staff to know what to look out for.

The onset of a hearing problem often produces symptoms such as lack of concentration, poor attention span, tiredness in class, listening difficulties, behaviour upsets and a fall-off in school performance. A child may frequently appear to be daydreaming, misunderstand directions through having misheard and forget to bring equipment and books, whilst requests may have to be repeated a number of times. A child may ask to sit closer to a sound source, such as a television or tape recorder, than is usual and fail to turn immediately when called by name. The teacher may have noticed a tendency to distract others and mess around in class, with a marked discrepancy in behaviour or 'take-up' of the classroom activities from one week to the next. The child with a conductive loss may have started to mouth-breathe, or have frequent absences with colds and catarrh. Complaints of earache, 'popping ears' or a visible discharge from the ear are obviously clear signs that something is amiss and may require treatment. Children with longer-term conductive problems may have difficulty listening in busy, noisy conditions, appear not to enjoy storytime and show delays in various aspects of speech, language and literacy.

Table 3.1 *Warning signs of a hearing loss*

Medical records or siblings showing a history of ear infections or failed screening tests, especially in winter. (NB Passing an audiology screen does not rule out the presence of a hearing-impairment.)

Frequent absences with coughs, colds and catarrh.

Complaints of earache, full or 'popping' ears, or a visible discharge from the ear.

Immature speech sounds, with some word endings omitted, and confusions between similar sounding words.

Speech limited in vocabulary or structure.

Louder or softer voice than is usual, with mouth-breathing or snoring.

Watching the speaker's face for clues and appearing to hear better when speaker's face and lips are visible.

Slowness in responding to simple verbal instructions, with frequent requests for repetition.

Giving inappropriate answers to questions, watching and following what other children do.

Misunderstanding if a sequence of directions is given.

Searching visually to locate a sound source or turning head to give one side an advantage.

Needing to sit nearer a sound source than is usual or asking for volume on TV, tape or record player to be turned up.

Daydreaming and drifting off, withdrawing, taking little part in discussion or conversation.

Inattention, restlessness, distraction of others, more responsive in quiet conditions or small groups.

Some irritability or atypical aggressive outbursts, more frequent behaviour upsets in school.

Little interest in following a story, especially in noisy conditions.

Failure to turn immediately when called by name unless other, visible signals are given.

Tiring easily, poor motivation, listlessness, lack of energy, difficult to reach, some stress signs such as nail-biting.

Particular difficulties in verbally related skills such as reading, 'phonic' work, sound blending and discrimination, and writing, with better skills in practical areas.

Periodic falling away of pace of learning, with shortening of attention span and greater demands for individual help.

In Table 3.1 many of the warning signs of a possible hearing loss are given, which teachers and parents can be alert to in their everyday encounters with children. It is imperative that children who show some of these signs are investigated further. Some common sense is required because features such as tiredness, behaviour upsets and concentration lapses may be due to a number of other factors apart from hearing. There is, however, no harm in eliminating deafness as the cause of a child's educational difficulties, by sharing any concerns about hearing with parents in the first instance, school nurse or medical officer, GP, or a visiting teacher of the hearing-impaired. It is at this point that some kind of audiometric test may be advisable. There is a range of audiological techniques to suit children of different ages and abilities. All audiometric tests attempt to give an accurate and reliable description of specific aspects of a child's hearing, information which is often displayed on an audiogram.

THE AUDIOGRAM

The audiogram is a diagrammatic record of the different levels of sound a child can just detect at different frequencies. The record refers to the child's hearing on the day of testing, bearing in mind the particular conditions in which the test was given. The results of a test administered in an audiology clinic may be different from a test given in school, for a number of reasons, including levels of background noise and sophistication of equipment or tester.

One aspect of a child's hearing sensitivity that it is important to know about concerns sound *frequency*. Sound frequencies are displayed across the horizontal axis of the audiogram shown in Figure 3.2. Frequency refers to the rate of vibration of sound waves measured in hertz (Hz). Slow-vibrating sound waves give rise to low sounds. The lowest tone audible to the normal human ear has a frequency of about 20 cycles per second, or 20 Hz. As the frequency increases we perceive a rise in pitch. Very rapidly vibrating sound waves produce high tones. Middle C on the piano has a frequency of 256 Hz, whilst the top note of the piano, four octaves above, has a frequency of 4096 Hz. The highest tones that children and young adults can detect are around 20,000 Hz (20 kHz), which is the kind of sound emitted by a TV screen.

The normal human ear does not respond with equal sensitivity to all frequencies. The bandwidth to which it is most sensitive is from 500 to 4000 Hz, the frequencies which are most important for hearing speech. If a sound has only one single frequency it is described as a pure tone. Speech contains a complex mixture of high and low frequencies. The complex nature of speech is partly explained by the fact that some speech sounds are produced by the vocal cords whilst others result from the tongue, lips and nasal passages.

It is possible to have defective hearing for high sounds and normal hearing for lower frequencies. A child with a high-frequency loss would have some difficulty in hearing the high-frequency components of speech, such as the consonants which begin and end words, plurals, and fricative sounds such as 'f', 'v', 'th', or 'sh'. The same child would be sensitive to the middle bits of words, usually vowel sounds,

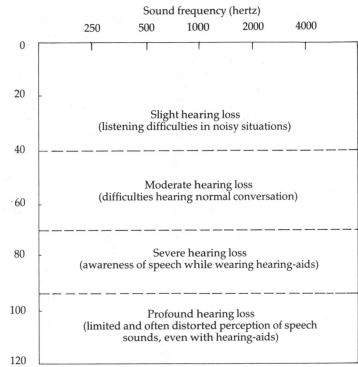

Figure 3.2 *Audiogram and categories of hearing loss (British Association of Teachers of the Deaf, 1981)*

which contribute to intonation and rhythm. As indicated, the most important frequencies for understanding speech are in the middle of the range shown on the audiogram, at 500, 1000 and 2000 Hz. For the child with a conductive loss, hearing sensitivity is usually dampened across all the frequencies, or, unlike most sensori-neural losses, it may be worse in lower frequencies. A mild hearing loss across all the frequency range will affect perception of the weaker, briefer or unstressed speech sounds, such as consonants, plural endings, fricatives, and nasal sounds such as 'm' and 'n'. In a noisy environment, such as a busy classroom, the child's sensitivity to speech sounds will be further reduced.

The second aspect of a child's hearing sensitivity that it is important to know about concerns *intensity*. The vertical axis of the audiogram records the intensity of the sounds that the child can detect at different frequencies. It will be recalled that the frequency of a sound is related to the rate of vibration of a sound wave. However, the intensity of a sound is related to the amplitude of the wave forms produced by a vibrating object. The greater the amplitude of the sound wave, the greater the disturbance of the air pressure, and the more intense the sound.

The physical properties of sound, such as frequency and intensity, have psychological correlates. An individual's experience of these dimensions is usually described in terms of pitch and loudness. The relationships between physical and psychological attributes of sound are complex. For example, a listener's judgement of the pitch of a sound will be affected by its intensity, whilst the apparent loudness of a sound, in turn, depends on frequency, as well as duration.

The physical attribute of sound intensity, the sound pressure level (or SPL) is measured in decibels (dB). The reference point for the softest sound which can be detected by a young adult with normal hearing is described as 0 dB SPL. The threshold of audibility varies across the frequency range and is at its lowest in the middle of the range at about 3 kHz. In other words, our hearing is at its peak at this frequency, but gets progressively less sensitive at lower and higher frequencies. In order to simplify things, the threshold level on the audiogram takes this into account and is represented as a straight line which does not vary with frequency. On the audiogram, then, the threshold of hearing of normal young adults is described as zero decibels hearing level, or 0 dB HL.

The human ear can normally deal with a tremendous range of sound intensities. A whisper is about 1000 times more powerful than a just-audible sound at threshold level. Conversation is about 100,000 times more powerful than a threshold-level sound. For this reason a logarithmic ratio scale is used to plot sound intensities on the audiogram. The audiogram charts the discrepancy from normal in the child's hearing sensitivity. Whispered speech is at a level of about 30 decibels. So a child with a 30-decibel hearing loss would just be able to detect a whisper. If the sounds of normal conversation are at a level of 50 to 60 decibels, then a child with a 60-decibel hearing loss would have difficulty hearing normal conversation. The noise of busy urban traffic is about 70 decibels, whilst a pneumatic drill at close quarters is about 90 decibels. In Table 3.2 the approximate intensities of a range of everyday sounds are given. Sounds above 100 decibels are extremely loud and can be painful to people with normal hearing sensitivity. Obviously, the further down on the intensity scale of the audiogram the child's thresholds of hearing are recorded, the greater the degree of deafness. Discrepancies from the audiometric zero indicate how much louder sounds have to be made at each frequency in order for the child just to detect them, compared with a person of normal hearing.

In testing hearing we need to know, for each ear, the level of hearing loss at each separate frequency displayed on the audiogram. Different audiogram configurations have different implications for the child's speech perception. We have noted, for example, that a high-frequency

Table 3.2 *Approximate intensities of common sounds*

Sound intensity (dB SPL)	Sound source
10	Rustle of leaves
20	Ticking of watch
30	Whispered voice, library
40	Quiet speech
50	Car at 30 metres
60	Normal conversation
70	Vacuum cleaner, busy traffic
80	Tube train, shouting voice
90	Pneumatic drill
100	Rock band
120	Jet aircraft

loss will have a different impact on what the child can hear of speech than a moderate flat loss across the frequency range caused by a conductive impairment. Clinical audiology uses the pure-tone audiogram extensively, although it is only one of several measures of hearing loss and not the best predictor of what children may be able to hear of speech in everyday listening conditions. Nevertheless, the audiogram is the one measure most likely to be available in the child's school medical records, and both teachers and parents should be able to interpret it.

In Figure 3.2 several broad categories of hearing loss are shown on the audiogram. One way of summarising the information on a child's audiogram is to average the decibel hearing losses over the five frequencies shown, for the better ear. In these terms, a 'glue ear' condition might give rise to an average hearing loss of 40 decibels across the frequency range. It should be remembered that the audiogram for a child with a sensori-neural loss may be uneven across the frequency range and between the two ears. A typical configuration is the 'ski-slope', which depicts an increasing fall of hearing sensitivity in higher frequencies. So the figure given as an average hearing loss for a child with a sensori-neural impairment may obscure important information. Nevertheless, deafness which averages more than 60 decibels can be taken to mean that a child will be unable to hear normal conversation without the use of hearing-aids.

HEARING TESTS

It is not always easy to test the hearing of young children, particularly if this is carried out at a hospital or clinic, where the child may feel anxious from the very start. Testing depends on the child co-operating and being capable of responding to a signal. Children who feel apprehensive, who do not understand the task requirements or who refuse to co-operate may fail a hearing test for reasons other than hearing loss *per se*. Traditional hearing tests are also subjective in the main. The Audiologist introduces some form of sound signal, such as a pure tone, into one ear and then interprets the response which the child makes. Some of the recent developments in audiological techniques have been towards more objective methods, which cut out human interpretation and error. Whilst there are several important advances incorporating computer technology, traditional hearing tests will be the norm for most children for some years to come. There is always the possibility that hearing tests will not reveal the true picture of a child's hearing sensitivity.

Distraction tests

A technique known as the distraction test is often used to screen the hearing of babies from about seven to eighteen months of age (Ewing and Ewing, 1944). In order to do the test, babies have to be able to sit up, with good back and head control, so that they can turn to locate a sound stimulus out of the field of vision. The baby is usually sat forward on the parent's knees, supported at the hips and facing one of the examiners, who engages the baby's attention with a toy. A second examiner presents a sound stimulus, which the baby must not be able to see or feel. High- and low-frequency sounds are presented separately at about 35 decibels in quiet conditions to both ears a number of times. If no response is observed at these levels, the sounds are made louder until a definite response is shown. A baby who does not turn to locate high and low sounds until they are presented at a 60-decibel level may be suspected of having a 60-decibel hearing loss.

Distraction testing is difficult to carry out, ensuring that auditory stimuli are only presented at the correct intensity. Conditions must be quiet and the infant must be contented and alert, but not too absorbed in the examiner's efforts to engage the child's attention. Scrupulous care is required to avoid casting shadows, moving into the child's line of sight or distracting the child with vibrations from footsteps. A severely hearing-impaired child who has become very visually aware may pass this test by responding to small visual clues, rather than sounds. Conversely, some normally hearing infants fail to respond in the expected way. When babies are developmentally delayed there are added difficulties in giving the test, although children with additional handicaps have an increased risk of hearing loss. Despite the drawbacks, distraction testing remains the standard procedure for screening infants (DHSS Advisory Committee on Services for

Hearing-impaired People, 1981), although it has been reported that as many as 41 per cent of infants with significant hearing-impairments are not identified by this screening procedure (National Deaf Children's Society, 1983).

Co-operative testing

From the age of eighteen months to about 2½ years, children's hearing may be tested using a co-operative technique. It is assumed that children in this age-range are capable of following verbal instructions and responding appropriately, although many parents would be less than optimistic about this. The examiner asks the child in a voice of carefully controlled intensity (about 35–40 dB SPL) to 'Give the dolly to Daddy', 'Put the brick on the chair' or 'Give the car to Mummy'. If a louder voice has to be used to get the child to respond, this may indicate a hearing loss. It may also indicate that the child does not understand the instructions, is inhibited or is simply not used to doing as requested. It can be difficult to be sure about the voice levels used in this approach. A current trend is to improve the testing of very young infants by using electro-acoustic signals, such as warble tones. Information gained from co-operative testing is not specific enough to determine whether the child has hearing difficulties in high or low frequencies, and other testing would have to be done to find this out.

Visual reinforcement audiometry

The basic principle of visual reinforcement audiometry is that children from the age of six months to three years can be trained to look in a certain direction wherever a sound stimulus is heard, by rewarding the looking response with the sight of a picture, animated toy or illuminated puppet. The child is usually sat at a small table and occupied with a toy. A sound stimulus is presented through loudspeakers located to the left and right of the child. As the child turns in response to the stimulus, a reward is given by the brief presentation of the puppet, toy or flashing light, close to the sound source. Here, too, the child must be contented, alert and responsive, but the technique overcomes many of the limitations of distraction and co-operative testing. When successful, the test provides fairly precise information about the child's hearing sensitivity across the frequency range. However, the test requires fixed apparatus, such as loudspeakers, which may be difficult to provide in some settings, for example, community clinics.

Conditioning techniques

Children who have reached a developmental level of 2½ years are usually capable of completing a performance test. The examiner 'conditions' the child to respond to a stimulus (such as 'Go') by dropping a brick into a box, or fitting a peg into a board. The test proceeds with a child continuing to respond to a variety of signals, such as the high-frequency sounds 's' or 'sh', warble tones or pure tones at controlled levels of pitch and intensity in free field. When a child does not respond to the sound stimulus at the level given, it is made louder until the child indicates that it has been detected, thus signifying a hearing loss.

Pure-tone audiometry

Children of 3 or 3½ years of age are usually capable of completing a pure-tone audiogram, which is a favoured technique from this age on because of the more specific information it reveals. An audiometer produces pure tones at different intensities across the frequency range. The child is trained to wait and listen for the sound stimulus, and then make a response, such as dropping a brick into a box. Each ear can be measured separately by presenting sounds through headphones, and the results are recorded on an audiogram. Audiometers are calibrated in a way that takes into account the varying thresholds of hearing across the frequencies when a large sample of normally hearing young adults is tested. The 'audiometric zero' (0 dB HL) is a straight line at the top of the audiogram which does not vary with frequency. This makes the interpretation of pure-tone audiograms simpler than free-field measures which are expressed in decibels SPL, where the baseline of hearing would be a U-shaped curve.

The audiogram in Figure 3.3 shows a severe sensori-neural hearing loss in both ears. Such an audiogram is characteristic of a child with a prenatal cause of deafness, such as rubella, where the development of the cochlea has been arrested, leading to a fairly uniform loss. We have followed convention by denoting results for the left ear with an 'X', and those for the right with an 'O'. When interpreting the scale showing hearing threshold along the vertical axis, remember that it is logarithmic and that the degree of hearing loss increases incrementally the further down the scale the child's threshold is recorded. A child with an audiogram like this has much useful residual hearing across the frequencies important for speech. Wearing appropriate hearing-aids, the child could be expected to hear the sounds of normal conversation in good listening conditions. The child's average hearing loss is 75 decibels HL in the better ear.

A severe high-frequency loss is shown in the audiogram in Figure 3.4. Selective loss for high frequencies is typical of deafness which results from perinatal factors, such as anoxia, because the nerve cells of the cochlea which respond to high tones are felt to be more vulnerable

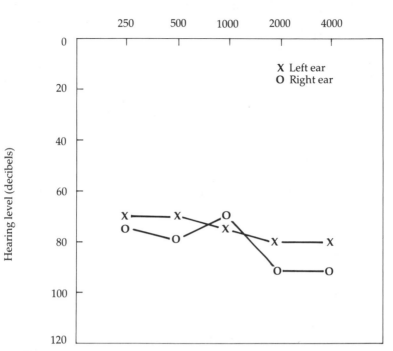

Figure 3.3 *Audiogram showing a severe bilateral sensori-neural hearing loss*

in any destructive process. A child with such a 'ski-slope' configuration would have considerable awareness of sound but miss many of the nuances and details of speech. A hearing-aid which amplifies high-frequency sounds more than low frequencies would need to be prescribed. Interestingly, this audiogram also shows an average hearing loss of 75 decibels HL in the better ear.

The audiogram of a child with a hereditary sensori-neural hearing loss is shown in Figure 3.5. This child's hearing loss averages more than 100 decibels in the better ear. Even wearing hearing-aids a child with such a profound loss would have limited access to the sounds of conversation. Uneven responses across the frequency range will result in a distorted experience of sound. At some frequencies, for example, there is no measurable hearing at all. It should be noted that there is no clear relationship between degree of hearing loss and how well the child will be able to develop speech and language, or cope with school. Obviously, a profound hearing loss is a tremendous obstacle to surmount, but there are many children with this severity of deafness who achieve well in mainstream school contexts, given appropriate support. In subsequent chapters we shall be looking in greater detail at

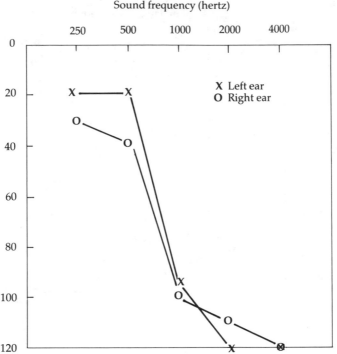

Figure 3.4 *Audiogram showing a severe bilateral high-frequency sensori-neural hearing loss*

some of the critical variables for success, but degree of hearing loss, *per se*, appears not to be one of them.

Bone conduction

The information revealed by a bone-conduction test can be very useful when an attempt is made to diagnose the underlying reason for a hearing loss. This test helps to locate the source of the hearing difficulty either in the middle ear or outer ear. When a pure tone is presented to the child through headphones, the signal travels down the ear canal, where it vibrates the eardrum and ossicular chain. The sound waves are converted into electrical nerve impulses by the cochlea and eventually perceived by the brain. In order to pass the pure-tone test the whole hearing system has to be in working order. Instead of pure tones through headphones, sounds can be presented through a small vibrator placed on the skull, usually the mastoid bone behind the ear. Signals produced in this way stimulate the cochlea directly through the bone, effectively bypassing the mechanisms of the middle ear. A normally hearing person will hear signals conducted through the air and bone at approximately the same levels of intensity.

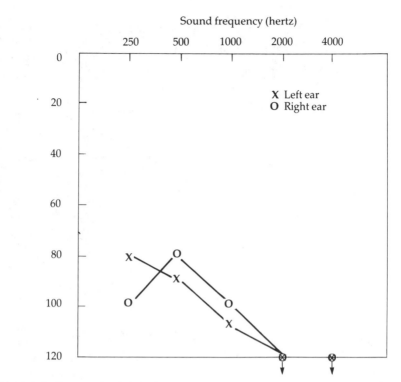

Figure 3.5 *Audiogram of a child with hereditary deafness, showing a profound bilateral sensori-neural hearing loss*

The audiogram in Figure 3.6 shows the results of pure-tone audiometry and bone conduction for a child's left ear. In order to achieve that, the right ear has to be 'masked off' by noise input. If the right ear were not masked, it would be impossible to say whether the results for bone conduction derived from the right or left ear, because the vibrator will stimulate both cochleas through the skull. The audiogram shows that bone-transmitted signals (marked by ']') are within normal limits across the frequency range. However, the pure-tone results through headphones indicate up to a 50-decibel loss. The hearing loss must lie in the outer- or middle-ear system because signals transmitted through bone to the cochlea are responded to normally. The loss is therefore a conductive one. If a child's audiogram were to show a loss for both air-and bone-conducted signals, then the results of the pure-tone and bone-conducted tests would look similar and a sensori-neural loss would be indicated. Where a child has a mixed loss, involving both middle and inner ear, bone-conduction levels would be depressed, with an additional loss of sensitivity for air-conducted signals.

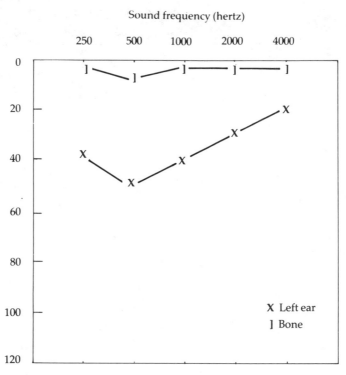

Figure 3.6 *Audiogram showing a conductive hearing loss*

Impedance audiometry

Although not a test of hearing, impedance audiometry gives important diagnostic information about the functioning of the middle ear. Put simply, the technique measures the amount of sound reflected by the eardrum when a sound wave reaches it. We have said that a hearing loss may arise from negative air pressure and a build up of fluid or 'glue' in the middle-ear cavity. In such conditions the eardrum is unable to vibrate freely and there is a general dampening of sound transmission across the ossicular chain because of the increased stiffness of the system. Impedance audiometry uses a simple but clever technique. A small plastic probe is placed in the child's ear canal for a few seconds. A tube in the probe feeds sound into the ear. A second probe has a microphone which picks up the sound reflected from the eardrum. A third tube allows the examiner to control the air pressure in the space between the probe and the outside of the eardrum.

In a normal ear, sound travels down the ear canal, through the eardrum and across the middle-ear cavity, with very little sound reflected back from the eardrum. Any inefficiency in the sound-conducting mechanisms, as a result of otitis media for example, will result in less sound conducted across the middle ear and more sound reflected back by the drum. This is picked up by the microphone and recorded on a graph. The test is less subjective than others because the child simply has to sit quietly and still. The examiner gains useful information towards deciding whether a child has a conductive disorder. For these reasons it has been argued that impedance audiometry should be used for the routine screening of children.

Speech audiometry

Whilst the audiogram may give fairly precise information about a child's ability to hear pure tones, it may not be a good predictor of hearing for more complex signals, such as speech. We can hazard a guess as to the components of speech which might be difficult to discern, such as 's' and 'f' sounds for a child with a high-frequency loss. However, speech consists of a complex mixture of tones. Speech audiometry is designed to assess what a child can hear of spoken language. In one approach the child may be asked to listen to a live voice in free field. A more controlled test is to present words or sentences through loudspeakers or headphones. Word or sentence lists are used containing the spread of vowel and consonant sounds found in speech. More recently, children have been asked to listen to specially constructed sentences which contain representative proportions of the different speech sounds in familiar vocabulary (Bench and Bamford, 1979). The child is asked to repeat what is heard and from the proportion of correct responses a judgement can be made about how clearly the child can discriminate between speech sounds at different intensities.

Electric response audiometry

This survey of hearing tests would be incomplete without some mention of the newer developments in audiology. A major problem we have noted is the difficulty in getting reliable responses from young children. The child has to respond clearly to sound stimuli, as opposed to inadvertent visual or tactile cues. A few children with significant hearing losses are missed because of the subjectivity of traditional hearing tests: there are many ways in which children give misleading information to the examiner about their ability to hear. It would be extremely valuable to have alternative methods of assessment which are less vulnerable to human error.

One recent development, available in specialist centres, is electric response audiometry. It is known that tiny electrical events occur, physiologically, in the cochlea and auditory pathways in the brain, when a sound stimulus is presented to the normal ear. Using computers, these nerve impulses or action potentials can be measured. The process may involve the child having a general anaesthetic so that an electrode can be passed through the eardrum to the covering of the cochlea. More often the test uses non-invasive electrodes, attached to the skin behind the ear, when the child is asleep. Information derived from this technique is not very specific. Severity of hearing loss may be indicated but not the pattern of frequencies involved. Electric response audiometry can be used to confirm a suspected hearing-impairment in children who are handicapped or unco-operative, and unable to participate in conventional testing. As such, it is an important supportive means of identifying hearing loss.

The auditory response cradle

Another innovation, currently being evaluated in maternity hospitals, is the auditory response cradle which tests the hearing of newborn babies. A computer is used to present a moderately high-frequency noise at about 85 dB SPL to the baby in a cradle. Sensors in the cradle identify changes in bodily activity, head movement and breathing in response to the sounds. The computer works out whether these physical changes are random, or indications of hearing loss compared with the normal response patterns of an infant. The auditory response cradle has been heralded as the screening method of the future for early identification of hearing loss in babies, but it is not entirely problem-free and other techniques, such as auditory brain stem response screening, may come to the fore.

HEARING-AIDS

For a child with a severe sensori-neural hearing loss, the only significant 'treatment' available is the provision of hearing-aids, together with appropriate family advice and educational support. We shall be considering some aspects of hearing-aid management again in Chapter 5, when we look at the listening environment in relation to effective teaching and learning contexts. In this book a broad view of the impact of deafness on development is expressed, not one restricted to the child's ability to hear sound. Nevertheless, most authorities would agree that the whole purpose of early identification and diagnosis of deafness is to provide whatever treatment is necessary to reduce the consequences of a hearing loss at source. There are very few children whose deafness is total. By the same token there are very few children who derive no benefit at all from hearing-aids, and many who benefit a great deal. The sooner a hearing loss is discovered and, where appropriate, hearing-aids fitted, the more likely it is that auditory factors will become a meaningful part of the child's growing experience and discovery of the world.

However, hearing-aids do not restore a child's hearing to normal, in the way that spectacles might be considered to correct poor vision. Hearing-aids make sounds louder. The 'gain' from hearing-aids may be about 30 to 40 decibels, but can be as much as 60 or 70 decibels in certain frequencies. How well a child uses hearing-aids depends on a number of factors: the configuration and nature of the hearing loss; the type of hearing-aid prescribed; the age at which aids were introduced; the listening conditions in which the aids are used; and a host of less specific factors, including the motivation, attitude and ability of the individual. Obviously, an important variable is the degree of hearing loss. The child with a profound loss, even wearing powerful amplification, may not receive very much useful auditory information. Such a child may not, through aided listening, have access to the sounds of natural conversation. In some instances, the child with a very uneven audiogram configuration may be difficult to fit with aids. A high-frequency loss, for example (see Figure 3.4), requires the higher frequencies to be amplified by greater amounts than lower frequencies. If this were not achieved, frequencies already better perceived would be amplified to levels of distortion and perhaps discomfort. Conversely, the frequencies where there is least sensitivity would still remain below thresholds necessary for perceiving speech sounds.

There are several ways of evaluating the gain in auditory sensitivity which hearing-aids bring to the wearer. Speech audiometry completed whilst the child is wearing aids would give some indication of the benefits of aided listening, compared with unaided. Assessment of hearing or hearing-aids usually takes place in the controlled acoustic conditions of a clinic. The conditions in which aids are used are often not ideal acoustically. Unfortunately, hearing-aids do not select the sounds which are most important for the child to hear. Aids pick up and amplify every detail of sound in the environment, irrespective of its relevance. Also, the impaired auditory system is less good at filtering relevant sounds. The noisier the listening context, the more likely it is that unwanted sounds will be amplified to the detriment of important sounds, such as the teacher's voice. Technical problems may arise such as 'recruitment', which leads to the blurring of highly amplified sounds so that they are less easily discriminated from their backgrounds. (Recruitment is the condition whereby a relatively slight increase in sound intensity results in a much greater increase in the sensation of loudness as perceived by the child.)

From these introductory comments about hearing-aids it should be clear that they are not, in any sense, a panacea. Hearing-aids are an indispensable part of the resources available to help children over the obstacles to learning which deafness presents. It is important for all adult caregivers, including parents and teachers, to be aware of the proper and effective use of aids, the acoustic conditions which are most sympathetic to hearing-aid wearers, and the strategies which can be adopted to maximise their effectiveness, for example, in the classroom. Hearing-aids, of themselves, do not provide solutions to such complex problems as the nature of adult interactions with deaf children. But that does not mean that we should be complacent about their management.

CONVENTIONAL HEARING-AIDS

The basic components of every conventional electrical hearing-aid are a microphone, an amplifier and a receiver (or speaker). The microphone picks up sound energy and converts it into electrical impulses which reproduce the pitch and intensity of the signal. The amplifier increases the electrical signal, which is then delivered to the receiver. In turn, the receiver converts the impulses back into sound. Conventional aids fall into two main types: those worn on the body and those worn behind the ear. Within these two basic designs there are many models available. The particular choice of aid depends on the age of the child, the nature of the hearing loss, the degree of amplification required and the effectiveness of the aid for the individual. Ideally, a hearing-aid should provide the user with access to speech sounds and good-quality reproduction, together with secondary considerations such as low cost, long battery life and limited maintenance requirements.

Body-worn aids

Body-worn aids are capable of giving good quality and very powerful amplification across a wide frequency range. In the body-worn aid (see Figure 3.7), the case houses the microphone, amplifier and batteries, and is worn high up on the child's chest. These aids are robust, the controls are easy to handle and, because of their size, batteries last longer and are easy to change. The receiver which delivers sound into the child's ear canal is separated from the amplifying system by a long cord. The receiver clips into the earmould which fits into the child's ear. This gives an important advantage to the body-worn type of aid: feedback is less of a problem. Feedback occurs when amplified sound leaks out around the earmould. The earmould is made from an impression of the child's ear, usually taken by syringing a soft silicone rubber solution into the ear and leaving this to harden. The mould manufactured from this cast should provide a good seal when fitted in

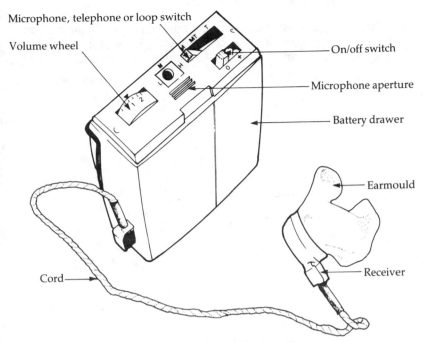

Microphone, telephone or loop switch

Volume wheel

On/off switch

Microphone aperture

Battery drawer

Earmould

Cord

Receiver

Figure 3.7 *Body-worn hearing-aid*

the child's ear. If the earmould is not a good fit, sound is picked up by the microphone of the aid again, giving a disturbing high-pitched whistle. However, because of the greater distance between the microphone on the body and the receiver at the ear, the feedback cycle is less likely to occur.

Body-worn aids have several drawbacks. Because they are worn on the torso the speech signal is not detected at the normal ear position. The body absorbs some sounds, whilst clothing may cover the microphone or produce unwanted sounds by rubbing against the microphone aperture. Body-worn aids are hard to conceal and children may reject them on cosmetic grounds. Their bulk and position, high up on the chest for a good 'ear–voice' link, mean that they may get in the way of an active youngster. Many parents find they have to keep the aid in a harness, cover the microphone aperture with a thin film of cellophane to keep it clean, and feed the cords through the child's clothing to keep them out of reach.

Post-aural aids

Post-aural aids sit behind the auricle and are small, inconspicuous and less inconvenient to wear. Since they are worn close to the normal location for hearing sounds, some of the normal functions of the ear are replicated, such as the detection of sound direction. In the post-aural aid, the case houses all the components, including microphone, amplifier, receiver and batteries (see Figure 3.8). Amplified sound is

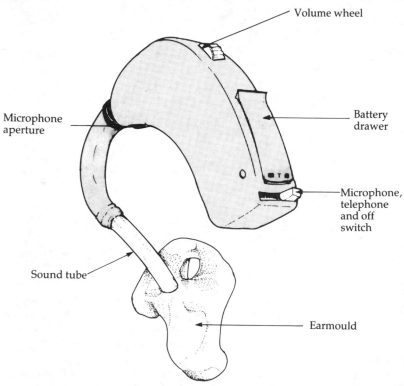

Figure 3.8 *Post-aural hearing-aid*

delivered to the ear via a small plastic tube which connects the hook of the aid to the mould. Until recently, it proved difficult to produce small but sensitive components, such as microphones and receivers. Although post-aural aids now incorporate efficient microchip circuitry which provides the same range of amplification as body-worn aids, there may be a narrower frequency response and more distorted sound quality than is possible in the larger aid. Post-aural aids are more easily lost, submerged or dropped, and less easy to repair. Controls can be difficult to manipulate, whilst batteries are expensive and have a shorter life. Some children have difficulty wearing the aids if they have small auricles, and parents may need to have recourse to sticky tape. But the major drawback of post-aural aids is the problem of feedback, given that the microphone and receiver are so close together. Even so, post-aural aids are prescribed for the majority of children, including small infants.

A recent development of the post-aural aid is the even smaller 'all-in-ear' aid. The entire components are contained within the earmould and inserted into the ear. 'All-in-ear' aids may be more expensive and few children are currently prescribed them, usually those with more moderate hearing losses. Their principal advantage is that the microphone position allows the auricle to play its normal physiological role in sound reception. They are not often recommended for young children because of feedback problems. Children need to have earmoulds replaced three or four times a year as their outer ears grow. The early 'all-in-ear' aids had to be restructured in new moulds as the child's ear grew, although nowadays a module including the 'all-in-ear' aid is more easily transferred to a new mould.

Adult caregivers and children must be aware of the strategies which can be used to increase the effectiveness of conventional hearing-aids. There are two major aspects to consider. First, the child's ability to hear using aids will depend on distance from the sound source. The further a speaker is positioned outside a range of about 2 metres away from the child's aid, the less likely it is that the voice will be picked up by the microphone. Secondly, as the communication distance increases, other nearer or louder sound sources will be picked up by the aid. So the child's ability to listen will be affected by the level of competing background noise in the environment. The implications of these factors for conventional hearing-aid use are important. In Chapter 5 more specific suggestions are made about optimum acoustic conditions for listening, and where to position the child in a learning context in order to avoid noise interference.

In general, speech perception is usually better in an environment with soft furnishings, carpets and sound-absorbent materials such as cork wall tiles. Sound reverberates and creates noise interference in rooms with hard-plastered walls, tiled floors, high ceilings and sparse soft furnishings. Adults should also be careful about where children are seated, preferably away from noise sources such as a sink, play or cupboard area in a classroom. It is a common misconception that hearing-aid users need to be shouted at, with slow, laboured and overarticulated speech. In fact, many of the strategies for communication that we shall be outlining in this book are designed to normalise how children and adults interact. A further point about aided listening: children fitted with two hearing-aids are not necessarily more severely handicapped than those who wear only one. Children usually find advantages in listening when two aids are prescribed because it is much easier to locate a sound and focus attention on it with binaural listening. This is especially true of noisy situations where children are expected to listen for protracted periods. Parents, and sometimes children themselves, may resist two hearing-aids as though this signified a double handicap.

RADIO HEARING-AIDS

Radio aids have been designed to overcome some of the problems associated with conventional hearing-aid systems, namely by providing a better signal-to-noise ratio at the child's ear. A radio system comprises a microphone and transmitter unit, which is worn by the speaker, and a radio receiver, which is worn by the child. Several variations are available. However, the basis of these systems is that a microphone is attached to the speaker, within about 20 centimetres of the mouth. What the speaker says is picked up by the microphone, converted into a radio signal and then broadcast on a permitted radio frequency range. The child's radio receiver is tuned to the transmitting frequency and picks up the radio signal. The output is amplified by the child's own hearing-aids and fed into the child's ears. Since the speaker's voice is transmitted via radio waves to the child's hearing-aids, what the speaker says is heard just as well across distances of many metres, without any interruption to the signal. However far the child is from the speaker, up to about 100 metres and through walls, the signal should be heard clearly by the child, regardless of other interfering sounds or background noise.

Undoubtedly, radio hearing-aid systems are a major factor in the successful integration of hearing-impaired children into mainstream classes where acoustic conditions may be very unsympathetic. By overcoming the problems associated with the communication distance in conventional systems, children using radio aids can receive clear speech signals in noisy listening conditions. For very young children, freedom of movement and exploration does not have to be sacrificed. It should, however, be remembered that radio aids cannot improve the child's hearing thresholds. The first generation of these systems has also been relatively expensive, occasionally unreliable, and cumbersome for the child to wear. Radio aids require appropriate management in the classroom to maximise their effectiveness. Care is required over their routine maintenance. Where children are able to use radio aids only at school and not at home, adjustment to two systems has to be made. More detailed guidelines on the use of radio hearing-aids are given in Chapter 5.

PROFESSIONAL RÔLES

This chapter has covered some of the physical facts of deafness across a broad spectrum, as a basis for understanding the ways in which hearing losses arise, how these may be identified and diagnosed, possible treatments, and the auditory significance of different forms of hearing loss for the individual. We have stressed the view that the technical aspects of deafness, such as perception of sound, have only limited power to account for the impact of deafness on childhood development, with little direct correspondence between how well children achieve in aspects of language, learning and literacy, and the degree of hearing loss. It should also be borne in mind that, when deafness presents significant developmental obstacles to children and their families, these are rarely experienced in just one dimension. The effects of a profound hearing loss on a child may be obvious in terms of speech and language development, but spill over in more subtle ways to affect the child's confidence, maturity and emotional well-being, and disrupt social encounters with others. For every hearing-impaired child there is a responsibility to discover as much as we can of the strengths and weaknesses of the individual, and not to let children become victims of their handicaps, in the sense that deafness itself is held to account for the way the child responds, behaves or learns. In much that follows in this book we shall be highlighting factors in the child's social and educational environments which have important effects and are open to change.

In this section we shall outline the professional rôles of different agencies involved with hearing-impaired children, and with whom teachers may have contact. We shall also be summarising the teacher's own responsibilities in the identification and assessment process.

The Health Visitor

At the pre-school stage, community health services largely take responsibility for the early identification of hearing-impaired children. Health Visitors see families with young children periodically to give advice on care and management, and to make developmental observations. They are often the first professionals to whom parents express their concerns, they have oversight of siblings and are able to link up with other medical agencies. Their continuity of contact with the family puts them in a good position to recognise when a child is slow to react to sounds, producing a limited range of vocalisation, or delayed in speech. Health Visitors screen all babies at around eight months for hearing, vision and general development. Given the difficulties in screening babies objectively, using methods such as distraction testing, insights gained by Health Visitors from what parents have to say for themselves about their child's hearing are important to take into account.

The Medical Officer

Doctors who are likely to be involved in identifying children with hearing losses are the Clinical Medical Officers who work in well-baby clinics, schools and other community services. The precise rôle of doctors varies from one health district to another. Medical Officers play a key rôle in identifying early difficulties both in pre-school child health clinics and on school-entry, when most children are medically examined. It is at this point that the 'sweep frequency' test may be given, often by the school nurse. Using a pure-tone audiometer, the examiner sweeps through a limited range of frequencies at a fixed intensity level of 15 or 20 decibels HL. 'Sweep' testing is often done in unsatisfactory conditions, and will not detect very mild losses or identify fluctuating hearing losses in children who happen to pass the screen on the day of testing.

Children who are identified as having possible hearing difficulties may then be investigated in a Community Health Audiology Clinic, staffed by doctors trained in audiology. The next step may then be to refer the child to the specialist team in a hospital audiology unit. In some cases a GP may decide to refer a child directly to the hospital services. Senior Clinical Medical Officers liaise between hospital services and the education authority. They will indicate the significance of any medical findings for later educational provision. This is a particularly important link for children with hearing loss as part of a range of medical difficulties. Medical Officers who work in schools have an ongoing rôle in identifying undiagnosed hearing losses which may be the result of mumps, measles or other infections. Medical Officers who work in the community also contribute to the multiprofessional assessment and review of children whose needs may require special educational help under the terms of the 1981 Education Act.

The Audiologist

The Audiologist specialises in the testing of hearing and provides important information towards the diagnosis of deafness and the prescription and monitoring of hearing-aids. The Audiologist usually works in a hospital centre in close co-operation with the ENT Consultant and the community medical services.

The ENT Consultant

The ENT Consultant is a surgeon whose medical speciality is the diagnosis and treatment of disorders of the ear, nose or throat. The ENT Consultant works together with the Audiologist and other colleagues at a hospital centre in deciding the best way of intervening when a child has a hearing loss, and on the prescription of hearing-aids.

The teacher of the hearing-impaired

The first educational intervention for the pre-school hearing-impaired child is usually made by a teacher of the hearing-impaired who visits the home. As soon as diagnosis is made, parents will need much information and encouragement, particularly in coming to terms with the hearing loss and accepting hearing-aids. Teachers of the hearing-impaired must be sensitive family counsellors as well as sources of practical advice. They often have a background in normal classroom experience followed up by further training, or a qualification pursued whilst employed in a school or resource for the hearing-impaired. Many specialist teachers have clinical competence in carrying out audiological assessments. The precise responsibilities of teachers of the hearing-impaired vary widely from area to area, with some teachers specialising in the early guidance of families from the time of diagnosis, others employed in peripatetic services as support agencies to schools, and many working in special resources, such as schools for the deaf. For the non-specialist teacher working in the mainstream, the teacher of the hearing-impaired is a valuable source of advice about hearing-aid technology, as well as strategies for helping individual children.

Local Education Authorities look to teachers of the hearing-impaired for the provision of inservice training for other professional groups and sometimes parents. It is important that teachers of the hearing-impaired work closely together with parents and other agencies, such as Medical Officers and Educational Psychologists, in the assessment and placement of individual children and the ongoing monitoring of children's progress, as well as contributing towards policy discussions within LEAs, in working towards good practice and the efficient use of resources. A number of ways in which specialist teachers can support hearing-impaired children in mainstream school settings, either as companion teachers or by providing additional tutoring, are discussed in Chapter 5.

The Speech Therapist

Speech Therapists are responsible for the assessment, diagnosis and treatment of communication difficulties, in the widest sense of the term. Many Speech Therapists contribute valuable advice to the families and teachers involved with the hearing-impaired. Speech Therapists usually work for a Health Authority, but accept referrals from parents, teachers, doctors and other professionals. They are usually able to give detailed assessments of a child's speech and language abilities and may carry out a programme of treatment. It has recently been suggested that the traditional view of Speech Therapists 'correcting' children's speech on weekly visits to an outpatients' clinic is an outmoded one. In relation to children with hearing-impairments and to children generally, Speech Therapists can make significant contributions to the overall management of communication. Valuable suggestions can be made for both parents and teachers to use in the natural learning contexts of the home and school. Handing on skills and strategies to those who have day-to-day contact with hearing-impaired children is an essential aspect of effective working partnerships between families and professionals.

The Educational Psychologist

Educational Psychologists have a training in child psychology as well as in teaching, and often have a wide experience of ordinary children as well as those with developmental or learning difficulties. They are usually employed by Local Education Authorities and visit groups of mainstream and special schools, as well as providing a service to the children and families who live in an area. Increasingly, Educational Psychologists are called upon to provide inservice training on a wide range of issues related to children and schools. Most Educational Psychologists are competent family counsellors, whilst at the classroom level there is usually a close affinity with the teacher's point of view. Psychologists should be able to give advice on ways of working with individuals or groups. As officers of the LEA, Educational Psychologists share some of the responsibility for decision-making and policy. They are therefore able to advise on the availability of resources to schools and to take a key rôle in identifying and planning for children with special needs. Educational Psychologists contribute to, and often organise, procedures under the 1981 Education Act. All teachers should have access to the Educational Psychologist who visits the school in order to discuss any concerns about children or the teaching environment.

Until recently, few Educational Psychologists had training or experience in working with hearing-impaired children, although many more psychologists are aware of the needs of such children and a number of LEAs employ specialist psychologists. Yet another outmoded view is that Educational Psychologists spend most of their time testing children. Their rôle is often one of facilitator: co-ordinating advice and information provided by parents, doctors, specialist teachers and other professionals, and negotiating the response made by the LEA to meet the needs of the child. Some Educational Psychologists have developed a high degree of expertise in working with hearing-impaired children and are able to offer in-depth psychological advice on individual children. However, perhaps the most valuable contribution that Educational Psychologists can make is one which draws on their wider experience of appraisal and monitoring of children, the evaluation of particular classroom milieus, and the setting and achievement of teacher objectives. Educational Psychologists are in a good position to work out a language of analysis of teaching and learning processes with those who have more detailed and specialist knowledge than themselves.

The teacher

When a child with a severe hearing loss is placed in an ordinary classroom setting in a mainstream school, the major responsibility for the child's educational experience is shouldered by a teacher who may have no specialist training or experience of hearing-impaired children. The ordinary classteacher also has a major contribution to make to the processes of identifying children with hearing losses which are undetected (see Table 3.1). A wide spectrum of hearing loss affects children in equally diverse and unpredictable ways, and it falls to the classteacher to be aware of appropriate teaching strategies, to organise the environment in ways which help listening and communication, and to devise an appropriate curriculum. Not least of all, it is the teacher's responsibility to keep parents in touch with developments in school and to involve them in the learning process.

In every Local Education Authority a structure of support agencies exists upon which schools can draw for advice and help. Inservice programmes should be available and can be requested from advisory and support agencies. The 1981 Education Act has placed a general duty on schools to be more aware of children with special needs, to develop efficient screening and monitoring procedures, and to set appropriate goals according to individual strengths and weaknesses. It would be unrealistic to expect teachers to make radical changes to their teaching styles, or to devote great amounts of time to individual children, whilst somehow managing to teach the rest of their classes. However, the onus is upon the teacher to ask other agencies for help in planning and evaluating the child's learning experience. The teacher needs to know what supportive help will be available when a severely hearing-impaired child is integrated into the mainstream setting, and how this is to be accommodated within the day-to-day running of the class. Modifications to teaching style, for example in using hearing-aids effectively, need to be reasonable and practicable. If a programme of integration for a hearing-impaired child is to work well, the teacher has to feel firmly at the centre of a working partnership between family and supporting professionals.

LEGISLATION AND SPECIAL NEEDS

The 1981 Education Act[1] has much to say about relationships between professional agencies, the collation of information and ongoing process of assessment, openness and frankness with parents, and the possibility of intervention in the stages leading up to any formal procedures. Because of the number of professional groups likely to be involved with a hearing-impaired child and the family, it can be difficult to give consistent advice to parents and to ensure that services are co-ordinated effectively. Circular 1/83, which accompanies the Act, advocates that professionals should give advice which reflects their own areas of expertise. Clear lines of communication and close co-operation are important and, if separate agencies are to work together and recognise each other's skills, there must be a shared belief that no single perspective on the needs of children excludes all others.

A number of strategies are outlined in the article by Webster, Scanlon and Bown (1985) for identifying a core team of professionals, including doctors, specialist teachers and psychologists, who will meet together regularly to plan service-delivery. The sequence of involvement of professionals with families should be clearly outlined. The lead rôle in advising parents about the first educational steps is likely to be taken by the teacher of the hearing-impaired. However, in some circumstances it may be appropriate for early family counselling to be given by the doctor in the team, particularly where hearing-impairment is part of a range of medical factors and there may be a changing developmental picture of the primacy of the various aspects involved. In another situation the psychologist may elect to work with parents in the home, for example where behaviour difficulties are experienced, such as tantrums or poor sleep patterns. The core team might decide to ask for other advice to be given, for example by involving a Speech Therapist or social worker. Such a core team can achieve cohesion by sharing information routinely, meeting families together, providing inservice training and engaging parents at every point when decisions are made.

In Circular 1/83, schools are also asked to keep clear and effective lines of communication with outside agencies. The circular describes what it calls a 'progressive extension of professional involvement'. What this means is that schools should know whom to call on for advice should a teacher become concerned about a child's hearing or when a child with a known hearing loss comes into school. In many LEAs schools keep a special needs register of children, which is discussed regularly with support agencies. A record is kept of the time any difficulties were suspected, whom the school referred on to, and what was done to help. It is essential, if honest relationships with parents are to be fostered, that any misgivings about children's hearing, developmental progress or the level of support available to meet the needs of a child with a known hearing loss are shared with parents.

Formal procedures under the 1981 Education Act are usually initiated when there are grounds for believing that a child has special needs which cannot be met within the resources normally available to the ordinary school. This will vary considerably from area to area. In some LEAs all schools have access to peripatetic teachers of the hearing-impaired, to Speech Therapists, and to special needs support teams. If a child's needs cannot be met from existing support, the formal statutory procedures are initiated in order to ascertain more fully what the child's needs are and how they might be met. The child who requires classroom help additional to that already available, or the child who would benefit from more specialist teaching in a unit for hearing-impaired children, or the child who requires a special school environment, should be assessed formally and a 'statement' issued.

The Local Education Authority collects the views of parents, teacher, Medical Officer, and any other professional involved with the child, such as an Audiologist, teacher of the hearing-impaired, or Speech Therapist. The formal procedures are technically complex and give parents the right to request or object to assessment, to seek independent advice, to be present at any examinations and to receive copies of all professional advice submitted during the assessment process. There are statutory periods of notice at various points, and parents have the right of appeal. A 'statement' is issued setting out the nature of the child's special needs and how the authority proposes to meet them. Any extra or alternative provision, such as classroom support or special school, will be named in the statement, together with a date for review. The 'statement' is meant to protect the present and future interests of the child whose needs are highlighted in the assessment partnership.

At the time of writing, the government has set out new legislative proposals intended to raise educational standards and to increase diversity and parental choice. These are likely to have a significant impact on children with special needs. The Education Reform Act proposes a national curriculum which will define in law which core subjects must be taught to pupils for the major proportion of their time. National tests may be introduced at seven, eleven, fourteen and sixteen years to grade children against national targets. The results for schools will be made public. Other changes are planned, such as the delegation of financial responsibility to schools. 'Open enrolment' is intended to let schools admit as many children as they can accommodate, according to parental choice. Schools may be able to opt out of LEA control and be run by the governors as grant-maintained schools.

There are a number of misgivings about these proposals. In a free-market situation it is uncertain how willing schools may be to integrate children with special needs or to adapt the curriculum. How will schools which have 'opted out' gain access to support agencies? Children who are the subject of 'statements' may be exempted from certain parts of the national curriculum, but this runs counter to the view that the curriculum can be modified to allow all children to have access to as wide a range of experiences as possible. It may be wholly inappropriate and very demoralising if national grade testing is applied to special needs children. Little consideration has been given to the larger group of children with special needs who are not statemented (the 20 per cent of schoolchildren estimated in the Warnock Report). Paradoxically, the Reform Bill is intended to increase freedom of choice and improve the quality of education, but for children with special needs these very aspects appear to be at stake.

NOTE

1. The legislation referred to here applies in England, Wales and Northern Ireland. Different legislation applies in Scotland as a result of the Education (Scotland) Act 1981 and its governing regulations (1982). For details of the Scottish Act see Mackay (1986) or Ward (1985).

4

Deafness and the learning process

In this chapter we shall be examining the impact of a hearing loss on processes of learning and development. We have not adopted an overly simplistic view. The physical facts of a child's deafness interact in a largely unpredictable and uncharted way with a complex web of psychological, social and family variables. It follows that a hearing-impairment may give rise to special needs which span a continuum of educational priority, from the mild and short-term to the serious and long-standing. Not all hearing-impaired children experience developmental difficulties. When special needs do arise, they may not necessarily be a result of deafness *per se*. Wherever possible, we have preferred not to look for within-child factors to account for special needs without first addressing factors in the learning environment and in the behaviour of adults, since it is these factors which are within the teacher's control and which are more easily modified.

In keeping with the intentions set out in the introductory chapter, we shall not be providing further summaries of the generous literature on deaf children's development, and readers are referred to the sources indicated earlier for such reviews. We shall be highlighting the major areas of concern for development when, for example, a conductive hearing loss onsets early in infancy and persists through childhood. How might such a condition affect a child's interactions within the family? What aspects of language and learning may be affected? How will the child fare in school? Are any developmental effects offset by surgical treatment? These are some of the issues covered, on an empirical basis, drawing on research studies with which the authors have had a recent involvement. Similarly, the approach taken to the developmental obstacles associated with more severe, sensori-neural hearing losses draws on a body of research centred on the interactive processes which define the social and communicative contexts of deaf children, their parents and teachers. (For a more detailed coverage of aspects of this work see Wood, Wood, Griffiths and Howarth, 1986.)

All that is documented in this chapter should be read in relation to the groundwork of normal development provided earlier. This framework, culled from the generic literature on children, was designed to give some clear bench-marks or signposts. But it is evident that, in the ordinary course of events, neither the parenting nor the teaching process is a straightforward or simple affair. The circumstances and experiences of most children at home and at school usually give a sense of 'rich clutter'. The principles of effective teaching and interaction that we have drawn are easier to observe than they are to deploy. However, a sympathetic family counsellor has observed that there is no single challenge or emotion experienced by parents of deaf children which is unique (Luterman, 1987). This is in close accord with our own view that deafness often exacerbates and compounds the already hazardous course of parenting and teaching.

CONDUCTIVE HEARING LOSS AND CHILD DEVELOPMENT

The impact of a fluctuating hearing loss on childhood has been extensively studied. This is a fairly controversial area of research, with some claiming that conductive hearing loss accounts for a wide range of irreversible deficits in speech and language, together with longer-term intellectual and academic problems, for example in reading. On the other hand, some researchers are dismissive of any significant effects which can be directly attributed to a mild, intermittent hearing loss *per se*. The truth of the matter probably lies somewhere between the two extremes.

In preparation for a hospital-based study of children with chronic otitis media, one of the authors sifted through existing research in order to identify common findings (Webster, 1986b; Webster, Saunders and Bamford, 1984). There is widespread agreement that children who suffer repeated attacks of otitis media, particularly when these begin in the first year or so of infancy and persist into school age, are likely to compare poorly with unaffected peers in speech, language and academic progress. Factors such as speech phonology, breadth of vocabulary, grammatical maturity, comprehension, expression, linguistic concepts, auditory memory, listening skills, intelligence, literacy, numeracy, behaviour and social adjustment have all been implicated.

In speech phonology, for example, it is assumed that children who cannot hear the sounds of speech clearly and consistently in infancy will thus have more difficulty in interpreting and producing the sound contrasts, or phonemes, of the more mature system. Rapid development in speech phonology generally occurs from about nine months onwards, following a period when a wide range of non-specific sounds are practised. The units of speech which are most at risk are the phonetic features of brief or weak intensity, such as the fricative 'f' or 'v' sounds, plural 's', nasal sounds like 'm' or 'n', and unstressed word endings. When efforts have been made to replicate the effects of a conductive hearing loss in the laboratory, it has been shown that some speech contrasts begin to be lost at 10 decibels. For present purposes we can assume that a mild conductive hearing loss of, say, 15 to 20 decibels will affect a child's ability to listen and make sound discriminations in noisy conditions such as a kitchen, playgroup or classroom.

We have said that perceiving, organising and producing the sound contrasts of the adult system are only one aspect of the child's meaning-making. Apart from delays in phonology, research also highlights delays when tests of vocabulary are given, such as identifying the correct picture when a word is spoken. They may show a more limited range of words in use and, when measures of syntax are taken, by the time most children are acquiring complex sentence structures in speech, the child with a conductive hearing loss may be twelve months behind, say at Stage III or IV. In school, the child may have difficulty understanding what is said, may interpret questions wrongly and may be unable to put ideas into words in order to reply. As well as being poor at using syntactic structures, such as tense forms, plurals and rules which govern phrase and clause patterns, the child with a conductive hearing loss may also have a more limited explicit awareness of how the language is put together, required, for example, to detect alliteration or verbal 'puns'.

It is the more subtle effects of conductive deafness which have been given least attention. For example, less well known are the research findings which suggest that children who have had persistent otitis media tend to withdraw from social contact, are listless, poorly motivated and distractible, have a poor attention span and limited concentration, or show dependency on adults for taking decisions. Children with otitis media and associated communication difficulties may be perceived as unwilling, or of below average ability. Children rarely draw attention to the fact that they are having listening difficulties and the condition may go undetected. The hidden and inconsistent nature of the condition simply reinforces the problem because parents and teachers are less likely to compensate than if the hearing loss were known about, or more severe. In one study with a focus on the behavioural and social consequences of otitis media (Silva, Kirkland, Simpson, Stewart and Williams, 1983), the mothers of a group of 5-year-olds with a mean conductive hearing loss of 20.2 decibels HL were asked to describe their children's behaviour. Typically, the children were depicted as being socially isolated, restless, disobedient, fidgety and destructive.

It is not surprising that children with frequent ear infections and language and learning difficulties should also present management problems to their adult caretakers. In all children, behaviour, adjustment and learning usually go hand in hand. However, we also recognise that, when communication is difficult, adults become more directive and controlling, whilst relationships become more emotionally charged. These issues, concerning how deafness dislocates the patterns of social interaction between children and adults, have come to prominence in research with more severely hearing-impaired subjects. The important point here is that we may expect there to be secondary consequences of even very mild hearing losses which contribute to a child's special needs, over and above hearing loss *per se*.

In discussing the ordinary course of child development, much was said about the active, problem-solving enquiries of children, as they test out their environment with the support of facilitating adults. At the heart of learning is the nature of adult–child collaboration, dependent on the motivation of the child to initiate interaction with partners, and the sensitivity of adults as they respond. Both are required to be negotiators, without a sense of the adult dominating or overdirecting the child. Unfortunately, the consequences of a conductive hearing loss appear to be that the child becomes a more passive learner, difficult to engage, whilst the adult, in turn, also becomes less facilitative.

INTERPRETING THE EVIDENCE

A number of explanations have been put forward to account for the apparently deleterious effects of a conductive hearing loss in early childhood. Some authorities, such as Quigley (1978), have argued that children with mild hearing losses of less than 15 decibels HL show measurable deficits in language. Such hearing losses may escape detection through school screening audiometry, where a sweep test is given across the frequencies at an intensity level of 15 or 20 decibels HL. Others are more sceptical about the evidence. Why should conductive deafness have such an adverse effect? After all, such deafness is not usually present from birth, nor is it continuous. Such children enjoy periods of normal auditory experience. Unlike sensori-neural hearing loss, conductive deafness commonly affects all sound frequencies by a similar amount, leading to a general dampening of hearing rather than a distortion of the auditory signals. And, as we have seen, middle-ear losses are usually 25 decibels HL or less, rarely up to 50 decibels HL.

One explanation is that the fluctuating nature of the child's hearing loss confuses the child at a critical period. A mild but constant hearing loss might not have such an adverse effect as a loss which is intermittent and inconsistent. What children hear of the sound patterns being used around them undergoes slight changes. This makes it difficult to build up a memory bank, or reference framework of meaningful sounds. Instead of the child 'catching up' during periods of good hearing, a fluctuating loss interferes with the child's perceptual organisation. In Chapter 2 we mentioned that infants perceive some sound contrasts more easily than others. For example, acquisition of the tense marker '-ing' precedes that of '-ed' because it has more acoustic stress and is more audible. Cross-language studies support this finding. Similarly, evidence from children acquiring other languages suggests that some sound contrasts are lost if they are not present in the child's early speech environment. So, the argument runs that inconsistencies in the child's auditory experience delay the acquisition of the reference structure for the perceptual units of speech (Bamford and Saunders, 1985).

Some researchers have gone further to argue that intermittent hearing loss in the first three years of life may lead to auditory deficits of an irreversible nature (Downs, 1977). In effect, it is argued that the child's ability to process sounds and language is permanently damaged. This is a view which derives partly from studies of animals. It has been shown in experiments that, if you give an animal a conductive hearing loss for a period of time when the auditory pathway is immature, abnormal development follows. Small anatomical changes take place in the nerve structures, accompanied by disruption in listening and sound localisation (Clopton and Silverman, 1978; Webster and Webster, 1979). On the basis of this evidence, claims are made that children with persistent conductive hearing problems will also be affected in their ability to listen to sounds, discriminate between them and blend sounds together. They may be poor at remembering sounds, and in putting sounds into sequences. On tests of more global language skills, such as vocabulary and sentence use, they may show immaturity. In order to show that such problems have a physiological origin, some researchers have tried to monitor auditory electric brain stem responses in children affected by otitis media (Folsom, Weber and Thompson, 1983).

There is another explanation for the effects of conductive hearing loss on development. This concerns the extent to which middle-ear disease is the *causal* agent. Evidence has usually been sought from the comparative study of two populations: one containing children known to have histories of otitis media, the other free from the condition. If subjects are not matched in every other relevant respect apart from hearing loss, findings will be difficult to interpret. Unfortunately, many of the existing studies have flaws in their experimental design. For example, children in the otitis media and control groups may not be matched for age, sex and intelligence, as well as for other factors which contribute to individual differences in learning, such as home background and school environment. When children are not well matched in these important respects, it is impossible to say definitely that any difference between the two groups on, say, a vocabulary test is due to hearing loss, rather than to some other factor, such as home background.

The commonsense view is that delayed language development does accompany conductive hearing loss. However, children subject to repeated attacks of otitis media may be at risk of developmental delay due to other factors. We can identify a number of factors which contribute to developmental delay and also predispose children to otitis media: poverty, poor nutrition, general ill-health, inadequate housing and overcrowding, low birth weight, quality of parenting and family circumstances. Any one of these factors may contribute towards a child's learning problems, as well as increasing the risk of middle-ear disease. The fact that they are often associated should not be interpreted causally, as the one bringing into being the other.

INTELLIGENCE AND ATTAINMENT

Besides looking for the effects of conductive hearing loss on verbal processing and language skills, researchers have also tried to identify more global sequelae of otitis media, such as effects on intelligence and school achievements. Evidence here has been sought in three ways. The first source comes from studies of children known to have early histories of conductive hearing loss, but no current hearing difficulty. Children with resolved middle-ear disease have been compared with control groups on a variety of measures. These include tests of non-verbal intelligence, visual perception, reading comprehension, sight-word recognition and mathematics. Findings vary, with major differences reported between groups on tests such as the Verbal Scale of the Wechsler Intelligence Scale for Children — Revised. Differences are often found on tests of phonic skills, such as sound blending and analysis, spelling and reading. Fewer discrepancies tend to be found between groups on tests of non-verbal reasoning, such as the Performance Scale of the WISC–R, which uses a selection of picture-sequencing, design, jigsaw and block-puzzle type tests and is less dependent on language for completion. Similarly, arithmetic is less likely to be affected. For further details of all this research and the test items used, see Webster (1986a).

The pooled findings of this work suggest that some long-term effects may be associated with early hearing loss, but these are unlikely to be permanent or insurmountable. Any pervasive effects are likely to be highlighted in verbal processing and language-dependent skills. They may not last throughout a child's school career. In support of this, one study gave children with early conductive hearing problems a battery of tests, which was repeated five years later. At the first assessment, all the children compared very badly with normally hearing peers on the verbal tests. But by the time of the second assessment, besides showing improvements in their hearing, the children had caught up with their peers in overall school performance and no longer gained poorer test scores (Hamilton and Owrid, 1974; Dalzell and Owrid, 1976).

In a second research category, studies have been made of children with current, long-standing hearing losses, which have not been resolved. Some groups, such as Eskimo children, appear to be particularly prone to middle-ear disease. When these children have been given a range of tests, including reading, spelling, computation, mathematics, verbal reasoning and intelligence, a consistent association is found, linking degree of hearing loss with lower attainment and Verbal IQ scores. There can be much less argument about this group. For many children, a persistent, ongoing hearing loss is an obstacle to effective learning and is very often accompanied by depressed academic achievement. For this group, the teacher's awareness and the strategies adopted to compensate are critical in enabling the child to realise full potential in school.

The third and final source of research evidence comes from studies of children who have been classified, by separate and very diverse criteria, as having learning difficulties. Researchers have looked, for example, at children referred to centres for the teaching of remedial readers. The aim of such studies is to determine how many children have symptoms of past or present hearing loss, what their profile of strengths and weaknesses is like, and how a hearing loss might account for the learning problems experienced. Some figures for the prevalence of conductive hearing deafness in children categorised as having learning difficulties were given in Chapter 1. Broadly speaking, a current or earlier history of fluctuating hearing loss is reported to be more than twice as common in children with reading difficulties, with some estimates much higher.

It is very tempting to ascribe reading difficulties directly to a hearing loss. Usually, the cause of a child's reading or spelling problem is attributed to the child's mastery of phonological skills: the rules which relate the sounds of speech to the written units of print. The assumption which is often made is that good sound discrimination is essential in learning to read. Obviously, if reading is taught in the early stages using a 'phonic' method, the child with conductive deafness may find a lot of confusions. Studies of children who read fluently before school age usually highlight good auditory discrimination as an important factor for success (Clark, 1976). When comparisons have been made of good and poor readers, children who are skilled at categorising and recognising sounds tend to become better spellers and readers (Bryant and Bradley, 1985). All this evidence has been parcelled together to support the argument that a reduction in hearing acuity often results in reading failure because the child is unable to recognise sounds in written words.

We shall be discussing reading at some length in later sections and again in Chapter 5. In our view, a good example of an oversimplistic approach is to seek single-factor explanations of a process as complex as reading. A more balanced view is that children bring a range of auditory, linguistic and cognitive skills to reading, together with a wealth of experience in problem-solving and meaning-making. It follows that a much more reasonable interpretation of how children learn to read will be multifactorial, including aspects such as sound-symbol information but also syntax, picture clues and story context. How well children succeed in early reading will depend to some extent on whether their resources as active questioners and problem-solvers are utilised. By the same token, we would argue that a fairly diffuse relationship exists between hearing loss and learning to read. If children with hearing difficulties struggle to read, this is likely to be due to a spectrum of language and behavioural factors, and not simply to an inability to distinguish sounds in words.

In almost all of the reported studies of the sequelae of conductive hearing loss, problems of interpretation arise because factors which predispose children to otitis media are also implicated in developmental delays in speech, language and learning. Some of these factors have already been mentioned, such as family environment and quality of parenting. For example, the effect of family size and the child's position in a family will be important both in determining the risk of respiratory infections and in influencing language development. Children who are frequently absent from school because of infections, who have long periods feeling unwell or who are adversely affected by medication may thus score lower on IQ and achievement tests. Prematurity, anoxia, neonatal asphyxia and any other environmental factors which detract from overall health and well-being may be associated with both otitis media and developmental delay.

Controversially, it has been suggested (Black, 1985) that some parents are much more active in seeking treatment when there are learning difficulties in school, or behavioural problems to cope with.

In other words, parents ask for (and often receive) medical treatment to solve what is really an educational or child management problem. It is this interpretation which has been proffered to account for the very wide regional variation in treatment patterns for otitis media from one health district to another in the UK. (For example, the rate of middle-ear surgical interventions in Oxfordshire, 79.9 operations per 10,000 of the population aged from zero to nine years, is over three times that in neighbouring Cheltenham, 23.7 per 10,000.) The general rise in middle-ear surgery, particularly in higher social groups, seems to reflect parental awareness and concern, not prevalence. If this view is correct, then this would increase the likelihood of researchers finding more children with learning or behaviour difficulties who had also been diagnosed as having middle-ear disease.

Recently, a study was mounted to try and sort out some of the controversies of previous research, surrounding the long-term sequelae of otitis media (Webster, Bamford, Thyer and Ayles, in press). A group of children was selected from hospital records with long and well-documented medical histories of chronic secretory otitis media, from early infancy onwards into the school years, but no measurable hearing loss at the time of the study. A control group was matched for age, sex, intelligence, school and social background, but with no history of hearing loss. A battery of tests was given to all the children who took part, including the Verbal and Performance Scales of the WISC–R, reading, spelling and phonic blending. A questionnaire was completed covering a variety of behavioural problems, such as withdrawal and poor concentration. A range of audiological tests was carried out in hospital, including pure-tone audiometry, bone conduction and listening in noise. Electric brain stem responses to a series of click stimuli were also recorded, using electrodes attached to the scalp to give a physiological measure of central auditory processing.

Were any differences identified between the two groups of children? On the auditory measures, no significant differences were found in the tasks requiring listening, or in brain stem recordings. Despite the claims made that early otitis media leaves children with long-term listening and auditory processing difficulties, we did not find any statistically significant effects in this study. On the psychological and educational tests there were small, but consistent, differences. Tests of vocabulary, reasoning, comprehension and short-term memory, on the WISC–R, all showed small differences in favour of the control group. Measures of phonic processing, reading, spelling, behaviour and adjustment again showed small, though non-significant, differences between the groups. The small effects observed suggest that factors such as family background and teaching environment are more powerful determinants of children's educational progress than a history of otitis media. In studies where selection, matching and experimental procedures are not rigorously controlled, much larger effects have been reported, but these are difficult to interpret with confidence. In fact, there were some very large differences in the educational test scores achieved by different children in the present study: a few were barely reading, whilst others were way ahead of their peer group. However, these were differences *between* matched pairs, not *within* them. In other words, children examined from some particular schools, irrespective of a hearing loss, tended to do better than children from other schools.

What conclusions can be drawn from this work? For the target group of children, that is, children with long-standing histories of otitis media but whose hearing is currently unaffected, there may be some small, pervasive effects on language and literacy. No specific auditory processing deficits could be found. Since a more rigorous experimental method seems to have excluded the major discrepancies between otitis media children and controls, we can perhaps correct the priority of issues associated with early conductive hearing loss. There are potentially harmful effects of conductive deafness, even where this is identified and treated, when the condition recurs and persists. But the children most at risk of developmental underachievement would appear to be those whose hearing loss is part of a nexus of disadvantaging factors associated with school and family environment, which conductive deafness exacerbates. We also know that these are the children least likely to be identified and treated, but most in need of teacher-vigilance and the kind of educational strategies recommended in Chapter 5.

APPROACHES TO READING

The links which have been made between reading difficulty and hearing loss highlight a number of misconceptions. The first set of misunderstandings concerns what reading as a process entails. The second set of confusions relates to the characteristic skills and strategies which hearing-impaired children bring to the reading task. In fact we do not have a complete research picture of either of these issues. But we do know that an oversimplistic approach is likely to mislead teachers who are looking at practical suggestions for the classroom.

In recent years a radical reappraisal has taken place of how children become readers. A number of important insights are to be gained by approaching the first of these issues — what the reading process demands — from the research on early spoken language interaction reported in Chapter 2. Written language has many specific features of its own, but remains one of the uses to which language is put, and is therefore best understood with reference to other aspects of language. However, one of the tendencies in textbooks on the teaching and remediation of reading has been to treat this narrowly, as a decoding process.

One of the basic principles we outlined in Chapter 2 is that children do not acquire spoken language for its own sake, but that meaning, function, purpose and relevance to everyday life are critical factors. In spoken language contexts, children construct meaning from situational clues and adult intentions, together with what words themselves signify. In the same way, the print of our society always has a context which supports its interpretation — unless, that is, reading is introduced to children in a way which strips it of context and renders it remote. The planning of a literacy programme, and the materials and methods chosen, ought to take into account the expectations and experiences children bring with them into school.

A second principle we highlighted is that children are active problem-solvers, who make sense of their experience by abstracting rules and regularities for themselves. Children generate hypotheses about written language, just as they do about spoken language. These considerations were drawn together in our model for the optimal learning environment, which enables children to share initiatives, plan, explore, review their findings and be creative in their questioning. If reading is introduced to children as a linear and mechanical decoding activity, they may be discouraged from testing out their own hypotheses about text. The shared partnership which young children enjoy with adults, who facilitate learning by well-tailored responses and a familiarity with the child's social world, underlines the importance of shared reading approaches. It is here that adults can help children by discussing reading strategies, and reviewing and repairing their meaning-taking from text.

In an article on reading, Bruner (1984) suggests that we should regard the process as a collaborative effort, whereby adults and children enter 'possible worlds' in drama and story. Reading should not be treated as an assembly line of bits and pieces, where sounds, letters and words are fitted together. The simplification and repetition of rote exercises and reading schemes is deprecated, in favour of the shared reading and writing of genuine messages, which serve a real social action. Importantly, children are introduced to the 'how' of reading from the outset, by sharing books with good readers, digging out meaning from text and reading to learn rather than learning to read. Another way of expressing this is to say that hitherto many schools have valued the products of teaching reading, rather than emphasising reading as a process of meaning-making.

This approach to literacy leads us away from models where the skills of reading are broken up into component parts. Examples of such 'flat earth' or 'bottom-up' approaches to the subskills of reading have been given in Webster (1986a, 1988b). 'Bottom-up' approaches begin at the level where the reader perceives visual features, such as letter-shapes, and builds these up into larger units such as words or phrases. An alternative route might be to convert letters into corresponding speech sounds, so that print is decoded into recognisable units of the reader's spoken language. The focus of teaching then becomes the learning of rules which relate the 40 or so distinctive phonemes of speech to the spelling patterns of English print ('phonics' or phoneme–grapheme correspondences).

The fact that poor readers sometimes show letter reversals and visual confusions in spelling and reading, or may have poor phonic awareness, is usually cited in support of 'bottom-up' approaches to reading. However, there is a strong possibility that experience of reading itself provides the child with insights about the visual and phonic features of print, and not the other way round.

In contrast, the 'round earth' or 'top-down' view of reading argues that what children learn in their active discovery of spoken language, in purposeful and meaningful social contexts, is then applied to making sense of print. Where the 'bottom-up' approach tends to draw its evidence from experimental studies, involving letter discrimination or word recognition skills, 'top-down' theorists reject these as unauthentic reading situations. In real life, children start to recognise print in familiar contexts, in just the same way as first spoken words relate to everyday objects and people. In the study by Payton (1984) of her daughter Cecilia's growing awareness of print, the child refers to a price tag whilst queuing at a supermarket checkout and remarks, 'That says Co-op'. In another context, Paul Bissex (1980) devised his own writing system as a pre-schooler, in order to give his mother messages like 'RUDF' when she refused to look up from her book and pay him attention. Both examples show children generating hypotheses about the way print works, intercalated with the 'here and now' of their lives.

Alongside encounters with story books, most children read adverts, signs, notices, menus, labels and cereal packets. Children's contacts with literacy occur within family contexts where shopping lists, cards, bills, maps, brochures, newspapers, TV guides, football coupons, tickets and mailshots serve to connect the family with the outside world. In Chapter 2 we reported the finding of the Bristol

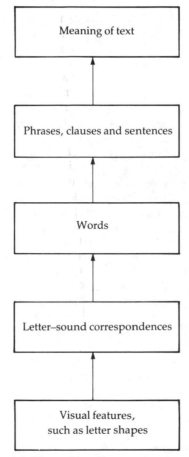

Figure 4.1 *'Flat earth' or 'bottom-up' model of reading*

studies that the most powerful predictor of later academic achievement in school is how frequently books are read with children at home. It could be said that children with book-reading experience have already learned a great deal about the function and meaning of print, which happens to coincide with the kind of literacy valued highly in school. However, there are many other domains of everyday literacy with which children are familiar, and which can also be capitalised on in school.

Reading begins for many children, then, by asking questions of print in different contexts, in order to make sense of it and relate meaning to existing understanding. The work of Ferreiro and Teberosky (1982) stresses the underlying logic of literacy development, as young children piece together how print works from the evidence to which they have so far had access. For example, some

4-year-olds in their study appeared to require a minimum of three letters before a word would 'say' anything, whilst five letters would be required for a set of five objects. Children may assume that names of adults are always longer than those of children, whilst long objects, such as a train, will have correspondingly long representations in print. For many children, too, reading is synonymous with writing: the conveying of messages in meaningful social contexts. Interestingly, having started at school, young children begin to get other ideas about print, for example that neatness, correct spelling and decoding letters into sounds are important to 'proper' writing and reading.

Several examples of the 'top-down' view of reading have been given by Webster (1986a, 1988b). All of these put the child centrally in the reading process, making predictions about what will be found in a text, sampling the different sources of information in order to check or revise interpretations which are made. Because the child's existing knowledge of language and the world guide what the reader looks for, the reader is said to *bring meaning to* text, rather than *deriving meaning from* it. All kinds of clues are present in text. These include the printed letters on the page and 'sight' words or phrases, together with information from pictures, headings and the layout of a text. Other clues come from the story context, or general experience of the language of books and how stories are likely to unfold. Expectations of likely meaning may also come from the child's knowledge of spoken language and life as it is lived.

As children interact with text, responsive adults are able to facilitate the child's active reaching for meaning by providing appropriate feedback and suggesting alternative ways of interrogating print in order to gain the message. The main difference between the 'flat' and 'round' earth models is that one holds reading to be a static decoding progression through a series of stages; the other holds reading to be a continuous sampling and testing cycle, whereby questions are asked of print, which are checked out and give rise to new questions. In actual fact, there is evidence that making up hypotheses all the time about text may use up much of the child's thinking space for other processes, such as relating what is read to what is already known.

There is a compromise position. An interactive model accepts that some clues arise upwards from the page, whilst others act downwards, as the reader makes predictions and looks for expected meanings. Good readers may well develop a lot of automatic skills. They may access words directly, on a straight visual recognition basis. When they ask questions of print, good readers ask the most efficient questions for reducing uncertainty. Poor readers' skills are less automatic, and when they interrogate

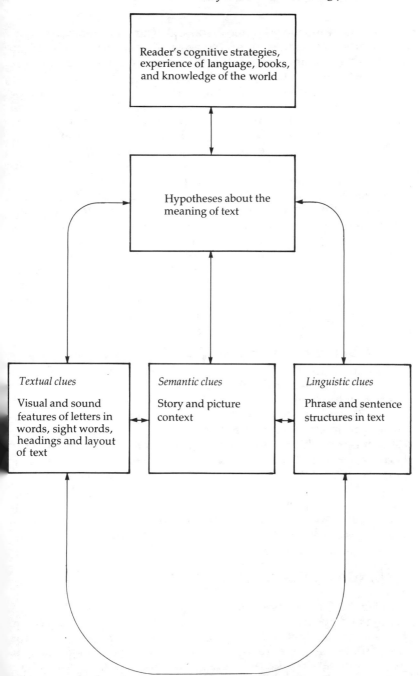

Figure 4.2 *'Round earth' or 'top-down' model of reading*

text they draw on more limited resources of language or experience, and ask the wrong questions. One possibility, especially relevant to the hearing-impaired, is that the classroom experience teaches the child not to ask questions at all.

In Chapter 5 we shall be considering further the kinds of strategy for fostering reading development which accord with our optimal curriculum model. This line of enquiry will take us into some of the differences between spoken language and print. Increasingly, the written word extends the child's ability to handle language into the disembedded, context-free mode. As text becomes more sophisticated, many of the clues to meaning are located within the conventions of print. Features of spoken language, such as pitch, intonation, rhythm and stress, are poorly represented in text. The reader has to take into account the abstract devices which link sentences together in narrative and discourse, and how time sequences are indicated, together with a wealth of information carried in word endings and phrase and clause structures. Conventions change according to the form, so that stories will be different from diaries, plays or textbooks. However, as readers progress they are able to deal with written language which is more self-contained and coherent, and less reliant on the immediate context.

Later on in school, children continue to form hypotheses and apply rules to see if they work, but the language of text has become a thinking- or problem-space in its own right. Vocabulary, syntax and nuances of meaning and usage are encountered, specific to written text. Children gain access to forms of language which outstrip the capacity of spoken language to handle complex, creative or abstract ideas. It is this which has prompted theorists to say that the tools of learning shape and change those who use them. Whilst the child's learning and reading start out linked to familiar surroundings and adults, eventually language and thinking are turned in upon themselves. Children with 'literate minds' are able to stand back from experience to reflect on events, manipulate ideas and infer logical relationships, beyond immediate boundaries.

READING AND CONDUCTIVE DEAFNESS

The idea that a mild hearing loss is a detectable and treatable *cause* of reading and spelling difficulties is neat and attractive. It hinges on the assumption that auditory discrimination plays an important part, at least in the early stages of reading, in helping children discover the 'alphabetic principle': that units of sound map on to symbols in print. If children have difficulty discriminating between vowel sounds, plurals, word endings and sounds like 'f', 'th' or 'm', they may find phonic rules difficult to master. Children with mild hearing losses may have problems in articulating, blending and sequencing sounds. In a 'bottom-up' model of reading, such children are stuck at the preliminary level of hearing sounds in words.

Exercises designed to help children categorise and recognise sounds are commonly introduced to children in school in order to get them *ready for* reading. A number of reasons have been put forward in defence of the 'alphabetic principle'. Children are helped to discover the meaning of new words by decoding print into recognisable speech sounds. Spelling-to-sound mappings give the child independence to tackle the many unknown words encountered in the early stages. A number of studies have shown that phonological awareness in young children is a good predictor of later reading success, whilst poor readers are usually much less effective in applying phonic rules than more able peers.

We discussed some of the problems of this linear, decoding model of reading, particularly as it fails to take into account other aspects of the child's meaning-making in other language contexts. A 'round earth' approach integrates aspects of the child's wider social and linguistic experience, styles of learning and problem-solving with the child's book-reading encounters. Apart from confusions at the sound level, children with conductive hearing loss may have poorer vocabularies and a more limited range of concepts than peers. They may have immature syntax, reflected in their use of word, phrase and clause structures. They may misunderstand instructions and be poor at framing their responses. Apart from this implicit problem with using the system, children with mild hearing losses may not achieve competence at the explicit level, which comes from a richness of language experience. It is the explicit awareness which enables children to experiment with, and think about, spoken and written language as a problem-space in its own right.

We have also drawn attention to differences in learning styles between children with conductive deafness and their peers. Children with mild hearing losses are often perceived as withdrawn and distractible, less inquisitive or creative in their problem-solving, less easy to engage as active, independent learners. The resources and experiences which mildly hearing-impaired children bring to reading, and to school generally, may be broadly disadvantaged. Inevitably, if there are listening difficulties in the classroom environment, full participation in the learning activities of the school is also affected. It is not surprising, then, that many children develop less effective strategies for learning, such as poor attention span, low motivation and adult-dependency.

The compounding factors associated with conductive hearing loss in childhood, highlighted in our own recent research, also serve to exacerbate children's learning difficulties in school. If conductive hearing loss tends to occur more frequently in environmental and family circumstances which are themselves less conducive to academic achievement, then these factors, secondary to the effects of hearing loss *per se*, must also be taken into account. Instead of posing questions such as 'Do children have a specific *site* of their reading problem, or a particular auditory processing deficit?', one might explore other relevant issues, such as 'How often are children with conductive deafness read to at home?'

A recent review of individual differences between readers has been given by Stanovich (1986). The conclusions he draws from this wealth of research evidence are far from straightforward. In many aspects of reading, a 'Matthew effect' can be observed: 'rich-get-richer' and 'poor-get-poorer' patterns. For example, many children in school are taught pre-reading skills, such as letter–sound correspondences or sight words, before they are allowed to tackle the first books of a reading scheme, with a controlled exposure to vocabulary and sentence structures. Children who remain at these preliminary stages because of difficulties are thus exposed to far fewer 'real' books than peers. Unrewarding early experiences lead to less involvement in reading-related activities.

Good and poor readers differ in how automatic the child's decoding becomes. Good readers may have been taught to decode from print to sound, but soon move on to quick and direct recognition of words. Good readers are then freed from decoding, to focus on meaning, calling on resources of language and general experience. In turn, reading itself contributes to the child's vocabulary, syntax and knowledge of the world, as the child reads to learn. Poor readers have much of their energy and thinking-space taken up at the decoding level, whilst this kind of activity contributes little to the child's understanding. The 'Matthew effect' is that poor readers tend to be given more practice at the low-level preliminaries, such as phonic skills, and are denied access to the kinds of reading experience which would enable their reading for meaning.

The 'Matthew effect' accounts for much of the evidence we have cited which shows that children with mild hearing loss often fail to make good reading progress. We have discovered a nexus of associations which accounts for some children's poor early development and progress in school. There are many reasons why some children come less prepared for school than others, participate less well and are slow to progress. Mild hearing loss appears to accompany a complex of disadvantaging factors which contribute to a 'poor-get-poorer' effect.

MODERATE OR MONAURAL SENSORI-NEURAL DEAFNESS

There is very little research evidence which addresses the consequences of slight-to-moderate sensori-neural deafness, or deafness which affects one ear only. However, it should not be presumed that we can be complacent about any child with a hearing loss. The few studies of children with permanent losses of up to about 60 decibels HL are summarised in Ross (1982) and Bamford and Saunders (1985). Compared with hearing children, a moderate hearing loss is associated with immaturities in speech, vocabulary, linguistic concepts and syntax. Speech consonants, particularly at the end of words, may be omitted, with delays in acquiring many of the sound contrasts. Speech discrimination may also be affected. In expressive language, children with moderate losses tend to use shorter sentences, with fewer features at the phrase and clause level. For example, there is a general lack of development, even in school-leavers, of the recursive features such as co-ordination and subordination which characterise Stage V. In Chapter 2, we described the later stages of syntax development as being the most creative and inventive, which enable children to link their ideas together and have access to an unlimited range of expression. Many hearing 4-year-olds may have already reached this stage. A worrying aspect of the research evidence is that progress towards more complex language appears to tail off as children with moderate hearing losses get older, so that they may never 'catch up' with hearing peers.

Ross (1982) lists some of the concepts with which moderately hearing-impaired children have difficulty, leading to further problems in understanding academic tasks in school. Directions such as 'separate', 'above' and 'between' are often misunderstood. Even a mild hearing loss reduces the amount of incidental language overheard, for example, in the conversations of others, whilst words may be used or 'explained' in more restricted, face-to-face settings. Children come to know the multiplicity of meanings which words can have by a richness of exposure to their use in different contexts. Metaphoric or non-literal usages, such as 'cutting through the red tape' or 'feeling under the weather', may lead to confusions. Every area of the school curriculum has its own specific lexicon which may be unfamiliar, such as the workshop, gymnasium or laboratory ('clamp', 'trampoline', 'alkali'). A wide range of underachievements in school subjects (for example, more than two years' delay in reading) is attributed to listening difficulties, poor classroom management and the language of instruction. Ross (1982) also draws attention to the poor self-image and social adjustment of some mildly hearing-impaired children, who may resent wearing hearing-aids and feel like 'outsiders' amongst hearing peers.

The educational obstacles associated with monaural listening are by no means as severe as those linked with bilateral sensori-neural losses, or with conductive impairments. Permanent damage to the nerves of one ear is most often the result of a viral infection, such as mumps, during childhood. The condition may not be treatable and hearing-aids may be inappropriate. Most children with one good ear cope well in school, so long as adults are aware of the implications. The child's listening ability is most affected in noisy, reverberant conditions. Over a distance from a sound source and in high levels of background noise, a monaural child may be slow to respond and be unclear about the message. There will be a loss of directional location which comes from stereoscopic listening, so that a child may need to search around to identify a speaker. The most practical help that can be given is to sit the child in a class position with the good ear towards the sound source. A fall-off in academic performance, an avoidance of social situations or a loss of confidence usually indicate that the monaural child is under stress. For this child, some thought may then have to be given to the intervention strategies covered in Chapter 5, particularly with regard to listening conditions, classroom management and supportive help.

CHILD DEVELOPMENT AND SEVERE SENSORI-NEURAL DEAFNESS

The effects of a more severe sensori-neural hearing loss on childhood can be devastating. The case notes provided in Chapter 1 were chosen to depict the complex, but largely unpredictable, course of events as families cope with the obstacles which deafness presents. However, it should be said from the outset that it is a mistake to assume that all hearing-impaired children face the same problems, inevitably have limited linguistic and academic achievements, or can be guaranteed to benefit from a particular communication method or educational philosophy. In a group of hearing-impaired children any sense of sameness is likely to be illusory.

Although the numbers of severely hearing-impaired children are relatively small, this is a population which is differentiated by many varied factors. It is generally agreed, for example, that deaf children of deaf parents (approximately 10 per cent of all deaf children) encounter fewer behavioural or emotional problems, and may progress better academically, than deaf children of hearing parents (Meadow, 1980). In the latter situation, every family has to rediscover all the difficulties associated with deafness completely anew. Adjustments must be made and expectations revised. How well families are able to do this varies considerably. It is also well known that children whose deafness was caused by maternal rubella are much more likely to have special needs arising from intellectual and visual anomalies. In addition to degree and cause of deafness, a range of socio-economic factors which contribute to differences in achievement in hearing children, such as parental occupation and income level, also influence the achievements of deaf children. It is for reasons such as these that caution is urged in making generalisations: the 'all deaf children ... ' trap.

The research studies on which we have drawn in this section of the chapter were largely carried out with children who have severe to profound impairments. Deafness, as far as could be ascertained, was present in early infancy, with no other significant handicap (such as a visual-impairment). Undoubtedly, the special needs associated with profound deafness may be more marked, both in kind and degree, than those associated with more moderate deafness. In line with the spirit of the 1981 Education Act, we have shifted our focus away from categories of handicap and factors within the child's disability towards processes of teaching and learning. In the end it is a teaching response geared to individual needs, within the restraints imposed by classroom resources, which is advocated. What we have done is to use current research findings to underline important points about the effects which contrasting strategies and responses may have, as adults interact with deaf children.

EARLY INTERACTION

There is no reason to believe that deaf babies come into the world any less prepared than hearing infants in their orientation to socialise, explore, act on the world, achieve goals, seek out regularities or read intentions and meanings in adult behaviour. The infant's early contacts with people and the environment include touch, taste, smell, sight and sound, which is perhaps why sensory handicaps are so difficult to detect in young babies: they have many ways of coming to know the world and of interacting with it. Because infants are involved in shared exchanges with adults in familiar settings, where intentions are inferred and events anticipated, 'conversations' can be said to take place well before first words. The interest which babies and adults have in each other is extended into turn-taking dialogues, where the mutual attention of the participants is sequenced and alternated in games such as 'Peek-a-boo'. An important step is taken when the outside world is brought into the joint attention of adult and child. In Figure 2.1 this was depicted as a triangle of reference, in which a shared visual experience is suffused with language.

When observations have been made of severely deaf babies and their mothers, a number of aspects are different. In one study (Gregory and Mogford, 1981), mothers had much greater difficulty establishing turn-taking. Instead of smooth vocal exchanges, when first the mother then the infant responds, there were many more vocal clashes, when mother and infant vocalised together. Mutual attention and joint reference were harder to establish with hearing-impaired babies. Normally the adult's commentary, intonation and tone of voice are tied to familiar events, so that when attention is drawn to a particular object the relationship between words and their referents is emphasised. When the deaf baby turns to look at a shared object or event, the accompanying 'voice-over' is missing. The triangle of reference is disrupted because the social experience lacks the dimension of spoken language.

Adults find it much more difficult to integrate their vocalisations, gestures and expressions with the experiences shared with the child. Mothers of deaf children did not play anticipation games, such as 'Round and round the garden' or 'This little piggy', which introduce children to language in predictable formats of interaction. Where parents of hearing children might be observed discussing and negotiating play activities, mothers of deaf children tended to direct and command.

The early encounters between parents and hearing-impaired babies may be seen as unrewarding, frustrating and emotionally charged. One consequence is that parents may feel it is not worth talking to the child, if the child cannot hear. Another reaction may be that the parents will try and flood the child with talk. Some parents end up deliberately trying to teach the child words. They may turn the child's head towards them in order to draw attention to new things. They may take a toy from the child to bring it close to their own mouths, so that the child can 'see' the object and what is being said together. Each of these responses results in a more directive, intrusive style of parenting. The adult exercises much higher levels of external control over the infant's experience.

By the age of about eighteen months, hearing children are engaged in dialogue with parents as genuine partners with something to say. Adults interpret the child's utterances and make them explicit. In Table 2.1 we listed a range of features which characterise adults' speech to infants as they hold the child's interest by special voice-pitch, tone, rhythm and intonation patterns. Adults simplify what they say and clarify meaning, using devices such as repetition of key words and sentence frames for new vocabulary. There is a sense of the fine-tuning of adult speech to the child's own, as the adult paraphrases or expands what the child says, which in turn provides a better model from which the child can learn.

In the Gregory and Mogford (1981) study, video-recordings were made in the homes of eight deaf children of hearing parents, from the age of about fifteen months until their fourth birthday. The first words of the deaf children tended to be deliberately elicited and rehearsed. Rather than emerging within a natural context of interaction, where words reflected experiences shared, words were taught and performed: 'We're working on "Mummy" at the moment'.

In Chapters 1 and 2 we discussed the importance of contingency: adults pacing and timing the help they offer to children, by taking cues from the child's moment-to-moment understanding. The child is allowed to take the initiative, whilst the adult's rôle is to structure the task by prompting, making suggestions, thinking things through with the child and providing feedback. Contingent reactions are part of a collaborative partnership where the adult facilitates rather than teaches. In these early interactions with deaf infants, adults tend not to make their reactions contingent on what the child does. Instead, they often demand that the deaf infant attends to them. In effect, infants are asked to adapt their behaviour to the intentions of the adult, rather than the other way round.

Deafness does not merely restrict what the child can hear. It is also likely to disrupt some of the social-interactive processes which lay the foundations for communication. Early diagnosis of deafness and the provision of powerful hearing-aids help to offset these problems. The greater the child's auditory awareness, the more easily adults and children collaborate in meaning-making.

FROM HOME TO SCHOOL

A number of research projects have highlighted important changes in the social, linguistic and learning experiences which normally hearing children enjoy, as they move from home to school. The Bristol studies (Wells, 1981; 1985; 1987), described in Chapter 2, demonstrate how everyday activities at home provide the stimulus for questions from the child. Adults engage children by agreeing topics, taking turns in which elements of the child's previous utterance are included in response and leaving the child time to reply. Adults take up the child's meaning by expanding and paraphrasing, adding useful vocabulary, information or 'social oil'. Many conversations are initiated by the children themselves, and are sustained, with a sense of partnership, over many turns. Tizard and Hughes (1984) confirm the richness of talk and intellectual challenge observed at home.

At school, the range, depth and frequency of interactions with adults diminish. Adults ask more questions which require a limited response, or use questioning to test out what children know. Children initiate less, get fewer turns and are less likely to have their utterances taken up or extended in response. Teachers' moves become more highly controlling and didactic, with children expected to take a more respondent, passive role. What staff say to children in school often reflects a concern to organise materials and resources. Teachers' ignorance of the child's social world beyond school, pressure of curriculum objectives and demands on adult time in large groups of children are some of the reasons put forward to account for these home–school differences. Clearly, the typical classroom milieu is geared to different kinds of learning activity and adult-responsiveness from those observed at home. Some children flourish at school, others do less well. There are grounds for assuming that children with special needs in language and listening require a learning milieu which is more interactive and collabora-tive. In Figure 2.2 we have suggested an ideal learning environ-ment, which attempts to specify the kinds of co-operative learning experience which appear to be most facilitative.

How does the deaf child fare in moving from home to school? There is a range of current practice, in terms of educational placement for severely hearing-impaired children, which varies from area to area. We shall explore this issue further in Chapter 5. In many cases children attend specially resourced nurseries, where additional adults are on hand to help. The underlying intention of nursery placement, perhaps at an earlier age than usual, is to enrich the child's social and linguistic experience, perhaps through exposure to new toys, materials and activities, or through linguistic interactions with other children.

A number of studies (reported in Wood *et al.*, 1986) have looked at the nature of interactions between adults and deaf children in nurseries which have a more favourable adult–child ratio. Deaf children may have many more contacts with adults during a typical day. However, these are usually very brief, lasting no more than two or three turns. Similarly, encounters between deaf children and peers are often brief and limited. The pattern of activities is comparable, in many respects, to that found in ordinary nurseries, with children enjoying long periods of free play, interspersed with adult-directed activities, such as listening to stories and group conversations. Once again, the emphasis tends to be on managing equipment and, when adults do become involved in children's play or activities, interactions are often adult-dominated and revolve around question–answer exchanges. So, whilst the intention of nursery placement for the hearing-impaired child may be to enrich the child's play and language, in fact interactions may be restricted in depth and quality. This is true of 'special' nurseries, but is much more likely to be observed in ordinary nurseries which have been given additional resources for a hearing-impaired child, unless a great deal of thought has been given to how those resources are to be used.

In another Nottingham study, twelve children with severe to profound hearing losses were filmed at three-monthly intervals, from when they came into school at age three until they moved into primary school (Tait, 1987; Tait and Wood, 1987). More detailed attention was paid to the nature of the deaf child's behaviour and the strategies which adults use, during interactions observed longitudinally. At the start of the study some of the children showed no evidence of being aware of speech addressed to them, and produced no recognisable words. In other words, children were arriving in school at stages of linguistic development reached by many hearing infants before their second birthdays. The study focused on three aspects felt to be critical to communicative competence: turn-taking, joint visual reference, and awareness of the adult's speech. The important implication of this work is that, if children have not established the foundation skills for conversational interaction at home, they are unlikely to do so in the interactive encounters they will probably meet with in school.

A series of stages have been outlined which represent an increasing awareness of spoken language and a growing ability to participate in verbal interaction. It should be said that this work did not include children who were using sign, although it would be very relevant to have an equivalent body of data for children using sign-supported methods of communication. The following stages are also given in Table 5.3, alongside some suggested strategies for intervention.

(1) Disengaged

At this stage children are unaware of being spoken to, attention wanders fleetingly from place to place and any turns left by the adult in conversation for the child to fill are missed, while the child's own vocalisations appear random.

(2) Engaged

The child is beginning to look at a shared object of reference and attends partly to the adult when spoken to. Turn-taking may be possible in a clear game format.

(3) Structured attention

By now there is a better match between the onset of the adult's speech and the child's attention. The child reads meaning and intentions in context, takes turns readily and vocalises at appropriate points in dialogue, although the words may not be clear.

(4) Structured vocalisation

Vocalisations are more word-like and predictable, and conversational turns may be filled even when the child has not been looking at the adult at the end of the previous turn. In other words, children are filling turns through having heard what was said.

(5) Growth of autonomy and initiative

This stage can be described in terms of equal conversational partnership because the child actively initiates dialogue which serves a wide range of functions. The child is able to add new information and offer more than is asked. By now the child interrupts, changes the topic, contradicts, asks questions, teases and argues, and is able to refer beyond the 'here and now'.

This framework of analysis has a number of potential uses: first, to make a more detailed assessment of a deaf child's progress in transition from pre-verbal communication to speech; second, to plan an educational programme based on our knowledge of normal patterns of interaction between adults and children at each stage; and finally, to evaluate the effectiveness of an educational placement, in terms of the depth and nature of interaction which adults are able to offer children in the early stages of development. In Chapter 5 we shall be suggesting a number of ways in which children in these early stages can be included by the teacher as a conversational partner, where meaning and significance arise as much from the social context as from what adults say.

CONVERSATION AND THE SCHOOL EXPERIENCE

As we saw in Chapter 2, schools are not places where children can easily develop their basic communication skills: the nature of adult–child responsiveness in the classroom serves purposes largely to do with the handing on of information, the practising of skills such as the 3Rs, and the management of resources. Observation studies often report a sense of busy purposefulness in primary schools, but few teachers adopt collaborative or problem-solving approaches to learning, whereby children are stimulated by discovery and self-questioning, in shared enquiries.

In the ORACLE study (Galton *et al.*, 1980), an average day in a primary class was spent with children working independently at assigned tasks, and the teacher managing, leading, questioning, monitoring and 'talking at' the class group. There was a great deal of interaction going on between the teacher and the class, but only a minor part (about 2 per cent) of this involved individual pupils. The Bennett study (Bennett *et al.*, 1984) confirms that the role which most teachers adopt is one of handing over materials and exercises for the child to work on. This image of the learning process as one of adults setting goals which children passively pursue falls into the north-east quadrant of Figure 2.2.

Of the 'key factors' identified by the Mortimore study (Mortimore *et al.*, 1988) as being positively associated with effective schools, a number relate to classroom interaction. Perhaps the most critical factor in determining children's progress is the nature of adult–child talk. We know that adult–child conversation serves a number of important developmental ends. At one level, children are acquiring social conventions, such as turn-taking, how and when to maintain visual attention on a speaker, asking questions, agreeing a topic and relating successive turns to an agreed theme. At another level, children negotiate ways of using language to make intentions clear, in purposeful contexts where meanings and intentions are easily read. Through dialogue, children are able to make sense of their environment by testing out hypotheses, discovering the rules and systems which operate, as well as many cultural and value markers.

Through negotiation with responsive adults, children are able to achieve insights which they would not attain if left to their own devices. By planning, discussing and reviewing tasks with children, adults focus attention on relevant aspects, gauging the child's understanding and giving more help when needed. It is through conversation that children are exposed to a wide range of complex functions served by language, and are introduced to more adult ways of thinking and managing their learning. So, in the course of using the language system with more mature partners, children not only refine their control of language, they also develop their wider competence and understanding.

One essential ingredient of productive linguistic encounters is that talk emerges, almost transparently, from experiences and activities shared. What happens when teachers are conscious of the fact that they are expected to focus their energies on improving children's speech and language? In fact, many teachers react in the way that parents sometimes do, when a child is perceived as a poor communicator. There is a natural reaction to elicit vocabulary or 'teach' grammar, and to rehearse correct structures. The child may be expected to work on language forms in situations devoid of any real social function or purpose. When children are asked to imitate or repeat correct language models, the form of language is highlighted, rather than its meaning: speech becomes an object of attention in its own right. For a wide range of children with special needs in speech and language (see Webster and McConnell, 1987), efforts to train or drill language forms are usually unproductive. In the Nottingham studies a great deal of research attention has been paid to the structure of dialogue between teachers and deaf children. At the heart of this research is the question: 'How do aspects of a teacher's conversational style influence the child's communicative competence?'

An important developmental principle, which was introduced in Chapter 2, concerns the issue of conversational control. Some adult 'moves' in conversation are much more likely to be followed by children taking the initiative, adding something new, asking questions and making active contributions of their own that either sustain the dialogue or move the topic on. Other adult moves have a very inhibitory effect and are unlikely to be followed by an extended contribution from the child. Examples of different levels of control are given in Table 4.1. The most controlling move is to follow a child's turn with a demand to repeat a better formed model: 'Say "I *did* painting", not "I *done* painting"'. Examples given earlier show that this is an ineffective strategy, and one rarely used by adults with hearing children in the home context. At a second level, two-choice questions simply provide slots for the child to fill, with a limited range of options, such as 'Yes' or 'No': 'Have you had your milk?' The next move, questions beginning 'Where ... ?' 'When ... ?' or 'Who ... ?', also dictates the nature of the child's response, since the speaker holds control of the direction and content of the dialogue: 'Where did you go at the weekend?'

Table 4.1 *Levels of conversational control*

Adult move and level of control	Example
1. Enforced repetition	Say 'I *went*', not 'I *goed*'.
2. Two-choice question	Is it a blue one or a green one?
3. Wh- type question	What did you do at Scouts last night?
4. Personal contribution, comment or statement	I love going on the big dipper too.
5. Phatic or 'social oil'	Ooh, really, goodness me.

The examples of conversational interaction given in Chapter 2 show that adults at home are skilled at handing over initiative and involving children as equal partners in dialogue. Moves which promote this include those at the fourth level, personal contributions or commentary, which are often followed by the child taking the initiative: 'I had a nice surprise for my birthday', 'When I was small I went to Margate'. Finally, 'phatic' moves, or social oil, confirm the adult's attention and interest, and encourage the child to say more: 'Hmm, nice', 'Ooh, how lovely'. The child still has the option of keeping hold of the conversational floor.

There are a number of reasons why hearing-impaired children have an increased likelihood of experiencing more high-control conversational moves from adults. If the child's speech is difficult to understand, because of either poor articulation or lack of a supporting context, adults may resort to seeking repetition or clarification of what the child has said. Another source of high control is inherent in the belief that deaf children must be taught, and work at language. There is a double disadvantage for deaf children. Teaching styles in most classrooms, geared as they are to 'pedagogic' purposes, are unlikely to provide children with a language environment which fosters development of their mother tongue. But when teachers recognise a need to focus on language, the strategies they are likely to adopt to teach language in a *deliberate* manner may steer even further away from the kind of facilitative interactions that we have depicted in some detail in Chapter 2.

In the following example, taken from a textbook on the teaching of language to deaf children (Van Uden, 1977, page 263), a group of children are discussing going home from school for the holidays:

Cora: Some ...
Teacher: *Ssss*, say your *ss* better!
Cora: Some girls, Bernie and Lea and Cora, ... I, ... is ... are allowed to go home tomorrow.
Teacher: Yes ... are allowed to go home only tomorrow ... Elly say it!
Elly: Some girl ...
Teacher *(interrupting)*:   Some girl*s*, plural form!
Elly: Some girl*ss*, Bernie and Lea and Cora, are allowed to go home tomorrow.
Teacher: That is correct.

The teacher steps into the dialogue in order to correct pronunciation and grammar, but at some cost to the conversational flow. The teacher's approval at the end of the exchange seems to be aimed at the well-formed sentence the child has produced, rather than at the child's meaning. This is a good example of the teacher exerting a high degree of control over conversation, where strategies such as imitation and repetition of correct language figure highly. The sense of negotiation between adult and child is absent, the style is directive, the children are put into the rôles of passive assimilators. They are aware that the aim of exchanges like this is to practise their speech.

In one study (Wood and Wood, 1984), teachers were asked to change their styles of conversation with deaf children. Observations of deaf and hearing children show that the more control the teacher exerts in dialogue, the less likely children are to take the initiative or to address other children, and the briefer the child's turns become. At the start of the study, the teachers relied mainly on questions to get children to respond or to think further. Opportunities were often taken to 'improve' a child's contribution or to 'repair' any misunderstandings that arose. For example, if a breakdown in conversation occurs because the teacher finds something ambiguous or unintelligible, the dialogue might be halted and a clarification sought: 'I don't understand, did you say *bike* or *kite*?'. The more immature the language and the poorer the intelligibility, the greater the likelihood that breakdowns in conversation will occur, and the more the teacher resorts to stepping into the dialogue to patch over misunderstandings and make teaching points.

Using the five categories of control listed in Table 4.1, examples of adult moves were demonstrated to the teachers involved in the study and they were encouraged to bias their language towards each of the move-types in turn, as they interacted with children. Could the teachers change their style at will? It did prove possible for the teachers to adopt more- or less-controlling strategies, with corresponding effects on the child's own contributions. When teachers used high-control moves, children were far less likely to take the initiative, sustain a topic or make an extended contribution than when low-control moves were used.

Example 1   Enforced repetition

Teacher: What's the matter with his Mummy?
Child: Fed up of work.
Teacher: Yes, she's fed up with working. Can you say that?
Child: He, he fed up working.
Teacher: Not he ... *She's* fed up with working.
Child: She's fed up.

Example 2   Two-choice question

Teacher: Is your doctor a nice lady or a horrible lady?

Child: Lady nice *(nodding)*.
Teacher: A nice lady?
Child: Yes.

Questions need careful consideration. We know that questioning is an important aspect of language interaction, more so when it is the child who initiates the enquiry. In the Tizard and Hughes (1984) research, children were observed as persistent questioners. In joint activities with adults they asked how things work, where people are going, what things costs and so on. However, when the adult asks many two-choice questions, conversation is heavy going because children become increasingly passive and inhibited. Wh- type questions are often used for 'teaching' purposes, asking children to think further on a teacher-prescribed issue. This is a good example of 'non-contingent' adult behaviour because the child is asked to respond to the intentions of the adult, and not the other way round. Confusions may then arise about what is being asked. In the following extract, there are further difficulties because of a mismatch between what the teacher does and what she says.

Example 3   Wh- type question

Teacher: What colour does the lady wear when she gets married? What colour *(points to ring finger)*?
Child 1: White.
Teacher: White, yes.
Child 2 *(points to ring finger)*: ? No, yellow.

In the low-control sessions, teachers concentrated on avoiding questions and either telling children about their own experiences or commenting on what the children had to offer. In consequence, children took more of an active part and were more talkative.

Example 4   Personal contribution

Teacher: I don't like crabs.
Child 1: Eee? Eee? *(gestures beating them to death)*
Teacher: Oh! Do you kill them?
Child 2: —? Blood, dead.
Teacher: Oo, how horrible!
Child 1: Mrs, my father, shop, holiday, shop eat it!
Teacher: Crab?
Child 1: Open *(gestures scooping out crab)*.
Teacher: They're lovely to eat.
Child 2: I saw, and saw, swimming(?), holiday, I saw—, I saw fish—

Teacher: A real one?
Child 2:   *(Draws 'J' in the air, for 'Jaws')*

Despite the obvious limitations in the verbal language that these children use, the teacher's moves give a sense of equal partnership, which enables the children to contribute freely, to introduce new information and to change the topic. In the final, phatic session, the teacher is sharing a picture book with a group. Relinquishing control altogether and simply oiling the conversational wheels results in much more animated talk from a number of children.

Example 5   Phatic

Child 1:   And he's going to fall in *(pointing to picture)*.
Teacher: Oh!
Child 1:   He's fell in, an't he?
Teacher: He's falling *(points)*. Look.
Child 1:   And he's fell in.
Child 2:   Uh, it's dirty water!
Teacher: Oh dear!
Child 1:   Look how he's going in that water!

What conclusions can be drawn about productive conversations between adults and deaf children in the classroom? A balance has to be sought, recognising that classroom dialogue may be put to many uses, besides improving children's communication. Where the teacher aims specifically to engage children in dialogue, certain styles will be more effective in enabling children to take turns, assume the initiative and make extended contributions. The ground rules discussed here will be taken up again in Chapter 5, when we discuss intervention strategies. The Nottingham research shows that it is possible to avoid an overquestioning, controlling kind of conversation. The teacher is more likely to be successful with poor communicators if a mutual experience, activity or project, can be found, so that interaction is context-based to begin with. The more talk surrounds a known topic which is familiar and relevant to the child, the greater is the momentum to participate. The teacher needs to give something from personal experience, to comment on the child's own contributions and to hand conversation back to the child, allowing ample time for a reply. Both adult and child have to be able to enter the dialogue as equal partners, and this needs to be reaffirmed with phatic comments from the teacher.

When teachers question less, avoid jumping into dialogue to correct or repair the form of a child's utterance, and generally pay more attention to what children are trying to mean, then children tend to reciprocate by making more frequent and longer contributions. Too much control stifles, but too little also robs the teacher of opportunities to negotiate meaning with a child, when help is needed to make intentions clear. This is not to imply that teachers should never question or give signals about the clarity or coherence of what the child is trying to say. However, questions are much more effective when they arise genuinely out of a topic or theme which is already well established in a shared dialogue, and not used simply to test a child's knowledge. Where ambiguity arises, the adult can respond by putting the child's assumed meaning into words — 'You're upset because you've missed your bus, are you?' — as opposed to cross-examining: 'What did you say?', 'What does that mean?'

Although conversations with immature children often arise out of the 'here and now', ultimately talk serves to share memories, objects and events not immediately present, and plans for the future. This has been described in terms of disembedded thinking (Donaldson, 1978): a change from attention to what is without, to an awareness of events within. We have said that there are a number of children with profound hearing losses who do overcome obstacles to learning and interaction in order to develop 'normal' speech and language. They are able to use language to think about, manipulate and infer relationships between ideas and events which have no immediate context. We have provided some explanations which account for differences between teachers who work with deaf children in a variety of settings. Some styles constrain the linguistic and cognitive demands made upon children, such as questioning, enforced repetition and imitation. Other styles expose children to greater challenge and complexity of language in the classroom, whilst engaging the child as an active partner. In order to move children forward in their linguistic development, the teacher has to find ways of talking about hypothetical situations, inviting speculation about cause and effect, and invoking imaginative experience, whilst also sustaining the child's urge to know more.

SEVERE DEAFNESS AND LANGUAGE DEVELOPMENT

The vast majority of the research literature on the severely hearing-impaired is concerned with the evaluation of *products*, rather than *processes*, of learning. The purpose has often been to establish how far behind normally hearing peers deaf children fall, in terms of their achievements. This descriptive approach is linked with the 'deficit model' of handicap, which tends to attribute any difficulties in learning which may arise to the child's disability

(Webster, 1986a). We shall not be referring in any detail to this evaluative literature. Rather, we shall be highlighting some widely agreed findings, in order to set the scene for the remainder of this chapter: recent studies which have thrown new light on the acquisition of skills, such as literacy and numeracy, in severely hearing-impaired children.

Some very early observations of deaf babies in the first six months suggest that they do vocalise, coo and cry like hearing babies. At the babble stage, when the child begins to produce the significant sound contrasts which are used around them, deaf babies produce a reduced range of sounds, in less quantity and with flatter tones. The speech sounds of deaf babies are thus slower to become language-specific than those of hearing counterparts. When features of speech have been isolated which make 'deaf' speech different from hearing, speech rhythms, vowel distortions, omission of consonants, and slow, laboured or breathy speech are reported. Speech intelligibility has also been used as a measure of educational success. Untrained listeners are often able to understand less than a fifth of deaf children's speech. In the study of deaf children's speech by Dodd (1976), for example, 11-year-olds were using less than half of the 44 sound contrasts, or phonemes, of English. Difficulties in mastering the sound system are ascribed to the incomplete or distorted nature of the child's auditory experience, even when powerful hearing-aids are worn.

A critical question concerns the kind of language *internalised* by the child with a severe hearing loss. Normally hearing children are thought to have inner speech-like experiences which correspond to their outer use of speech sounds. When thinking or reading, for example, most children have a covert speech code which is just used for themselves: an internal symbol system which enables the child to represent and work over aspects of their experience. Access to an inner speech code has been held by some to be the foundation stone for literacy, determining whether a severely deaf child will be able to read. This argument has also been used to explain the reading difficulties of children with conductive hearing loss, assuming that children must be able to decode text into speech sounds in order to discover the meaning of words. The lack of an internalised language, or the alternative use of an inner thinking code based on signs, gestures and other symbols, such as finger spelling, has been cited as the major cause of the deaf child's literacy problems. We shall be examining this argument again later in the chapter. Suffice it to say at this point that, as in the case of conductive deafness, we do not believe a single-factor explanation has the power to account for deaf children's reading problems.

There is also a body of literature on the grammatical development of deaf children. In Chapter 2 we set out the features of successive stages of syntax growth, which linguists use to describe the course of normal development. The consensus view is that there are many similarities, as well as differences, between deaf and hearing children in the early stages. For example, in the Gregory and Mogford (1981) study of early interaction between deaf infants and hearing parents, two-word combinations, such as 'Not hot', 'More sock' and 'Mummy gone', start around the time the child has acquired about 50 words, which is the same for hearing children as they move into Stage II. A major difference is that deaf children take much longer to acquire words: the two most severely hearing-impaired children in this study had fewer than ten words at four years of age.

Gregory and Mogford (1981) take issue with the view that deaf and hearing children develop along the same lines, albeit at different rates. They feel, from the patterns of interaction observed, that it is not just a matter of reduced exposure to speech, but that deaf children come to know language from a different set of 'taught' experiences. This is very much in accord with our own view, that many deaf children are expected to assimilate, rather than generate, language. Whichever view is correct, deaf children do continue to construct a system of grammatical rules as they pass through school. The most comprehensive studies of the syntactic structures which deaf students can use and understand were carried out by Quigley and his colleagues (Quigley, Wilbur, Power, Montanelli and Steinkamp, 1976). Deaf children from ten to nineteen years were tested on a wide range of sentence forms, such as negation, determiners, use of pronouns, question forms and verb processes. They found that deaf children generally make slow but consistent progress throughout the age-range on almost every aspect of syntax tested.

There are particular sentence structures which continue to pose problems for deaf individuals into adulthood. One of the processes normally acquired at Stage V is the embedding of one clause within another. Whilst deaf pupils might understand simple structures like 'The boys worked with Dad' and 'The boys liked airplanes', they would be unable to respond correctly to 'The boys who worked with Dad liked airplanes' (believing that it was Dad who was keen on planes, rather than the boys). Similarly, passive sentences cause confusion. Whilst hearing youngsters also misinterpret sentences like 'The boy was pushed by the girl' until about eight or nine years, deaf students of seventeen or eighteen years might continue to think that the girl, and not the boy, was pushed. The rule which deaf children apply to both active and passive sentences is one of straight left-to-right processing of word order: subject–verb–object.

When children approach reading, the mismatch between the grammatical structures controlled by the child and those found in text has also been specified as a source of reading failure.

Finally, whilst many deaf children appear not to be engaged in productive language interaction, where the 'to and fro' of conversation is experienced, it may also be supposed that deafness denies children access to the richest data available for grasping the flexible range of meaning in language: overhearing idioms being used in a multiplicity of social contexts. There may be similar consequences of exposing children to taught or drilled language, where word-meanings are acquired in limited classroom contexts and lack a supporting social framework which suffuses the language with meaning. So, for example, whilst a child may use and understand prepositions in sequences like 'on the bed', 'under the table' and 'by the roadside', less literal meanings may be more elusive: 'on the whole', 'under the weather', 'by Christmas'. Metaphoric usage may, in fact, lead to some bewilderment. Expressions such as 'caught in the middle', 'the baby threw a tantrum', 'drenched to the bone' and 'down in the dumps' are likely sources of comprehension breakdown.

BEHAVIOUR AND PERSONALITY

Another example of the deficit model in action is the assumption that there is a special style of personalilty and behaviour which is attributable to deafness. In this book we have steered well away from the notion of a special psychology for deaf individuals. We have preferred not to locate obstacles to learning, or the source of any developmental anomalies, within the children themselves. However, one argument which is sometimes used is that, because deaf people cannot hear, they develop different ways of perceiving information and making sense of the world. In consequence, deaf individuals are thought to be more rigid and literal in their thinking, unable to deal with abstract concepts.

Quigley and Kretschmer (1982, page 76) report on a technique used with deaf children to evaluate the ability to infer meanings which are not explicitly stated. In the following example:

> The shirt is dirty
> The shirt is under the bed
> The cat is on the shirt
> The cat is white

it can be inferred that the cat is under the bed. Deaf children may understand the individual sentences but have difficulty in making this inference. It could be argued that more limited language experience and restricted contact with print causes this kind of inability, rather than a qualitatively distinct learning style, which cannot cope with inference or hypothesis. Whichever interpretation is correct, inferencing ability has also been cited as a major cause of reading problems in the hearing-impaired.

Severely hearing-impaired children have been variously described as socially immature and impulsive; lacking self-direction and motivation; showing low incentive to achieve; unable to reflect on their own behaviour and weigh the consequences of their actions; having poor persistence and attention span; poor at making relationships; unable to see other people's points of view; slower to respond to change and ask for explanations; lacking social adaptivity; rigid and egocentric; poor at seeking information; restricted in general knowledge and experience; dependent on adults and unable to care for their own needs; lacking self-esteem; and more compliant and less creative, buoyant, confident or happy than their hearing peers. The stereotyped picture of the unique 'deaf personality' is one of passive dependency on others, unquestioning styles of learning, and unenquiring, self-centred and naïve assumptions about the world.

This is a classic example of the deficit model, which attributes behaviour traits and learning styles to the child's disability. A much more optimistic view is that it is not deafness *per se* but the indirect effects of deafness which affect social maturity, emotional adjustment and learning strategies. Many of the behaviours listed above are similar to those associated with an external locus of control or 'learned helplessness'. Individuals with an *inner* locus of control assume responsibility for their own behaviour: they are more confident and active in their planning or decision-making. Individuals with an *outer* locus of control tend to blame events on forces outside themselves and see themselves as powerless.

The roots of an external locus of control in deaf children are not hard to find. Many parents have unresolved feelings of guilt, or a sense of the child's vulnerability, leading to overprotection. The parents of a 5-year-old deaf child may be terrified that the child will get lost and be unable to explain where he lives. Or a child may not be allowed to ride a bike for fear that she will be unable to hear traffic. For children to grow by taking responsibility, parents have to stand back at times, and allow the possibility of failure. Heightened direction and control at home may lead to passive reactions and a feeling of being unable to influence events. The child's passage into adulthood may also be limited by the nature of adult–child interactions at school. Here, too, we have seen that deafness seems to elicit more managerial, directive and controlling styles from adults, where children are often expected to take the role of passive assimilator rather than active enquirer in the learning process. They may be exposed to more rote learning and teacher-prescribed assignments, without the sense of partnership or negotiation which leads to a sharing of responsibility.

Finally, we should recall the principle presented in Chapter 2, which highlights social interaction as the means by which children experience the power and function of language, discover ways of self-regulating their behaviour and thinking, but also have access to a wide range of shared cultural values and attitudes. The point is that typical behaviours and learning styles in the severely hearing-impaired may be a product of early home experiences and of schooling, rather than inherent in a 'deaf personality'. Less nurturing styles of interaction will lead to slower generation of speech and language, but will also have effects on the child's take-up of more mature ways of problem-solving and self-organisation. Where the child is not involved in conversation with peers, or is unable to overhear the interactions and discussions of others, it will be more difficult to absorb general knowledge and keep up with trends in dress, 'in' slang, jokes and nicknames. We also arrive at a considered view of events by discussion, listening to opposing points of view, and gauging the reaction of others to what we say. This, too, may be more difficult for the hearing-impaired child.

The deficit model leads to a pessimistic view of what can be achieved, given the restricted 'condition' of deafness. The alternative view locates many of the child's difficulties in the learning environment. The way forward is to find routes around the obstacles to learning and to productive social interactions that deafness often creates. In Chapter 5 we shall be considering the positive strategies which teachers and schools can adopt to modify their own typical behaviour and teaching styles.

READING AND SEVERE HEARING-IMPAIRMENT

Earlier in this chapter we discussed a number of approaches which have been made to the reading process, as we currently understand it. Previous thinking tended to dissect reading into subskills and stages, in line with a linear, 'decoding' model. The 'flat earth' or 'bottom-up' view is that reading is superimposed on the child's base language, and that the task is to learn the rules for deciphering one to the other. In teaching terms, this is often expressed as the practising of skills for relating the visual symbols of print to the sounds of speech.

More recently, the 'round earth' or 'top-down' view of reading takes into account what children learn in their active testing out and reinvention of the language system, as they interact with adults in meaningful social contexts. To become readers, children apply their hypothesis-forming and rule-using to the reconstruction of meaning in text. Reading is an integral part of the fabric of experience and problem-solving, shared with facilitating adults.

There is a compromise position which takes into account that some clues to meaning arise upwards from the page, whilst other clues are brought to reading in the form of predictions and expectations that children have of print from their knowledge of language, books and the world.

It is widely agreed that children with severe sensori-neural hearing losses may face formidable problems in becoming fluent readers. When large-scale evaluative surveys of reading attainment have been mounted, both in the UK and in the USA, children with severe hearing losses are unlikely to have achieved a reading age of nine years by the time they leave school, on tests standardised on hearing children. (For further discussion of attainment levels of deaf children and some difficulties of interpretation, see Webster, 1986a.) A single-factor view, expressed for example by Conrad (1979), is that deafness traps children at a pre-phonetic stage of reading. Lacking internal speech sounds, children are unable to utilise the 'alphabetic principle': that units of sound map on to the visual symbols of print. Similar arguments have been put forward to account for the reading difficulties associated with conductive hearing loss.

In fact, we have to take into account a number of aspects of the reading process in order to understand how reading may be more problematic for the hearing-impaired. At the sound level, children may have difficulties mastering the sound system and using a large proportion of the phonemic contrasts of English. Focusing on another 'bottom-up' route, some researchers claim to have identified visual-perceptual deficiencies in deaf children, required for perceiving and discriminating letter shapes (Cooper and Arnold, 1981). In effect, the core reading problem is said to lie at both ends of the process of decoding from print to sound.

In contrast, other work shows that there are few developmental differences between deaf and hearing children in identifying letters, discriminating and matching letter shapes, and acquiring a basic sight vocabulary (Kyle, 1980). One distinct possibility is that any differences in 'bottom-up' skills thrown up by research simply reflect the child's growing experience of print. The very fact of being more proficient at reading may lead to greater insights about features such as letter shapes and letter–sound correspondences, rather than the other way round.

At another level, the nature of the child's inner language code for thinking is important. It is held by some that, at least in the early stages, children cannot access meaning directly from print, but that the visual symbols must first be converted into the child's inner thinking code. Whether or not a child develops an auditory-based inner language system will depend on the kinds of interaction and experience enjoyed with adults, as well as on the preferred mode of communication adopted. There is no reason why other kinds of inner recoding strategy could not be used to mediate between print and meaning. Deaf children may integrate aspects of gesture, sign language and finger spelling, together with speech sounds, in their inner coding system. Children who sign, for example, may think in signs and 'read aloud' in signs (Quigley and Kretschmer, 1982).

One possibility is that inner thinking codes based on anything other than auditory symbols may be at a disadvantage in processing print. The reason for this is that an auditory code is especially geared to the rehearsal and storage of a sequence of verbal items, necessary, for example, when discerning the meaning of a long embedded sentence, where information at the beginning has to be held over until the end. However, these issues are to some extent speculative, and there are other, more obvious aspects of the reading process to consider.

Syntax provides the organising structures of language which relate sound to meaning. In Chapter 2, we considered the relationship between the development of syntax and the use of language in communication and social interaction. In the same way that children acquire concepts such as conservation of quantity through 'hands-on' pouring and doing activities, we argued that dialogue provides children with living evidence of how syntax works, in the changes sentences undergo as they are handed backwards and forwards in conversation. Severely hearing-impaired children are less likely to enjoy facilitating social and linguistic interactions with adults. They are slower to generate the rules of syntax. They also adhere to rules like subject–verb–object word order, which are misleading when applied to passive or embedded structures. Even when competence is achieved at the *implicit* level, in the sense of being able to use language structures functionally, there may be limitations in the child's *explicit* awareness of syntax: a knowledge of how the code is put together and how it works. Written language increasingly draws on the child's ability to stand back from language, to experiment with and think about features of the system, as a problem-space in its own right.

In consequence, when the child approaches reading there may well be a mismatch between the syntax of reading materials and the structures the child controls. Most hearing children come to reading with a fairly sophisticated language base, including complex syntax. When many deaf children come to reading, they find a dual problem: not only the printed code but also the language which the code represents is unfamiliar. Discovering how to read becomes a language learning process at one and the same time.

We have also said that a richness of language use in interactive contexts provides children with evidence of the semantic flexibility of language. Many teachers comment on the literal interpretation of language by deaf children and the apparent lack of metaphoric expression. For example, the meaning of phrases like 'a biting wind', 'clean as a whistle' or 'take your time' may evade many children, for the same reasons that verbal puns in jokes do not characterise 'deaf' humour. Nuances of form, structure and meaning may also be a source of comprehension difficulty as children approach reading.

This leads us to a final aspect of the deaf child's experience and development which has an impact on how text is approached and how the child becomes printborne: social interaction and styles of learning. One of the secondary consequences of deafness is that children are very early put into the position of being passive assimilators of language. In one of the Nottingham studies (Howarth, Wood, Griffiths and Howarth, 1981), adults were observed sharing books with deaf children. Even in this context, the experience was different from that normally enjoyed in shared book-reading. Adults tend to use the occasion to teach the child, draw attention to new vocabulary or correct pronunciation, and generally step into the reading flow more often to test understanding or make a point to the child. As a result, story continuity suffers and the meaning of a text may be more elusive. These changes in adult–child interactions in shared reading reflect the more directive, controlling styles of adults in conversation with deaf children.

In school, language may be taught in a decontextualised way, devoid of real purpose and function, and isolated from real experience of the world. Rote vocabulary drills and grammatical exercises, which characterise many 'structured' teaching programmes, lead to passive, unquestioning styles of learning. If children are not expected to enquire, initiate questions, seek out rules and reconstruct their own models of how language works, they will be poorly prepared for actively reading for meaning. The lack of inferencing ability mentioned earlier — going beyond the literal to infer meanings not explicitly stated — is as much to do with the child's development of active strategies for meaning-making as it is to do with linguistic awareness. In trying to help deaf children read, teachers may have to address additional problems, moving children towards independence in learning, awareness of how to go about their own study, learning how to learn.

WRITING, SPELLING AND SEVERE DEAFNESS

Writing can be considered an integral part of the language curriculum for any child, one which should not be taught separately as an isolated skill. This is the view we have put forward in relation to reading. Both reading and writing should grow out of interactive encounters in meaningful social contexts, and be part of the child's overall language enquiry and problem-solving. Another overly simplistic view is that writing is a linear activity: encoding information in letters, words and phrases to make whole sentences and paragraphs. Both writing and reading involve far more than transcription from one set of symbols to another (Perera, 1984).

In fact, writing shares many of the features discussed earlier in relation to spoken language and reading. In the early stages, for example, children may write squiggles and marks as pretend shopping lists, stories or notes to granddad. Children are also aware of adults' writing: cards, forms, cheques, letters, crossword puzzles and notes to the milkman. Writing is rooted in familiar contexts, with specific purposes. To begin with, the form of writing is linked with its meaning: some children feel that only content words, such as 'Mummy' or 'house', are real, whilst words with fewer than three letters or without a concrete image, such as 'if' or 'but', are not considered to be real words. Names of adults may be thought to be bigger or longer than names of children. By five or six years, many children become aware that written language is a system separate from the objects and experiences it can represent. Increasingly, written language in school becomes decontextualised, self-contained and a medium for thinking and learning. In Chapter 5 we shall be returning to some of the differences between spoken language and the formal structures of writing, as a basis for planning classroom strategies.

There are generally three distinct stages in any act of writing (Webster, 1986a). The first is really a pre-writing phase, when the writer collects ideas together and decides what is going to be said, before putting pen to paper. In the second stage, ideas are reconstructed using the conventions of print. A network of skills is required here, such as legible handwriting and spelling, which affect the ease with which a reader may respond to a person's writing. However, the more central aspects which affect the meaning of what is written include choice of vocabulary, phrase and clause patterns, and the devices used to link sentences to form a cohesive text. The third stage is one of subsequent review or reinspection of what has been written. Without this final phase of reappraisal it is hard to imagine how writers could tie sentences together by cross-reference, pronouns, conjunctions and other kinds of textual link. These writing stages provide a convenient framework for discussing the writing of hearing-impaired children, and are the points of reference when we come to consider helping children to write.

The written language of deaf children has probably received more research attention than any other aspect because it is easier to study than, say, speech recordings. Many hearing-impaired children have difficulties at the first stage, thinking what to write. They may have a limited fund of experience or language to draw on. Writing may have been approached as a mechanical chore or exercise, in the same way that spoken words are sometimes 'worked on' by adults who are not sure how to proceed with a deaf child. Paradoxically, frustration may be experienced because there is a mismatch between the level at which a deaf child thinks and feels about an issue, and the linguistic means the child has for expression.

At the second stage, writing draws on the vocabulary, syntax and sentence-links the child knows. Research shows that deaf children use shorter, simpler sentences than hearing peers, with more errors and non-standard usages (so-called 'deafisms'). They use more content words, such as nouns, verbs and adjectives. Least frequently used are function words, such as articles, conjunctions and prepositions. Sentences are said to be more rigid and stereotyped, sticking to a well-rehearsed pattern. There may be a poor awareness of the rules which govern how words are used with each other, whilst juxtaposition may connect ideas together, dispensing with formal grammar: 'With girl boy mother play', 'I is was very good eat food', 'Hair wash and baths tomorrow school'.

A sample of free writing by a 13-year-old profoundly deaf girl of average intelligence is given in Figure 4.3. Most of the sentence patterns used are at Stage III or IV, with three or four elements of structure. Noticeably lacking are those devices which children use to extend and link their sentences together, such as 'and', 'but' and 'so'. However, there is a reaching out to more mature ways of connecting clauses together, such as subordination ('because'), and an indication of time sequence ('Then morning...', 'when the ...'). Some phrase structures are mastered, such as preposition–determiner–noun ('in the shed'), pronouns ('my'), intensifiers ('very') and auxiliary verbs ('will be'), with some features almost correct, such as possessives ('My Dad cows'). However, there are many 'errors' and omissions, such as verbs ('The mountain lot of

The snow come down The mountain from the sky. The sky will be a white. The mountain lot of snow because The mountain too higth. Then morning I saw The grilled and salted lorry ~~what~~ Past my house all The round road make a safe stop slippy The round road. My farm very very cold. My Dad cows in The shed keep warm this morning. I wake up this morning a 8 oclock want The Tiax come my house for me going to school. The Tiax diver show becoren The snow will be a slippy. When The Tiax stop The Tiax will a move down The hill.

Figure 4.3 *Free writing by a 13-year-old girl of average abilities with a profound hearing loss*

snow'), whilst some unusual rules appear to be applied ('will be a slippy', 'will a move', 'make a safe'). There are few spelling mistakes, a point we shall take up later. At a number of points the child has some complex ideas to express, but lacks the syntax to put them into a sentence and simply places the important words close together ('make a safe stop slippy the round road', 'want the tiax come my house'). Because some of these language patterns are atypical, and not observed in the writing of hearing children, the written language of deaf individuals is considered to be both delayed and deviant.

Many deaf children appear to write sentence by sentence, with little awareness of how to connect sentences and how to achieve cohesion by cross-reference or the use of pronouns for subjects already introduced. This brings us to the third stage, reappraisal. Most writers rehearse their ideas internally, as they think out and subsequently reinspect their writing. Such rehearsal would be impossible without some form of inner language code. We have already discussed the potential significance of an auditory-based inner language code for the reading process. An inner speech-like code seems especially geared to the rehearsal and processing of a succession of verbal items. (A visually based system, such as sign or finger spelling, is arguably more effective in storing and processing simultaneous sensory input.) By the same token, children with good inner speech may be at an advantage when composing long, embedded or interconnected sequences of verbal information. (For further discussion of the implications of different inner coding systems for short-term memory and language processing, see Webster, 1986a.)

There are a number of explanations for the apparent immaturity in deaf children's writing, and for some of the more unusual or 'deviant' patterns which are used. One view is that function words, such as 'if', 'so', 'that' and 'but', have only fleeting presence in speech, and are missed perceptually by children relying on residual hearing. Another view is that many function words are relatively late to appear in the normal stages of language development anyway, and so will not be 'in reach' until the child has a wider experience of communication. Problems of sustaining dialogue and enjoying conversational interactions with deaf children create secondary obstacles to learning, so that children are less familiar with discourse features generally: the sustaining of topics over stretches of conversational 'text'. For any one of these reasons, the end product is that, when hearing-impaired children write, ideas may appear to come bursting out of the language at the child's disposal, with a sense of unchecked disorganisation.

To summarise, there are a number of possible reasons why deaf children may experience writing difficulties, some experiential, some linguistic, some related to inner language. Children may have difficulty at the composing stage, at the stage of putting thoughts into sentence structures, and at the stage of review. The kind of writing which has often been associated with severe deafness may take the form it does because pressure of what the child wants to say comes flooding over the linguistic limitations of the child. In Chapter 5 we shall address the issue of engendering a writing momentum. There are a number of ways in which teachers can foster a genuine urgency to write, as part of a language curriculum in which listening, talking, reading and writing are integrated. The techniques for joint composition, reappraisal and review which are described should lead children to a greater awareness of the reasons for writing, the structural and functional characteristics of writing, and how a cohesive and coherent text can be worked up.

Spelling is one secondary aspect of the 'working up' of a piece of writing. Most authorities agree that spelling is not usually a major problem for deaf children, relative to achievements in reading or other aspects of communication. In spelling, children can utilise a range of strategies. In just the same way as there are many sources of information in reconstructing meaning in reading text, so there are many routes to storing and retrieving the way words are spelt. The early untutored writing of Paul Bissex shows a rudimentary awareness of some sound features of letters and letter names: 'RUDF', 'HAB BRTH DA', 'OWT UV ORDR', 'MI ZIPPR WONT ZIP' (Bissex, 1980). In school, children often begin to spell by using their knowledge of sound–symbol correspondences, particularly if reading has been taught using 'phonics'. At this point, mistakes such as 'apul', 'becos' and 'anser' are common. Children also incorporate visual strategies into their spelling, resulting in errors such as 'caght', 'cuople' and 'lahgfing'.

These examples show the child's flexible, testing-out approach, as different strategies are tried and rules formed, dispensed with or modified. Clearly, spelling is not a rote memory task. It is more than likely that children will attempt to copy, learn and construct spelling patterns by drawing on a variety of letter, sound and visual-whole features. Our present understanding suggests that spelling and reading act reciprocally to build skill in each other (Cataldo and Ellis, 1988). In other words, as ability in recognising sight words increases, children will modify their approach to spelling, and vice versa. Proficient spellers appear to make a shift towards visual strategies as they get older. In fact, most irregular words must be stored visually ('yacht', 'eye'); whilst an important need for most people who are uncertain about a word is to write it down to see if it 'looks right'. By the end of primary school, many children are able to work out how words are spelt from visual analogies. Faced with an unfamiliar word, they may try to recall features of related words, as a basis for spelling the new word: 'knee — kneel', 'light — alighted', 'decide — decision', 'advise — practise'.

In one of the Nottingham studies of children's writing (reported in Webster, 1986a) around 90 per cent of deaf children's spelling errors were of the visual recall kind: 'sicossors' (scissors), 'tiax' (taxi), 'becaren' (because), 'wiodow' (window), 'beauiful' (beautiful), 'ot' (to), 'clindren' (children), 'care' (car). A number of experiments on spelling conducted by other researchers (Dodd and Campbell, 1987) provide supportive evidence to our own. When pressed, many deaf children are able to use phonological information from lip-patterns in order to spell spoken words. The fact that the deaf children in these studies tended to rely on visual clues to recall spelling patterns aligns them with good spellers generally, since that seems to be the most successful route to accurate spelling. To reiterate, spelling is not often reported as a major problem for severely deaf children, relative to other aspects of writing, such as syntax. However, there are implications from the work discussed here for teachers who wish to help children improve their spelling, which we shall cover in Chapter 5.

REASONING, NUMERACY AND DEAFNESS

In an earlier section we discussed an idea that is sometimes put forward, that deaf individuals have a special, more rigid, egocentric and literal way of making sense of the world, which is also incompatible with abstract thinking. One class of children had been considering a prediction of Nostradamus that the world was going to end the following Saturday. After the weekend, a profoundly deaf boy was asked whether the world had, in fact, ended. The boy replied that he did not know: he had been at a football match at the time! This kind of reasoning takes account of personal reality rather than hypothetical possibility. Imagine a class of children set the problem: 'If it takes one man three days to put up a garden fence, how long will it take two men?' If children respond with answers like 'Two men would do the job a lot faster because one could hold the fence stakes while the other knocked them in the ground' or 'Depends how much you pay them', have the children necessarily gone wrong in their thinking?

There is evidence to suggest that the ability to solve these logical problems, where irrelevant personal or practical considerations are put aside, is a product of schooling and literacy. In the example above, children come to an awareness that, when asked questions of this kind in school, correct responses home in on the mathematical operations involved. Some researchers, like Bruner, have argued that individuals do not develop along a unitary dimension of thinking towards more abstract, formal logic. Rather, individuals learn a range of problem-solving strategies which are situation-specific. In non-literate, non-schooled cultures, making inferences from hypothetical reasoning about implausible situations is uncharacteristic and may not be called upon. In the study of an African tribe called the Kpelle, researchers posed logical problems of the kind:

Experimenter: Spider and black deer always eat together.
Spider is eating. Is black deer eating?
Subject: But I was not there. How can I answer
such a question?

Some time later, after the question had been repeated:

Experimenter: Black deer was eating?
Subject: Yes.
Experimenter: What is your reason for saying that black
deer was eating?
Subject: The reason is that black deer always walks about all
day eating green leaves in the bush ...
(Cole, Gay, Glick and Sharp, 1971)

It is because of cross-cultural evidence such as this that many reasearchers now disagree with Piaget's earlier claim (he later modified this view) that the *natural* culmination of children's intellectual growth is the stage of 'formal logic': thinking freed from its real world content. In school, children may be led progressively to the point where they can tackle formal prepositions and problems of the kind: 'If A + B = 20, and B is always less than A, what can be said about A?' This kind of problem transcends space and time, its relevance is not personal or immediately apparent. However, there are doubts about whether the majority of youngsters, even in late adolescence, ever achieve this degree of formal logic. What is perhaps more important is that the general utility of this kind of reasoning has also been queried, as it does not provide a plausible explanation of how people normally think (Wood, 1988).

One possibility is that the style of reasoning which is said to characterise the deaf individual arises from social experience and from schooling. We have highlighted a range of factors associated with severe deafness, which lead to qualitatively different learning experiences, including conversational interaction where talk tends to be less challenging, wide-ranging or hypothetical, more adult-controlled and directive, constrained to the concrete 'here and now'. If children have more limited exposure to print, to active problem-solving activities in science or mathematics, to self-initiated methods of enquiry in the humanities, or to the propositional thinking of design and technology, then it is hardly surprising if these thinking styles are not fostered. What we have, then, are not inevitable barriers to abstract modes of thinking in the hearing-impaired, but reflections of the fact that we have yet to find ways of teaching many deaf youngsters successfully, across the curriculum.

One set of studies has looked at mathematical reasoning in groups of hearing and hearing-impaired school-leavers (Wood, Wood and Howarth, 1983). One aim was to see whether the symbols of mathematics pose problems for severely hearing-impaired children. The 'special psychology' theory of deafness holds that all forms of abstract reflection involving the internal manipulation of symbols will be more difficult for those whose sensory loss has resulted in a shift in perception and cognitive processing. In other words, there may be 'theoretical' limits to what deaf children can achieve in subjects such as mathematics, irrespective of teaching. As a corollary, if deaf children's learning of mathematics has no theoretical limits, there is the possibility that some approaches to teaching mathematics are more successful than others.

A total of 1005 children were involved in the study, all of whom were in their last year at school. Of these, 540 were hearing-impaired, drawn from special schools, units and mainstream class placements, and 465 were normally hearing children, included for comparison and to provide a database for analysing score patterns and errors. All the children were given the Vernon–Miller Graded Arithmetic–Mathematics Test (1976). This test involves relatively little written language, but covers a wide range of abilities and processes, including addition, subtraction, multiplication and division, together with algebra, decimals and fractions, and problems using graphical representation.

The average hearing losses and overall mathematics ages are given in Table 4.2. Hearing children did significantly better than hearing-impaired children from all three school backgrounds, and tended to be about three years in advance of those in special schools or units. How important was degree of deafness in influencing test scores? Despite the fact that the hearing losses of children in the study ranged from 30 to 120 decibels HL, hearing loss *per se* accounted for very few of the differences between children's test scores (less than 10 per cent of the variance). So, degree of deafness was not a good predictor of maths age for individual children.

Table 4.2 *Mean mathematics ages for hearing and hearing-impaired school-leavers in different school settings*

Type of school	Mean hearing loss (decibels HL)	Number of children (n = 1005)	Maths age in years (Vernon–Miller)
Special school for the deaf	92	269	12.1
Unit in ordinary school	68	136	12.8
Mainstream-integrated setting	48	135	14.0
Ordinary school	–	465	15.5

What effect did school background have on test performance? When children with similar hearing losses in the different types of school setting were compared, the scores were about the same. In other words, type of school placement is not a significant factor. However, there were very wide differences between some schools and others. Children from one special school achieved maths levels equivalent to those achieved by those in mainstream classes with much less severe hearing losses. Other children in special schools had average maths ages well below nine years. This is a similar finding to the one reported at the beginning of this chapter, in the study of attainments of children with conductive hearing loss. It is not so much the hearing loss, or the subject area selected, which accounts for differences between children's attainments. Rather, it is factors *within* the teaching milieu which affect how well children progress.

Finally, analysis of the scoring and error patterns of hearing and hearing-impaired children on the Vernon–Miller Test shows that hearing-impaired children tackle the test items in the same way as their hearing counterparts, with no differences in the mathematical reasoning displayed. They were no more impulsive or less reflective. Their test performance was not indicative of a special learning style of the deaf. Whilst progress is often slower, hearing-impaired children pass through the same stages as hearing children, as they master mathematical processes. The reasons for slower progress are felt to lie in the teaching and communication process, rather than in any inherent cognitive problems associated with deafness.

MONITORING AND EVALUATION

At a number of points in this book we have stressed the professional responsibility which all those involved in planning and providing for children's special educational needs share, to ensure that a teaching programme is well tailored to the needs of the child. The part played by parents in contributing to appraisal and decision-making is crucial. Whatever teaching methodology is adopted, there is an ongoing obligation for all involved to ascertain how far the learning environment enables every individual to reach full potential. Teachers sometimes focus their energies and concerns on factors which it is hard to change, such as home circumstances, the child's ability to learn, or degree of deafness. At the same time, other factors may be neglected which have a real impact on the child's progress. Teachers exert a large measure of control over the environment in which learning takes place: the organisation of materials and resources, and strategies for teaching. A basic ingredient of most of the Nottingham research studies reported in this chapter has been the attempt to make an accurate appraisal and evaluation of processes within the framework of teaching and learning.

In contrast, the historical record of research on the hearing-impaired is marked by its preoccupation with the outcomes of teaching rather than the processes of learning. Research on reading, for example, has largely centred on evaluating the standards of literacy achieved by deaf children in relation to hearing norms. In this final section we shall highlight some of the pitfalls encountered when formal, standardised tests are given to hearing-impaired children, and also provide signposts for more effective methods of appraisal of both teaching and learning. At the time of writing, the government's Education Reform Act proposes major changes in the way the curriculum is organised, including national attainment targets at different age points. How these subject targets are assessed, whether children with 'statements' or identified special needs are included or exempted, and how 'disapplications' or modifications to the national curriculum can be made, are issues which will have to be faced. In our view, an important aspect of any educational provision is a planned and informed policy of appraisal and review, which both grows out of, and in turn informs, teaching strategy.

What are the hazards associated with formal testing of deaf children? Tests which rely on good rapport or verbal instructions, tasks which are timed, or material which draws heavily on the child's linguistic skills, will tend to reveal more about the child's or the examiner's communication skills than about problem-solving, mathematics, intelligence or whatever skill area is being assessed

(Webster, 1989a). A number of Nottingham studies have looked at the use of traditional reading tests with older deaf children (Webster, Wood and Griffiths, 1981; Wood, Griffiths and Webster, 1981). Briefly, these studies show that, when given a silent reading comprehension test (such as the Widespan or Southgate Test), patterns of right answers and errors made by deaf and hearing groups are different, although reading ages may be nominally the same. For example, deaf children make many more errors and tend to persist in providing answers to test questions well beyond their level of understanding: they often do not self-monitor or self-correct. In order to solve the linguistic puzzles of test materials, deaf children may resort to strategies such as key-wording, word association or non-verbal ploys. By utilising picture clues and the layout of questions on the page, some children were able to get systematically correct answers (although they made many errors as well) on reading tests, without reading the text.

The message of this work is that formal measures, such as reading tests standardised for use with hearing children, may tap very different processes in deaf and hearing groups. This makes the results of such assessments a poor guide to progress, or to the planning of a teaching programme. Severely hearing-impaired school-leavers who achieve a reading age of nine years on formal tests, for example, do not read like their younger hearing counterparts. At best, standardised testing of deaf children is misleading and non-productive. Taken at face value, formal test results are unlikely to lead to more effective teaching because they give no clear indication of what the child has achieved or what skills should be taught next.

In consequence, many teachers are turning increasingly to informal skill profiles as a basis for structuring observations, in order to set objectives and monitor children's progress over time. Profiles can be constructed in any behaviour domain and involve the setting out of a developmental sequence of observable skills which reflects the teaching curriculum. Along the continuum of 'listening', for example, early target observations might include 'turns head to loud sound' and 'responds to tone of voice indicating No'; whilst later observations might include 'takes a message through hearing only, such as over the telephone'. The principle of profiling is that observations of children's emerging strengths and areas of relative weakness are built up over time, using a clear reference framework. Importantly, parents and children themselves can take part in the appraisal process. Constructed with care, profiles of achievement give some definite indications of what the child needs to learn next. We shall be returning to the issue of profiling as a basis for planning, appraisal and review in Chapter 5.

A further signpost we shall leave concerns the turning of attention away from factors inherent in the child and towards the analysis of variables within the learning context. A great deal of the recent evidence presented here shows that the strategies which adults use as they interact with children have a significant effect on development, particularly in language and literacy. Using the system of analysis given in Table 4.1, teachers can assess the quality of adult–child interactions, for example by tallying the number of high-control moves observed over a time sample. In becoming more aware of teacher styles, it should be possible to move towards a more cognitively oriented curriculum for hearing-impaired children.

—5—

Strategies for intervention

One of the major aims of this book is to set out a coherent approach to the development and education of hearing-impaired children. In so doing we have drawn on a body of research evidence with a focus on the nature and role of interactive encounters in fostering language and thinking. We have been particularly careful to avoid fuelling old and unproductive controversies about which method of communication is best, or whether the needs of deaf children are best met in special schools or mainstream. Instead we have adopted a pragmatic approach, which replaces 'teachers should ... ' precepts with questions such as 'How can children and adults become more effective language partners?', 'What factors in the listening environment can be modified?', 'Which approaches to literacy are likely to be effective?' and 'How can extra support be organised within the ordinary classroom?' A basic assumption is that teachers exert a fair measure of control over the conditions created for learning, and will want to take responsibility for evaluating whether the approach adopted (whatever that entails) has had positive outcomes for the child.

At a number of points we have stressed the importance of the 'image' we hold of children as learners. Recent trends in developmental psychology have emphasised the active, problem-solving character of early learning as the child operates on the environment in the company of facilitating adults, in order to reconstruct a model of the world and how it works. Brought to prominence are features such as the importance of meaning, as children enjoy conversation and other shared activities with adults in relevant and purposeful social contexts. Awareness of the function and intention of learning is critical, in order for children to take a growing responsibility for their own enquiry, learning how to learn. A focus on meaning-making has direct implications for the strategies adopted to foster language and literacy. In early language experiences with a severely hearing-impaired child, for example, adults may be overconcerned with the quality of the child's speech or listening, at the expense of the range of communicative intentions expressed (see, for example, the work of Halliday described in Chapter 2).

At the heart of our philosophy is the notion of a cognitively oriented curriculum, drawn in Figure 2.2. This both summarises what we know of effective learning encounters for hearing and hearing-impaired children, and suggests how teachers can use classroom resources of materials and adult time to negotiate tasks with children. This model also encapsulates what we have gained from the 'effective schools' literature: learning as guided rediscovery, the generation and testing out of hypotheses within a cycle of 'plan, do and review', where teachers sequence and pace activities and make their own behaviour contingent on the child's. This contrasts markedly with the idea that teaching is the handing over of information to passive recipients, with the teacher 'performing', directing, managing and exercising high levels of control. Whilst not wishing to understate the learning obstacles which any degree of deafness may present to the child, there is very little sense in which the strategies put forward in this chapter constitute a specific approach to those who are hearing-impaired. In every case we have highlighted good generic classroom practice, which also turns out to be helpful for children with hearing losses.

SUPPORT SYSTEMS AND INTEGRATION

Recent data on the distribution of children with hearing losses in relation to educational placement (Figure 1.1) show that the vast majority of 'known' hearing-impaired children spend some or all of their time in ordinary school settings. Many of these children will have less than severe hearing-impairments, which are, nevertheless, of significance educationally. Surveys carried out by the Department of Education and Science in the 1960s (DES, 1967) showed that about a third of children supported by units and teachers of the deaf in mainstream settings had severe-to-profound hearing losses. This established trend towards integrated provision, even for children with profound deafness, has grown in momentum with the changes in philosophy and practice reflected in the 1981 Education Act, together with economic pressures, parental expectations, and technological developments which have facilitated the earlier diagnosis of deafness and the provision of more sophisticated hearing-aids. At the same time that these various influences have contributed to a growing number of severely hearing-impaired children in ordinary schools, we have also become more aware of the potential hazards to learning and development which are associated with mild and transient hearing losses.

There are a number of implications to be drawn from this current picture. First, the major responsibility for teaching hearing-impaired children falls, increasingly, upon those who have no specialist training or experience. The practical needs of teachers who are working with classgroups in which hearing-impaired children participate are considerable. Integration of children who are hearing-impaired in mainstream is one of a range of options and can take many forms. But it is not a 'soft' option, and a great deal of planning, careful collaboration between support staff, mainstream teachers and parents, discussion of appropriate curriculum options, and evaluation of children's progress over time is required for integrated placements to work successfully.

A second implication concerns the rôle of specialist staff, such as Speech Therapists, psychologists and peripatetic teachers of the hearing-impaired, and the nature of the supportive help they can offer. In Chapter 3 some of the traditional facets of support agencies were identified, such as advising about teaching strategies and hearing-aids, providing inservice training, helping to monitor children's progress, giving additional tutoring and companion teaching, or passing on information about resources and materials. Increasingly, schools are looking to support staff for advice which can be applied practically in the classroom, rather than, for example, a fortnightly visit when a child is removed from the classgroup for an individual session, which leaves the ordinary teacher none the wiser. There are implications, too, for those responsible for the training of specialist staff, if they are to be properly equipped for handing over skills and strategies to others.

The third implication concerns the status which is accorded to children with special needs, and to the teachers involved with such children, within the school community. A 'whole-school' approach starts with the premise that the responsibility for meeting children's educational needs is shared by all staff, whilst the children themselves are accepted as valued contributors to the school, rather than treated as visitors. A distinction has sometimes been drawn between integration which is locational, social or functional. The 'whole-school' approach is also concerned with the degree to which children with special needs participate in a wholly meaningful way in the school community, as opposed to merely sharing the site of the school, or simply eating together at mealtimes and joining up for assemblies or registration. Functional integration can be appraised in terms of the degree to which a hearing-impaired child has the opportunity to play in school teams, be included in plays and productions, have work displayed upon walls and in school magazines, and obtain as full access as possible to the school curriculum.

In Figure 5.1 a continuum of provision for hearing-impaired children is depicted, showing the variety and proportion of

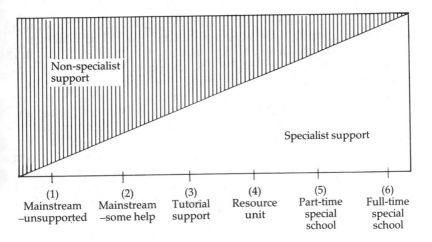

(1) Placement in a mainstream class – occasional monitoring and
    advice from a visiting specialist, such as a peripatetic teacher
    of the deaf.
    Classteacher and child are largely unsupported.

(2) Mainstream class with additional help in some areas from
    regular visiting staff, such as specialist teacher, Speech
    Therapist, special needs support teacher.

(3) Ordinary class with tutorial help – child is withdrawn or
    works alongside specialist teacher or classroom assistant on a
    daily or weekly basis across a range of subjects.

(4) Resource unit in ordinary school – special class with varying
    degrees of integration in mainstream classes and a reduced
    curriculum.

(5) Special school as a base, with part-time integration into
    selected ordinary classes with companion teaching or tutorial
    support.

(6) Full-time special school with intensive specialised teaching.

Figure 5.1 *Continuum of provision for hearing-impaired children indicating proportion of
specialist help*

specialist support available at each level. Ideally, a Local Education
Authority will have a broad range of resources available for
hearing-impaired children, which can be tailored flexibly to meet
the needs of individuals as these change over time. The idea behind
flexible support systems is to achieve a balance between the time
children are taught in the more demanding peer group context, and
that spent in individual work with an adult. Since the most scarce,
but potentially the most valuable, of additional resources are human
— the provision of extra assistance or teaching support, both in and

outside the classroom — the very first question that mainstream teachers tend to ask is just how much extra help will be available.

The overall responsibility for what is taught in an ordinary classroom should be taken by the classteacher. However, it is important for teachers to establish how a child's educational programme is to be planned, what kind of specialist advice will be available, how often a child will be visited, and how and when the adults involved are going to collaborate and share their thoughts. In some LEAs a multi-agency team, involving school staff, doctor, psychologist, Speech Therapist and specialist teacher, meets together regularly in school to discuss children's progress, the adequacy of resources, inservice needs of staff, strategies for teaching, the co-ordination of support in school, and future needs in relation to provision. The operation of such a team is described by Webster *et al*. (1984), in an article which highlights the importance of clear lines of communication with the officers in the LEA responsible for making provision, as well as with parents. Wherever possible, and particularly when any changes in placement are under consideration, parents should be centrally involved in discussions.

At a more detailed level, the classteacher may require a regular time set aside for planning and co-ordinating work with support agencies. If a child is going to spend time out of class for tutorial help, and if more than one adult is involved, then teachers must work carefully together. Some means of formal recording may be helpful, such as a work diary, which moves from place to place with the child and records work set and completed, or areas insufficiently covered. Detailed forward planning is perhaps the most difficult, although most useful, groundwork for supporting children with special needs across the curriculum. We shall be returning to a number of these ideas again when we discuss in more detail the setting of teaching objectives, curricular planning and record-keeping, later in the chapter.

UNIT PROVISION

The first units for hearing-impaired children were set up in four London primary schools in 1947. The original purpose of these classes was to provide the stimulus of 'normal' social experience and conversation to children with less severe handicaps who could be 'fitted in' to some of the lessons and activities provided for hearing peers. The expectation was that, by the secondary stage, children would transfer full time into ordinary classes without additional help. The unit teacher generally took care of the core curriculum with an emphasis on language and literacy work, whilst children integrated for social periods or less formal subjects. Specialist teachers who worked in such units often found themselves very isolated, both from other unit teachers and from the staff working in mainstream. There was often very little or no interaction between unit and mainstream staff, so that both worked independently, with little carry over of activities and considerable mistrust about the value of one another's work. Often, time was not set aside to explain the nature of children's difficulties to mainstream staff, or to explore ways of overcoming them (DES, 1967).

Units are an important part of the continuum of provision for hearing-impaired children, but their function has changed. It is now commonplace for profoundly deaf children to be placed in a unit resource within a mainstream school, particularly in the early years. Some units introduce children and parents to a supportive sign system, although there are restrictions in the utility of this approach if other children and staff in the mainstream school are not also familiar with the system. The advantage of unit provision is that some of the emotional and social consequences of very young children having to travel a long distance to get to school, or having to live away from home, are avoided. Even so it may be difficult for deaf children to sustain friendships made at school and to participate in out-of-school activities, if a unit serves a wide geographical area. Later on in this chapter we shall be examining some of the consequences of integrated placements for very young deaf children, in terms of the quality and nature of interaction with hearing adults and children.

Having the hindsight of the earlier efforts to put resources into ordinary school settings, many LEAs now appoint specialist teachers to the staff of the mainstream school so that they become part of the community, attend staff meetings and play a more vital rôle in raising the general awareness of the needs of deaf children within the school. Arrangements may be made so that the unit teacher works with hearing groups, whilst non-specialists take an activity with a group of hearing-impaired children. Companion teaching can be effective, where teachers pool their resources and work together in class. Reverse integration, whereby hearing children come into a unit to work alongside hearing-impaired children, can also be valuable. There is a recognition (or perhaps aspiration!) that all children benefit, in terms of tolerance and understanding, from growing up with others who are different from themselves.

If children who attend a unit for much of their time are to feel an integral part of the school, they need to be located in the main body of the school buildings, rather than in a 'terrapin' or portable classroom at the bottom of the playground. Similarly, communal

school hours, playtimes, lunchbreaks and assemblies are important, so that all children share the framework of the school day.
Many schools also feel it is important for all children to be included
in a common system of record-keeping, particularly at the secondary stage, to wear the school uniform and to be included in
after-school clubs, excursions and activities, and for all parents to be
invited to school events, such as fund-raising days, parent evenings
and sports days.

There are many hearing-impaired children, usually those with
more severe communication difficulties, whose needs cannot be
met entirely in mainstream classes with additional support. Some
children may feel comfortable only in a more protected, secure
environment with a predictable routine. The small scale of most
units means that the teacher has time to make close relationships
with all members of the group, and to be on hand to sort out any
difficulties which may arise during the course of the day. Some
children may need to spend the larger proportion of their time
within the unit, covering basic skills and more formal aspects of the
curriculum, such as mathematics. Integration into larger groups
may need to be broached progressively, starting with practical
subjects or areas where a child has already shown confidence and
skill, such as gymnastics, cookery, design, or computer work. A
balance has to be sought for each child between time spent in
demanding situations in school and more personalised, intensive
work with specialist staff.

The key issue is one of flexibility. A unit for hearing-impaired
children may function as a school centre for advice and materials. It
may be a refuge for those children who find the social stresses and
changes of a mainstream school daunting. For others, a unit may be
a quiet setting for concentrated work and extra teaching help. A
number of very successful units prefer to see themselves as
curriculum resources or supports. School booklets are sometimes
produced, setting out the rôle and aims of the unit, examples of
schemes of work followed by specialist teachers, and general
strategies for communication and use of hearing-aids. All the
teachers involved with hearing-impaired children meet regularly to
discuss children's needs, areas of the curriculum where extra help is
required, and how the unit can resource the teaching programme
effectively. The range of support may include inservice training on
the nature of deafness and associated learning obstacles, sign
language instruction, advice on teaching strategies, modification of
the text of worksheets or course books, and co-teaching. A
'whole-school' approach assumes that children are supported
within the ordinary classroom wherever possible, with a wider
sharing of the responsibility for meeting special needs.

SPECIAL SCHOOL

Another kind of provision for hearing-impaired children which has an important place within the continuum of resources shown in Figure 5.1 is the special school for the deaf. Many special schools have undergone a process of self-evaluation recently, rethinking their contribution and rôle. Special schools usually have a generous adult–child ratio. They may be expected to be staffed by teachers who are well qualified, up to date and enthusiastic about working with children who have more severe hearing losses or additional handicaps. Special schools operate on a day, part-time or residential basis. They are usually recommended on the basis that a child's personality, ability to learn, confidence in relating to other children, and communication needs are such that the ordinary school experience, even with unit support, would be overwhelming. In the special school, all the staff are conversant with the needs of hearing-impaired children. Increasingly, many special schools have become associated with a 'Total Communication' approach, where the whole body of teaching and ancillary staff are able to use a signing system. Many special schools would argue that they are better placed to meet the needs of children who require a sign communication system.

Residential schools tend to cater for more severely hearing-impaired children, children with additional special needs, or children in family circumstances which prevail against the child living at home. There are two exceptions in the shape of selective residential schools, which admit children on the basis of outstanding abilities and attainments. These selective schools are sometimes justified on the basis that many staff are recruited as subject specialists, who have also had training to teach the hearing-impaired. They offer academic opportunities to the most able deaf children, who may be unable to reach their full potential in an integrated setting.

A number of questions can be asked about all special schools for the deaf. Are they, in fact, centres of excellence and expertise? Should education prepare children for life in a 'hearing', as opposed to a 'deaf', community? Should we measure the success of deaf children in relation to how well they compete alongside hearing children? Is special school placement opted for as second best, when all else has failed, rather than as a positively planned opportunity? To some extent these are moral issues which we shall not pursue here. Suffice it to say that there are contrasting opinions, usually fiercely upheld, about the rôle of special schools and sign language in relation to the culture and identity of the adult deaf community, which do not always concur with the views of hearing parents or of specialist teachers.

When decisions are made about school placement, parents have a right to unbiased information and clear indications about the pros and cons of each particular course of action. Parents may more readily accept the reasons for recommending a residential placement at the secondary level, when the social and academic demands of school are greater, and the child is more mature. On the other hand, children placed in a special school at a young age may benefit from more intensive help early on, with the prospect of returning to mainstream. Always, the advantages for the child in a special school environment have to be weighed against the disadvantages, such as distance away from home, loss of contact with local children and perhaps a more restricted educational curriculum. One of the recommendations of the Warnock Report was that special schools could forge much greater links with mainstream, acting as resource centres, providing inservice initiatives, supporting some children on an 'outreach' basis and giving intensive help for others. Once again the key issues are flexibility to local needs and careful evaluation of whatever provision is made.

HEARING-AIDS AND THE LISTENING ENVIRONMENT

An important aspect of the educational programme for hearing-impaired children is the management of listening conditions and, when provided, of hearing-aids. For children with conductive hearing losses, the problems of maintaining attention control and perception of speech will be exacerbated in a noisy environment. When children are expected to listen for long periods and where there are competing sources of sound stimuli, children with difficulties in sound discrimination, speech comprehension and linguistic immaturity will be further disadvantaged if acoustic conditions are poor. For the more severely hearing-impaired child dependent on hearing-aids for useful auditory information, there are a number of factors which can enhance their effectiveness. Basic guidelines for the non-specialist are provided here, as a supplement to the information given in Chapter 3. For those who require more technical and detailed advice on the management of hearing-aids, comprehensive coverage is provided in the books by Tucker and Nolan (1984) and Webster and Ellwood (1985).

Good listening conditions are achieved in two main ways. The first is by keeping unwanted sound out. A room which is regularly invaded by noise from heavy road traffic, an adjoining workshop, dance studio or gymnasium, or voices and clattering feet running past will be less conducive to listening. Whilst double glazing and sound-proof doors may be beyond the resources of many schools, some thought can be given to the siting of rooms and any likely noise sources, when the timetable is planned. The second consideration is the reduction of noise within a room. Hard floors, high ceilings, concrete pillars, breeze-block walls and wooden cladding reflect sound and prolong sound interference. Sound-absorbent materials, such as acoustic tiles, carpets, soft furnishings, soft table-tops, curtains, rubber boots on chair legs, and cork wall tiles, cut down reverberation and unwanted noise.

Choice of seating position is important. Children will be able to listen more attentively to each other, to a story or to the teacher's voice in positions away from well-used areas such as a store cupboard, library area or passageway. Hearing-impaired children are often helped in their listening by being able to see the speaker. Present-day classes are often grouped around tables rather than set in rows, whilst the teacher may move around freely. In order to see and hear the contributions of other children, as well as listen to the teacher, positions to the side and a few rows from the front are generally best in mainstream groups. Key points are proximity of contact with the speaker, a minimum of noise sources or visual distractions from outside the room, and a reduction in the amount of noise generated within it.

There are many added considerations for children wearing traditional hearing-aids. These largely concern the intensity of a sound signal reaching the child's ear, in relation to the level of surrounding unwanted noise (signal-to-noise ratio). With conventional aids, the child's ability to hear a speech signal depends on distance from the speaker. As a general rule, a child wearing aids should not be expected to hear as clearly at distances more than about 2 metres away from the speaker. At distances greater than this there is more than likely a nearer and louder sound source, which will be picked up and amplified by the child's hearing-aids. It is worthwhile listening through an aid to the sorts of extraneous sound which the microphone picks up. Sounds we tend not to notice, such as a fan heater, projector, shuffling feet, sounds of crayons dropped in a box, or desk lids shutting, can be disturbing when amplified through an aid, and drown out relevant sounds.

As we stated in Chapter 3, hearing-aids are unable to select the sounds which are most important for the child to hear, whilst a child's impaired auditory system may be less good at filtering relevant sound signals. In a room that has high levels of noise all around, the child will require close proximity to the speaker. Turning up the volume control of the hearing-aids will not help, since that will amplify both the speech signal and the noise to levels which may be intolerable to the wearer. Not all of the child's day is spent in one particular classroom. For all the factors which have been highlighted in relation to listening conditions and hearing-aids, it is as well to be aware that different physical situations, such as the playing field, dining hall, laboratory or library, will make different demands on a child wearing conventional aids.

TAKING CARE OF HEARING-AIDS

Both body-worn and post-aural aids, described in Chapter 3, have adjustable settings which can make a significant difference to what the child perceives. For younger children particularly, it is important for the classteacher to know how the controls should be set for an individual, so that if they are accidentally altered they can be readjusted. All aids have an on–off switch so that the batteries are not wasted when the aid is out of use. Degree of amplification or gain is controlled by a numbered or marked volume wheel, and a recommended gain setting will have been made for a comfortable listening level about 2 metres away from a speaker. Tone controls, which alter the quality of the output, will also usually have been set. Other settings, which may limit the output of the aid at certain frequencies, should not be interfered with. In many instances these are tiny sunken screwheads which require a jeweller's screwdriver to adjust them.

Most conventional aids have a control switch marked M, T or M/T (see Figures 3.7 and 3.8). For everyday use the control should be set to the M position, which indicates that the microphone will pick up sound signals in the environment for amplification. Set to T, the aid no longer picks up environmental sound. The T setting indicates a loop pick-up coil facility, which was originally intended to allow individuals to use their hearing-aids with the telephone, although its main use is within an induction loop system.

A loop system is basically a wire installed around a room and then connected to a sound source, such as a radio or TV, which drives the loop. The loop works through the process of electromagnetic induction. Briefly, when a conductor, or wire, is carrying current, a magnetic field is set up around the wire. If another conductor is situated near to the first, then a current will be induced into this conductor whenever a change occurs in the strength of the current through the first. The pick-up coil in the hearing-aid is simply a tightly wound conductor which permits induced current to flow when a changing magnetic field is nearby. This induced current is then passed on to the amplifier, and the amplified electrical signals are converted back into sound by the receiver, for delivery to the ear.

Older-style telephones produce a magnetic field which induces a current into the pick-up coil of a hearing-aid, so that the telephone signals are amplified directly. (Modern phones may require an adaptor.) A classroom can be fitted with a loop system, which is then driven by a teacher's microphone and amplifier. As the teacher speaks, an electric current passes through the loop, setting up a magnetic field which varies according to the speech signal. Wherever the child is within the loop, a current will be induced in the pick-up coil of the child's aid, which is then amplified and converted back into sound. Some aids have an M/T switch which enables the use of a loop system together with the environmental microphone of the aid. Children can then hear the signals fed through the loop together with their own voices, as well as those of other children.

Every teacher should be aware of how to replace an earmould in the ear properly, and how to position the hearing-aid, particularly a post-aural aid, correctly. Eventually, even very young children can manage to fit their own aids and replace the moulds if they become loose. If the earmould is not a good fit or is loose, amplified sound leaks out from around the mould, is picked up by the microphone of the aid and produces an irritating high-pitched feedback whistle. Younger children need to have earmoulds remade three or four times a year as their outer ears grow and the seal becomes imperfect. Feedback problems are less likely to occur with body-worn aids because of the greater distance between the microphone on the body and the receiver at the ear. In replacing a post-aural aid, the mould is held on its outer edge and inserted into the ear canal with a backward, twisting movement. The parent or support teacher will be able to show how the mould is anchored in the helix of the outer ear. The hearing-aid is then slid over the pinna to sit neatly behind it, making sure the sound tube is not twisted in the process. The aid should be switched on properly, set at the correct output level and checked for feedback whistle.

Post-aural aids are less robust than body-worn aids and need to be well cared for, especially when they are taken off. When not in use aids should be switched off and stored in the hinged box provided. With a body-worn aid, the lead should be disconnected when not in use and coiled carefully to avoid stressing connections and sockets. Children must begin to take responsibility for their hearing-aids as soon as possible. Left in pockets whilst changing for games or swimming, aids can be lost, stepped on, or put through the washing machine. Children should be encouraged to complain if an aid is not working; however, there are some simple checks which the teacher can make. With a body-worn aid, if the aid is taken off, the receiver held at lead length from the microphone and the volume turned to full, there should be a strong feedback whistle. With a post-aural aid, if the aid is taken off and volume turned to full, there should again be a feedback squeal. There is a simple device, like a plastic stethoscope, which can be obtained through the specialist teacher, to listen to the output of a hearing-aid.

Teachers should know how to gain access to the battery compartment and make regular checks on the battery: the 'heart' of the hearing-aid. Different aids take different batteries and these should be supplied by the parent or specialist teacher, who will be able to demonstrate how they are replaced. Some batteries lose power suddenly, others drain slowly. Depending on the type of battery, routine changing times vary from once or twice a week, to once a month. An ample supply should be stored safely in school, in dry, cool conditions out of reach of small children. It is important to replace failing batteries immediately, with the terminals facing the correct way, so that the child does not have to cope with poor quality or intermittent signals.

Even if the hearing-aid itself is working, a sound tube (see Figure 3.8) blocked with wax will prevent the child from hearing anything. Visual inspection will reveal dirty or loose parts of the system. The mould can be washed in soapy water and the tube cleaned with a pipe cleaner or soft toothbrush. The tube should not be crimped, cracked or contain condensation. With a body-worn aid, the cord (see Figure 3.7) should be checked at the points where it connects to the aid or receiver. The microphone aperture should be cleaned of any dirt, food or other spillage. With very young children it is important to check that body-worn aids are securely harnessed and child-proofed, for example by a cling-film or commercially produced 'baby' cover to protect the microphone. A harness should be worn on top of clothes so that the aids are not buried under layers of clothing, whilst the leads must be kept from trailing to prevent them being pulled or chewed. Obviously, hearing-aids will work only if set to the appropriate controls and switched on.

If teachers are in any doubt about any of the issues discussed here they should consult with the specialist teacher of the deaf. It can be useful to keep a written note of the recommended settings for each of a child's aids, together with the telephone number of the support teacher, or the hearing-aid department of the local hospital for direct contact, should an aid go wrong and checking procedures not remedy the fault. The specialist teacher should be prepared to leave spare batteries, cords, receivers or a spare aid with the classteacher, and demonstrate how a new mould is fitted to the aid and the sound tube trimmed. At an early stage the supporting specialist should be asked to take the classteacher through some of the checking procedures listed in Table 5.1. It should also be remembered that

Table 5.1 *Checking post-aural and body-worn hearing-aids*

Control settings	Check on/off switch Ensure correct M, T or M/T setting Check volume setting Ensure tone control is set correctly (Keep a record of all settings for each aid)
Battery	Change batteries regularly according to guidelines Check battery inserted correctly (+ to +) Listen to output through plastic stethoscope Remove aid from child, switch on, turn volume to full and listen for feedback Replace battery if output is poor or distorted
Microphone (body-worn)	Check microphone aperture for dirt or spillage Check 'baby' cover in place or wrap aid in cling film Harness should be securely worn over clothing Check aid is high on chest for good 'ear–voice' link, with top of aid proud of harness for sound access to microphone
Lead (body-worn)	Inspect cord for looseness, fraying or breaks Talk into aid and wiggle lead at connecting points If no sound or output is intermittent, replace lead When in use, conceal leads in clothing or harness and prevent from trailing When not in use, disconnect lead and coil carefully
Earmoulds	Inspect earmould for wax, wash in warm water and dry Blow out any condensation in tubing Check tubing for cracks, crimping or twisting If feedback occurs, reinsert earmould for better seal Inform parents or support teacher if earmould fits poorly

two aids are often prescribed for children because of the advantages of binaural listening for locating a sound source and focusing attention on it. In collaboration with the specialist teacher, it should be possible to explore with the child optimal classroom positions for listening. The simplest way to do this is to give the child a familiar picture-pointing task to spoken instructions (e.g. 'Point to the ... '), repeated in varying locations.

RADIO HEARING-AIDS

The use of FM radio transmission in hearing-aid systems has effectively overcome many of the problems of conventional hearing-aids to do with the distance between the wearer and the speaker, and the likelihood of unwanted noise being amplified to the detriment of relevant signals. In other words, radio aids provide a better signal-to-noise ratio at the child's ear. Undoubtedly, radio systems have been a major factor in the successful integration of hearing impaired children into mainstream school settings. Used appropriately, radio aids provide children with clear speech signals even in very poor listening conditions, across distances up to 100 metres and without interference. However, radio aids must be used selectively if their full potential is to be exploited, and routines must be established for their care and maintenance.

In one variation of a radio system, the child wears a single unit which is a combined radio receiver and personal hearing-aid. The parent or teacher wears a transmitter unit, which comprises a microphone coupled to a radio transmitter antenna. Certain systems have a small lapel microphone which is attached within 20 centimetres of the speaker's mouth, so that the transmitter unit can be worn on a belt around the waist, rather than around the neck. What the speaker says is converted by the transmitter unit into a radio signal and broadcast on a radio frequency carrier wave. The child's unit houses a receiver (the hearing-aid transducer is also called a receiver) tuned to the same radio frequency. This decodes the radio transmission into an electrical signal which is then amplified and fed into the child's ear. The system can be used as a normal body-worn hearing-aid when the radio facility is switched off, for example during a group play activity when direct input from the teacher is not required. On the other hand, the child's microphone can be switched off so that only radio transmitted signals are received. This might be appropriate in situations such as a school assembly, where background noise is high and the child benefits from a clear, uninterrupted signal from the speaker's transmitter. Older students in school or higher education may use this mode in a lecture.

The combined unit can also be used as a conventional aid and radio receiver at the same time. The child receives information from transmitted signals as well as from the microphone on the aid itself, which picks up environmental sounds together with the child's own voice. There is considerable flexibility in the way the system may be used. The teacher can switch the transmitter on when it is appropriate to give a direct message to the child. However, not all that the teacher says will be relevant to the child wearing the aid, in which case the transmitter should be switched off, when the child retains use of the conventional aid.

It should be remembered that, when the transmitter and radio receiver are switched on, all that is picked up by the radio aid microphone worn by the speaker is transmitted to the child's ear. A child cannot be expected to be vigilant to things which are personally relevant if most of the input from the teacher's transmitter is directed to others. By the same token, it is not always the teacher who needs to be heard clearly. Where another class member is reading a story, relaying news or reporting back on a task, the transmitter can be handed over to this child to wear. Alternatively, the teacher may wish to repeat or summarise the key points using the transmitter. The rule of thumb is that the transmitter should be on when the teacher wishes to address a hearing-impaired pupil directly or as a member of a group, whilst other children can be asked to present their ideas via the microphone.

In a second type of system, a transmitter and receiver are used in conjunction with the child's personal hearing-aids, of either body-worn or post-aural type. When not required the radio facility can be dispensed with. The receiver is connected to the child's personal aids by a lead to an input socket. The hearing-aids must have an audio input facility, usually a plug connection or a shoe which slides over the bottom of the hearing-aid. Signals fed into the aid from the receiver are amplified in the conventional way and delivered to the child's ear. The hearing-aid's own microphone remains sensitive to sound while the system is in use, so that children hear their own voices and environmental sounds. Aids without direct input can use this type of system through the loop facility (T or M/T setting). A loop of wire is taken from the radio aid receiver and worn around the neck with post-aural aids, or around the aid itself with body-worn aids. The child's receiver picks up transmitted signals in the usual way, setting up a magnetic field via the loop worn by the child. A current is induced in the T coil of the child's aid, which is then amplified, converted into sound and fed into the child's ear.

Loop systems used in this way have some disadvantages. The performance of a hearing-aid on the T setting is often inferior to the normal M mode, particularly in amplifying low-frequency sounds. The orientation of the pick-up coil in a post-aural hearing-aid will vary with head movement in the neck loop, resulting in variations in the output of the aid. If the child's aid does not have an M/T setting then the system is much less flexible and the child will be unable to hear voice feedback or environmental sound, unless the receiver has an environmental microphone.

Radio aids can also be used to drive a wire loop fitted around a room, so that a number of children wearing hearing-aids on T mode can receive transmitted signals. One other kind of system which may be encountered uses infra-red light, rather than radio waves, to carry the speech signal from the teacher to the child. The advantage of using light as a carrier is that it does not spill over into adjoining rooms, but it cannot be used outdoors. The teacher wears a microphone and infra-red transmitter, which floods the room with infra-red light. Children wear a unit which functions as a conventional hearing-aid and infra-red receiver, and this recovers the speech signal. Alternatively, the direct input or T coil facility in the child's aids can be utilised. Infra-red systems may also be fixed in a particular classroom. It will be evident that, for many of these systems, ongoing specialist advice and oversight will be necessary. But there are some simple everyday checks which the ordinary teacher can make, listed in Table 5.2.

Table 5.2 *Checking a radio aid system*

Transmitter	Change batteries or recharge according to guidelines
	Check microphone is free of debris
	Inspect antenna for looseness
	Check microphone is within 20 cm of speaker's mouth
	Check on/off switch
Hearing-aid	Check separately before coupling to radio-receiver
	Check battery
	Remove aid from child, switch on, turn volume to full and listen for feedback
	Inspect audio-input lead/shoe connection
	If loop is used check connections, change loop if suspect
	Set mode correctly: M for direct input, T or M/T for loop
	Set volume correctly
Receiver	Change battery or recharge according to guidelines
	Check frequency code and match with transmitter
	Check leads and connections
	Set to receive radio signals, place transmitter in another room by a sound source, switch on transmitter and listen to reception through child's hearing-aids
Receiver and hearing-aid combined	Change battery or recharge according to guidelines
	Check frequency module code and match receiver with transmitter
	Check leads plugged in correctly
	Check system as a hearing-aid with radio facility off — see Table 5.1 for body-worn aids
	Set to radio facility, switch off environmental microphone, place transmitter in another room by a sound source, switch on transmitter and listen to reception

Obviously, if a radio system is used in conjunction with the child's personal aids, checks should first be made on the child's own hearing-aids, following the guidelines already provided, making sure that the transmitter and radio facility are switched off. A record should be kept of correct settings, connections and the frequency modules to be used. The radio units should be examined for loose wires or dirt in the microphone apertures. To check the radio facility, the unit should be set to receive radio transmission, with the environmental microphone switched off. The transmitter can be switched on and placed in another room by a sound source, such as a cassette player, and the quality of the reception assessed by listening through the child's aids. It is essential that batteries are replaced or recharged according to the manufacturer's guidelines. In making sure radio aids are used to peak efficiency and remain trouble-free, close collaboration is required between family, support teacher and school. An overall aim is that some responsibility for caring for radio aids, and for signalling when the system is working or not, should be taken by the child.

HOME–SCHOOL LINKS

Many hearing children benefit from careful preparation and introduction to their first days at school. Similarly, at points of transfer between schools, anxiety can be reduced by planning ahead and making links between families and teaching staff. For hearing-impaired children, first contacts with school are critical. In Chapter 1 we mentioned the feelings of loss, guilt and inadequacy that many parents feel when a diagnosis of hearing loss is made. It is for these reasons that parents may feel a heightened sense of apprehension when a hearing-impaired child leaves the secure environment of home. Similarly, parents may express a great deal of concern at the prospect of transfer to a large primary or secondary school. Home–school links are more straightforward if a hearing-impaired child is to attend a local nursery or infant school: there may be siblings or familiar neighbourhood children who already attend, and the family may be able to deliver and pick the child up themselves, having daily contact with staff. If the child is to attend a unit serving a wide area or a special school for some or part of the time, travelling is likely to be involved and ongoing contacts between home and school may be more difficult to sustain. Initial contacts and home–school links need careful thought when this situation arises.

With more severely hearing-impaired children, it may be difficult to explain and discuss plans for school. The best preparation may be for the parents to visit with the child in the term before entry, say one afternoon a week for half a term. In many LEAs, transition from home to school is eased by teacher-counsellor posts, whereby the specialist teachers who visit families at home also work part time in the special resources attached to schools. The important work of the professional counsellor in helping families towards acceptance and realistic expectations for a deaf child is thus extended into school.

The ordinary teacher in a nursery or infant group could also make this useful bridge by visiting the family of a hearing-impaired child at home, perhaps accompanying the specialist teacher initially.

Some other useful ways in which children can be prepared for school are discussed by Bishop and Gregory (1983). These include keeping a scrapbook to record important events in the pre-school years. Snippets relating to the pre-entry visits could be included, such as photographs of the teacher and class, or any drawings and paintings produced. The teacher should be given any important information, such as food preferences or individual ways of signalling toilet needs. Similarly, the family can be given information well in advance about parent groups, arrangements for parent–teacher liaison and, where appropriate, details of sign language classes.

Almost all teachers who have worked with hearing-impaired children acknowledge the daily diary which goes backwards and forwards with the child as the best home–school link, Very young children, or those with limited communication skills, find it hard to describe what they do at nursery or school. The parents have little way of knowing what the child has experienced, in order to talk over and reinforce any new ideas or concepts, unless there is an ongoing dialogue with the teacher. A note can be made of the main activities enjoyed during the day, a newly discovered name or item of vocabulary can be highlighted, and a drawing or photograph of a special event or trip appended. Parents, of course, can do likewise, using the diary as something of a forward planner to help the child look forward to impending events such as a hospital visit, expected sibling or birthday party. Further ideas along these lines are given in Bishop and Gregory (1984) and Webster and Ellwood (1985).

One important factor which was noted in Chapter 2 in relation to home–school transition is the marked change in the nature and quality of conversational interaction between adults and children, as children move from the culture of the home to that of the school. The home–school diary is one way of bridging the gap, so that experiences in school can enhance and reflect what the child does at home, and vice versa. Many secondary-age students use such a link, if only to indicate homework commitments.

First contacts with a new secondary school are also critical. Parents should have been fully involved in discussions about suitable alternatives, where any specialist resources are located and the kind of classroom support a child is likely to receive. Parents will be helped to make informed decisions if they are able to visit schools and are given unbiased guidance. Where there is mutual agreement about placement a child can be prepared confidently. Many secondary schools offer an orientation programme to children with special needs, so that they have an advantage over other new entrants to the school. This might take the form of visits to the school or resource base to meet other children and staff in the term prior to entry. Sometimes children with special needs are admitted a day early, or in the last week of the old term. This time is used to explore the geography of the new school, such as main teaching blocks, library or office. There may be an opportunity to experience the routines of registration or lunch in advance. Helpful arrangements might include the organised adoption of a hearing-impaired child by an older and sympathetic pupil, who is available in the first few weeks to 'show the ropes'. Some schools provide information booklets for children, giving very clear and basic information about the school, such as maps, timetables, rules and regulations, clubs and facilities.

For parents who are anxious about their own personal contacts with the secondary school, the name of contact staff can be given, with details of telephone extension numbers and good times of the day to call. It is important, too, that parents are given frequent opportunities to discuss a child's progress in school. Increasingly, secondary schools are adopting a profiling approach to record-keeping, to which both parents and the youngsters themselves can make a valuable contribution. We shall be taking up this issue of ongoing appraisal and assessment of children later in the chapter.

PRE-VERBAL STAGES OF DEVELOPMENT IN SEVERELY HEARING-IMPAIRED CHILDREN

In laying the foundations of language, the patterning of children's exchanges with adults prior to the emergence of speech is very important. Some of the complex developments of early infancy were highlighted in Chapter 2, as adults 'scaffold' their interactions with very young children in meaningful social contexts, bringing the infant's experience into juxtaposition with language. By six months, the infant is capable of following the adult's line of gaze to objects in the environment and, by making what they talk about contingent on a shared object of attention, adults begin to put the child's experience into words. Adults are quick to respond when the infant vocalises. They read meaning in the child's behaviour, leave long pauses after having spoken, and give the infant time to respond. From an early age infants are treated as though they are competent conversation partners, in social situations rich in regularity, repetition and structure. As the infant reciprocates by taking more deliberate and 'genuine' turns in interaction, the conventions of giving a message and eliciting a response are rehearsed, well before the child begins to talk.

Observations of hearing-impaired infants suggest that these early foundations are no less important for them, although they may be disrupted. Evidence suggests that mutual attention, joint reference, turn-taking and contingent responses are much more difficult for adults to establish with hearing-impaired children. Some deaf infants are offered early placement in ordinary nursery schools in order to enrich their interaction with other children and adults. Paradoxically, research points to a reduction in the quality and depth of interaction in such placements. A number of children arrive in nursery or infant school without the foundation skills for communication, which may only be developed in intensive and sustained encounters between adult and child. In Chapter 4 we outlined a series of stages which can be used to assess the child's growing awareness of spoken language and to plan experiences which should help participation in verbal exchanges. A summary of stages and teaching strategies is given in Table 5.3, based on the work of Tait (1987) and Tait and Wood (1987).

Table 5.3 *Pre-verbal stages to the beginnings of conversation in young deaf children*

Stage of development	Pattern of interaction	Adult strategies
(1) Disengaged	Child unaware of being addressed Looks fleetingly from place to place Turns left unfilled Random vocalisations No synchrony between child, adult and object of reference	Follow child's line of gaze and comment on object of reference Parallel play with commentary Use 'formats' for interaction (peek-a-boo, sharing picture book, turn-taking games) Adult modifications to speech (intonation, structure)
(2) Engaged	Child begins to look at object of reference Child attends partly to adult when talking Turn-taking in a clear format	Create contexts for talk in 'here and now' Encourage imitative play (play house, shop counter, dressing-up box)
(3) Structured attention	Match between onset of adult's speech and child's attention Reads meaning or intention in social context Takes turns readily Vocalises at appropriate point (words may not be clear)	Create opportunities for joint reference (finger puppets, small-toy play, construction toys) Adult responds contingently to child's glances, gestures or vocalisations

(4) Structured vocalisation	Few random vocalisations Vocalisations more word-like Conversational turns filled (even when following 'non-looking' at adult) Responds to auditory information alone	Allow child to initiate, give time to respond Take up child's utterances and respond to intended meaning Listening activities • listening for sound onset • effect of child's voice on others • awareness of adult's voice (fade physical prompts)
(5) Growth of autonomy and initiative	Equal conversational partnership Child actively initiates Child adds information Child interrupts, argues, teases and contradicts Child expresses feelings and needs, manipulates others Use of language to sustain social interaction, explore, question and fantasise	Facilitating strategies • paraphrase, expansion and clarification • phatics • personal contributions from adult • low-control exchanges

For children at the 'disengaged' stage there is little synchrony between the objects and sources of communication which form the reference triangle. At this stage, children with poor auditory awareness have yet to discover how to divide their attention between the person addressing them, the object referred to and what is being said. Initially there may be no awareness of being spoken to, and the child may look at many different things unrelated to what is being said or done. There is little evidence of understanding, since conversational turns are left unfilled. Teaching strategies for such children are based on what we know of normal parents and infants. Parallel play, with the adult joining in alongside and simply commenting on the actions of the child, gives opportunities for the adult to follow the child's line of gaze and introduce appropriate language.

Familiar play routines may help establish turn-taking and interaction. Tait (1987) gives examples of play sequences where the teacher feigns sleep until a child bangs a drum, or one pretends to be a police officer as the other drives a car, signalling and voicing directions to stop. The point here is to help a child discover that communicative acts produce anticipated responses. The adult fosters this discovery by responding immediately and contingently to any of the child's actions which can be construed as having communicative intent. Singing and nursery rhymes, such as

'London Bridge is falling down' and 'Ring a ring of roses', also provide opportunities for children to listen and join in at the correct moment.[1] Taking turns to post shapes, pick cards and shake dice to make moves in board games may reinforce a sense of 'first you then me', as well as more boisterous turn-taking in relays, musical stops and 'Simple Simon' action routines.

At the 'engaged' stage there is growing correspondence between where the child looks and what is said. However, the child may still tend to look away before the adult has finished talking. Interaction becomes much more structured when the child sustains attention on the adult, looking away fleetingly to the object of discourse. The child appears to understand more of what the adult is saying or doing, and begins to fill slots left in conversation by vocalising. Adult strategies are directed towards creating situations where there is some point in the child looking at the person who is speaking, such as through finger puppets, or shared play with a construction toy. It is only when attention patterns are well established that vocal interactions begin to develop.

In order to help a child move on to the stage of 'structured vocalisation', adults must treat every utterance as intentional communication and respond immediately. Mutual understanding is easier to achieve when talk arises out of a shared experience, picture-story or play activity in the 'here and now'. In most families, talk emerges from mundane, predictable and familiar social contexts. The adult leaves pauses following a turn which are long enough for the child to be able to fill. It is at this stage that the child begins to respond more to sound and that any physical prompts, such as touching to gain attention, can be faded to voice only. Some time can then be devoted to listening activities of the kind described later in the chapter. Interestingly, when the children in Tait's (1984) study began to respond more selectively to auditory information, hearing thresholds on the audiogram appeared to improve.

What characterises the stage of 'growth of autonomy and initiative' is really the very wide range of functions for which language is used. These include contradicting, questioning and disagreeing with the adult, interrupting and changing the subject, as well as adding information which goes beyond what the teacher has asked:

Adult: Have you got those shoes on today?
Child: Brush (*i.e. they have been cleaned*).
Adult: Did Mummy clean them? They look lovely!

When hearing-impaired children arrive at this stage without showing signs of autonomy or initiative — not negotiating, interrupting or introducing new topics — then we must examine aspects of the adult's conversational style. As we have already indicated, over-controlling, directive and managerial styles of conversational interaction may have a very inhibiting effect on the child's participation in dialogue, a topic we shall cover in greater detail later in the chapter.

Two factors deserve mention at this point. First, the stages of pre-verbal development are based on work with children in oral teaching environments, but a body of data on children in a signing milieu would be equally valuable. Second, an important educational implication of this work is that children who are not able to participate in meaningful and sustained interactions with other children or adults (before the stage of 'structured vocalisation') are unlikely to benefit from integrated placements with large groups of hearing children, unless a great deal of thought is given to the rôle of adults. From what we have said, the importance of contingent interactions with a responsive adult who has the time to engage the child in shared activities, with a sense of purpose and meaning, is inestimable.

EXTRA ADULTS IN THE CLASSROOM

For most teachers in mainstream, the most welcome kind of additional support for children with special needs comes in the form of extra human hands in the classroom. Policy varies from one LEA to another. Some schools welcome parents into classrooms to cook, read, sew, use computers or do craft work with children. Non-teaching assistants are sometimes appointed to work with groups or individuals on a more intensive basis, or to release the teacher to do the same. Where a teacher can call on specialist support from a visiting teacher or unit resource, it may be more valuable for help to be given within the ordinary classroom setting, rather than for children to be taken out for tutoring. It is easier to incorporate any individual work with the class curriculum when specialist support is given alongside peers. Communication between staff is eased and the stigma of removing children from classes is avoided. However, extra human resources within the classroom are rarely used effectively.

For very young children who are still at pre-verbal stages of awareness, the rôle of adults in sustaining intensive interactions with children, helping to structure attention and turn-taking, has already been highlighted. Extra adults in the nursery or infant group can develop the closeness and sensitivity of contact required with an individual, if only for some parts of the day. The evidence cited in Chapters 2 and 4 indicates that when children are admitted to school they usually experience marked changes in the nature and purpose of adult responsiveness. Adults tend to be more directive, managerial and controlling, with a consequent reduction in the depth and range of interaction, compared with at home. Moreover, deafness seems to evoke *less* rather than *more* facilitative behaviour from adults. Since effective interaction with adults appears to lie at the heart of learning, proper management of adult resources must be considered.

Thomas (1985, 1986) describes extra adults in class as the 'key to integration', and suggests clear definition of tasks and rôles: who does what, when and with whom. During an activity period the classteacher may wish to take the rôle of overall manager, maintaining discipline, presenting tasks to children as a group, organising resources and materials, and taking charge of aspects such as the amount of movement or noise within the class. Good managers will isolate the main features of the task and give clear expectations and instructions, for example about stopping and starting, together with regular feedback to children. An important aspect is the maintenance of flow through a session: keeping the majority of children engaged on task with a sense of purpose and impetus, without too many distractions or disruptions.

A second rôle might be defined as 'individual helper', where an extra adult concentrates on taking individual children for short periods of teaching. Work with individuals or small groups will have been planned in detail beforehand, specifying target activities with a rota of children over the activity period. This adult may also help sustain flow by dealing with interruptions, moving quickly from child to child to answer queries, providing information and feedback, and reminding a child of the point of the task. More individualised work might include sustaining a child's attention on relevant features, breaking a task into more manageable steps, explaining and clarifying, introducing additional activities and materials, 'fixing' a child's experience by supplying a useful word or underlining a concept, prompting a child when failure is met, sustaining listening, checking understanding, encouraging the child to reflect and relate new concepts to old, discussing ways of tackling a problem, providing rapid feedback and praise, and guiding children's thinking to the point where they are able to uncover solutions for themselves.

Where appropriate, part of the individual helper's rôle could be to engage the child as a conversational partner, providing the kind of intensive conversational interaction which characterises what have been called shared 'passages of intellectual search'. To put this another way, classroom resources can be organised in a systematic way, so that time and space are created for one adult at least to respond contingently to the child.

CONVERSATION STRATEGIES

The 'effective schools' literature referred to in Chapter 2 shows that an important determinant of children's general progress is the nature of adult–child talk. In the ORACLE study (Galton *et al.*, 1980) the children with poor achievements who would most benefit from adult engagement tended to get least teacher-attention, spend most time off task and receive little contingent help. Hearing-impaired children in a number of the Nottingham studies experienced less facilitating styles of adult–child interaction, often in the belief that for language to improve it has to be deliberately worked on. Since the nature of conversational moves has already been covered in some detail, in relation to both hearing and hearing-impaired children, a basic summary of helpful and less helpful strategies is included here and in Table 5.4. These strategies may also be shared with older hearing children and parents, as well as with school staff.

We have said that dialogue is usually embedded in a social context which has real purpose and significance for the participants. Adults and children do not talk about nothing: they discuss things of mutual concern which arise from shared activities. It is always easier for an adult to understand a child's utterances, and for the child to understand the adult, when talk is linked with a known context. For this reason the home–school diary is invaluable, both in helping teachers relate talk to home events and in enabling parents to extend and discuss school activities. In a community with ethnic minority groups, the sharing of experiences which are relevant to children's lifestyles is an important principle when stories, books and topics are chosen. A useful strategy to engage a child is simply to comment on the child's play or activity, showing an interest in what the child is doing and helping the child to explore a topic further: 'You're putting the seat in the car so the man can get in?' Practical, 'hands-on' activities provide an immediate context for talk. Eventually, as the child's linguistic competence increases, talk can be more free ranging, and used to refer out of context to other shared situations and events, as well as to hypothetical and abstract issues.

How do 'responsive' adults pattern their encounters with children? They rarely try to teach, drill or elicit new words, or to correct pronunciation errors. The child is allowed to question and initiate dialogue, whilst the adult responds to the child's lead, rather than pursuing themes which the adult considers to be important. The adult's responses reflect and develop topics, perhaps by adding further information or helping the child to question and search out possibilities. Responsive adults listen with genuine interest, hand conversation back to the child and invite a reply. The adult's turns often incorporate some aspects of the child's previous contribution and solicit a further response. Comprehension is negotiated as the adult restates, expands and clarifies the child's intended meaning. Sentences are tailored to the child's level of understanding, providing a more explicit and elaborate version, just beyond the child's in complexity. The child's involvement as a language partner is sustained by phatics, or social oil: 'Well I never!', 'Ooh, that's nice'. Similarly, when adults give something to the dialogue from personal experience, children are often stimulated to contribute further. A number of examples of this kind of adult responsiveness to children at different developmental stages have been given in Chapters 2 and 4.

Avoided are strategies with 'high control', such as interrupting, correcting faulty speech sounds ('crisp not cwisp') and asking a child to repeat a correct sentence ('Say "I went", not "I goed"'). Also avoided are talking for the child, not giving time for turns to be taken, and dominating dialogue. Display questions, whereby the adult requests information already possessed ('What colour is your pullover?'), are also inhibiting. Questions require scrutiny. We know from the Tizard and Hughes (1984) work that questioning is an important aspect of interaction, more so when it is the child asking the questions. Overuse of wh- type questions, such as 'What can you see in the picture?', leads to a decrease in spontaneous language: many children interpret such questions, quite rightly, as requests to speak. Adults may be more successful with reluctant or language-immature children if they offer questions which provide some help to the child in formulating a reply: 'Do you want to wear your pink tights or black socks?' Even so, research shows that, when adults ask too many two-choice questions, children become increasingly passive and inhibited, and dialogue begins to seem like interrogation.

Dialogue is put to many uses in the classroom. We know that teachers spend a lot of time using dialogue to present information, give instructions, find out what children know and develop children's thinking. For all children, including those with immature language associated with a hearing loss, there is research evidence to show that children are influenced by the teacher's conversational style. When teachers deliberately shift their styles to include more low-control strategies, such as personal contributions and phatics, there can be a dramatic increase in the spontaneous contributions made by the child. A balance has to be found, so that meaning and continuity are not sacrificed in order to teach, repair or correct 'faulty' speech or grammar. What we are suggesting is that classroom discourse often does not provide children with opportunities to explore a wide range of complex functions in language, since these rest on much more personal, sustained and intensive encounters.

It is through dialogue that children are exposed to adult ways of thinking and organising, and that, as a consequence of pursuing meaning together, children's hypotheses about the language system are raised and challenged. It is, in fact, in the 'to and fro' of conversational interaction that children are able to refine their own control of language, as rules are tested and adjusted in reciprocal turns, according to the feedback which adults provide. A comparison can be drawn between a child's experience of conversation and Piaget's classic water jar experiment. The changes produced in pouring liquid backwards and forwards between containers provides the evidence for the child's logical thinking. Similarly, the changes that sentences undergo as they are poured to and fro in dialogue provide the evidence from which the child reconstructs the linguistic system. (For further discussion of conversation strategies with hearing-impaired children, see Wood *et al.*, 1986.)

The conversation strategies discussed here are, of course, derived from work with hearing-impaired children in oral environments. Ongoing research with children in signing environments suggests that the same issues of control, use of questions, repair, personal contributions and the deliberate teaching of language out of context are just as important when signing is used. In other words, it is the quality of children's conversational encounters which is important, not simply the mode of communication used. Questions are sometimes raised about the teacher's response, should a child generate signs in class. In some instances, a child may be encouraged to use signs within the family. Teachers need to be clear in their minds about parental expectations, and whether they are going to respond to the child by signing. No general statement can be made about this since individual needs, motivation and circumstances vary. Some teachers attend classes so that they are familiar with basic signs. Some specialist support services hold sign classes in schools. In a few schools, specialist staff, deaf adults or signing interpreters work within mainstream groups. For some deaf children, undoubtedly, where a classteacher is able to reciprocate the child's use of sign the possibility of meaningful interaction is enhanced. However, there are marked differences of opinion on this issue, and classteachers will need to work in concert with the views of family and colleagues.

ATTENTION AND LISTENING SKILLS

Attention control features highly in the early stages of conversation with young, severely hearing-impaired children. One of the factors

Table 5.4 *Conversation strategies in the classroom*

Helpful

Creating a context for conversation: sharing activities which are relevant and
  meaningful to children's lives.
Commenting on the child's play or activity, showing an interest in what the child is
  doing and helping the child to explore a topic further.
Talking *with*, not *at*, children. Remember that the focus, at all levels, is the sharing
  of meaning.
Encouraging the child to question and initiate dialogue.
Providing social oil to sustain interaction: 'Hm, that's interesting'.
Expanding, clarifying and restating the child's intended meaning.
Incorporating some aspect of the child's contribution in the adult's response to
  ensure topical continuity across turns.
Listening to what the child has to say, handing conversation back to the child each
  time and allowing time for a reply. Avoiding dominating the interchange.
Giving personal contributions: 'I had a surprise today ... '
Using low-control moves to encourage spontaneous contributions from the child.

Less helpful

Deliberate teaching of vocabulary or grammar out of context: 'Today we're going to
  learn the names of things you find in a bathroom'.
Using display questions: 'How many fingers am I holding up?'
Enforcing repetition, asking children to imitate a correct model: 'Can you say torn,
  not teared?'
Stepping in to improve pronunciation: 'Make a better *ss* sound '.
Overusing two-choice questions: 'Is it blue or green?'
Overusing wh-type questions: 'Where did you go at the weekend?'
Talking *for* the child, not giving time to respond.
Using managerial, dominating and controlling comments.

---

most frequently associated with conductive hearing loss is poor
auditory discrimination, particularly when children are asked to
listen in noisy conditions, such as a busy classroom. For all children,
the ability to attend to a stimulus, to ignore distractions and to listen
over a stretch of time involves a complex hierarchy of skills. At a
very basic level, children have to select the significant sound
contrasts out of the stream of speech used around them. Children
are helped to do this by sharing a frame of reference in which visual
attention to objects is integrated with a meaningful social context
and appropriate linguistic input. But attention is disrupted in a
number of ways, apart from the sensory input level. Difficulties in
making sense of information leads to problems of motivation and
competing interests. Since language itself serves to direct attention
and mediate experience, children may be caught in a spiral in which
improvements in attention and growth in language are interdepen-
dent.

Most approaches to attention and listening (see Webster and McConnell, 1987) trace a developmental sequence in which the transfer of attention from one stimulus to another gradually comes under the child's own control. In the early stages, infants tend to be extremely distractible, paying only fleeting attention to every new stimulus. At this stage tasks should be kept short, and material and activities should be presented separately, with clear stopping and starting points and as few distractions and interruptions as possible. Before initiating conversation, many adults feel the need to catch a child's attention by touching the child's elbow, calling the child's name or gaining eye contact. Children may need help to shift from one activity to another, and would not be able to listen to instructions while also concentrating on a toy. There is a danger of adults inserting themselves into a child's focus in an overly controlling way, for example by holding an object in which the child is interested up to the mouth whilst speaking. Parallel play, commentary on the child's current activity and the turn-taking formats discussed earlier offer less intrusive ways of gaining attention.

Later on, when the child is able to switch from listening to looking, a number of group games can be enjoyed which foster auditory awareness, starting with simple location and identification tasks. Children can be asked to indicate, with eyes shut, where a specific sound is coming from, such as a drum, tambourine or loud clock. Children can identify sounds of different objects or instruments, using a tape recording of running water, bacon frying, washing machine, doorbell or alarm clock. Attention can be drawn to any interesting environmental sounds, such as a telephone, a passing motorbike or ambulance, a toilet flushing or workmen in the vicinity. A variation of hide-and-seek or hunt the thimble can be played, where the adult makes sounds softer and louder as the child approaches or goes further away from a hidden object or child. For some very hearing-impaired children, games can be played involving the onset of sound produced by the children themselves. Variations of 'Dead lions' or 'Musical statues' require children to sit down, dance, pass hats and form statues or dead lions at the onset of a drumbeat or when the music stops. Many nursery rhymes have actions to accompany them, which involve varying levels of listening in order to join in, such as 'Five little mice came out to play' or 'I can hammer'.

As children's attention control matures they are able to work alongside others in small groups and can tolerate more distractions and interruptions. Adults may wish to decrease the number of physical prompts to gain the child's attention and use verbal prompts instead, such as the child's name, 'Listen' or 'Watch me'.

Similarly, the child may increasingly be expected to cope with an instruction or question whilst absorbed in something else. Listening activities can then be more complex. For example, a one-element instruction can be given without gestures, such as 'Fetch your coat', whilst children can give simple messages to one another. Children can ask one another to select items or toys from an array, and then follow an instruction: 'Make the black dog sit'. In 'Eligibility' children are asked to perform an action, such as raising a hand, if they have black hair, red shoes, blue eyes and so on. Listening out for silly mistakes in a story, rhyming words in a jingle or references to animals or colours as a story is read can be fun. Children also like to model a rhythm or sequence of sounds, claps or drum beats produced by a partner.

Finally, adult support to attention-focus can be faded, as children integrate their attention across sensory channels and concentrate for longer periods. At this stage children can work in large groups, follow a sequence of instructions and listen to a greater information load, whilst also engaged in another activity. Popular listening games at this stage include 'Chinese whispers', where a message is passed from child to child, or 'Gossip', where a story is passed on with each child adding a bit more to it. Another activity starts with an adult giving a sequence of directions for drawings which increase in complexity, such as 'Draw a house with two windows, a blue door and a number 8 on the gate'. There are a wealth of sound games, such as 'I spy', identifying specific sounds at the beginning or end of words and detecting or making alliterations, blends and spoonerisms. At a more advanced level, children might be asked to extract the main concept or a sequence of ideas from what is said, to evaluate a speaker's purpose and to make judgements about tone of voice, mood or attitude.

CLASSROOM TECHNIQUES

Factors such as the academic organisation of a school, curriculum content and staffing levels have an effect on the learning opportunities available to hearing-impaired children in ordinary classes. However, teachers have most influence on what happens *inside* the classroom. There are a number of ways in which conditions for learning can be modified so that hearing-impaired children can participate more easily. Important aspects such as acoustic conditions, seating positions and the effective management of hearing-aids have already been considered. There are some additional 'enabling strategies' for teachers to take into account, which do not call for radical adjustments to teaching styles. Basically, these fall into three main categories: preparation of subject material, presentation of information to pupils, and interaction amongst pupils to foster learning. What can the ordinary classteacher do differently?

Where there is regular planning and liaison between the classteacher and support staff, a child can be prepared for some lessons beforehand. Pre-tutoring is particularly useful for older children following a subject-based curriculum, who spend only a part of their time in selected mainstream groups. A coursebook, lesson profile or written summary can be produced, highlighting key content and vocabulary, and any new or technical information. This could take the form of a handout, setting out the lesson content in terms appropriate to an individual's level of understanding. In a science lesson, for example, a hearing-impaired child might be given a simplified set of instructions to accompany a textbook, giving step by step instructions on how to conduct an experiment, the equipment needed and how to record findings. A preview of lesson material, worked over in a tutorial session by support staff, is very helpful for building confidence in older children joining academic groups, so that they have an advantage over others in knowing what to expect. *— personal reflection*

Teachers usually find that planning lessons in this way helps other pupils, since it means that material is thought through carefully and in detail. Handouts and lesson plans can be stored for future use and have a wider application for other children with comprehension or learning difficulties. Post-tutoring by a specialist teacher or classroom assistant depends on there being a summary of lesson material and content. Back-up teaching time gives opportunities for a child to review concepts and their application and to go over vocabulary and ask questions, as well as providing feedback about how much the child has absorbed.

How a topic is presented to pupils depends on how it has been prepared. Long stretches of unpunctuated listening without any visual illustrations, practical tasks or concrete examples can be very tiring for hearing-impaired children. Multi-media methods of presenting material to a class group can be used to reinforce key points and sustain interest. Most schools have access to an overhead projector, video-recorder and television. Flip charts, picture illustrations, diagrams, graphs, summaries and lists are all ways of presenting information which are visually accessible to a hearing-impaired child. New concepts or essential vocabulary can be highlighted during a lesson by writing on an overhead transparency or blackboard. Ideally, a lesson plan, class discussion and written clues will provide an integrated and meaningful whole. Class assignments and homework can be written down on a 'job-sheet', detailing materials, tasks and length of time to be spent on each activity. It may be part of the rôle of the 'individual helper' to make frequent checks on a child's understanding of lesson material and give feedback on the child's efforts as the 'job-sheet' is worked through.

If a hearing-impaired child is able to see a speaker's face, there may be additional clues in the facial expressions and natural gestures which accompany speech, as well as in the few speech and sound patterns which are visible on the lips. Lip-reading is not a very efficient method of understanding speech on its own because so many speech sounds look alike on the lips and others are not visible at all ('g', 'k' and 'h', for example, have no visible lip-shape). Undoubtedly, people who have a good grasp of the underlying patterns of language, and who can predict what a speaker is likely to say, make better lip-readers. However, lip-reading may be useful as a support to listening, alongside other clues. A hearing-impaired child therefore needs to be able to see the speaker's face clearly. Those who are more easily lip-read do not shout, slow down or overarticulate their speech, since such tactics tend to distort normal lip patterns. Speakers who hold pens, books or their hands in front of their mouths, or who have very heavy moustaches and beards, make for more difficult lip-reading. Similarly, teachers who talk whilst writing on the blackboard, address a child from behind or silhouette their faces by standing against a light source minimise the supportive clues from lip-reading. Children dependent on lip-reading cannot take notes and watch a speaker's face, which is why prepared handouts for a lesson or lecture may be helpful. Lip-reading can only occur effectively in *en face* situations.

Many hearing-impaired children can also be helped to participate in ordinary classes by being 'adopted' by another child. Prior to topic changes or important listening points, the teacher may give alerting signals to the group, such as 'Now we are going to move on to … '. But a classmate can be asked to cue a child into any lesson changes, announcements or important information by a nudge or brief word. Situations which the majority of hearing-impaired people find difficult are large group discussions. By the time a speaker has been identified in a group, the message may have been missed. The teacher can step in by summarising each contribution. Where a radio-aid system is used, the microphone can be handed to new speakers, or the main content repeated by the teacher into the microphone. Rather than repeating what is said, confusion may be avoided by paraphrase and breaking more convoluted ideas into smaller steps. Some teachers avoid these large group difficulties by co-operative class grouping.

One of the findings of the ORACLE study (Galton *et al.*, 1980) was that, even when grouped for an activity, children in ordinary classes tend to work independently, and their interactions are not task-related in the main. Children can learn a great deal from each other when tasks are matched to small group work. What tends to happen is that small groups are asked to follow *individual* assignments. Tasks can be structured so that they do involve children in co-operation and mutual assistance, and this is a particularly useful approach for hearing-impaired children in mainstream. For example, during a primary class project on animals, the observation had been made that rabbits always seek dark corners to hide in. Subsequently, the class was divided into groups of four and asked to make long tunnels for the rabbits, using cardboard boxes, glue and scissors. In other sessions designed to foster co-operative learning, children were set problem-solving tasks, such as making a structure from a set of materials which could be propelled up an incline using wind power through a straw. An essential part of such group work is defining who does what: ideas giver, plan drawer, helper, maker, observer or writer. The social and academic benefits of co-operative group work in the context of integration are discussed further by Johnson and Johnson (1986).

EARLY READING EXPERIENCE

In Chapter 4 we outlined a number of different approaches to reading which have important implications for all teachers, including those with hearing-impaired children in their classes. Reading is defined as the generating of ideas and questions about print within meaningful contexts which support their interpretation, rather than as a linear decoding exercise. There are parallels to be drawn between reading and the way children construct and test out the rules of spoken language. In both processes the child is admitted, albeit by a 'privileged' route in the hands of helping adults, to a community of language users. For hearing-impaired children there appear to be sources of reading difficulty at many levels. These include sound-confusions; immaturities in vocabulary, syntax and concepts; differences in cognitive processing; and secondary difficulties, such as passive learning styles and unhelpful reading experiences, which contribute to 'poor-get-poorer' effects. For many hearing-impaired children, learning to read becomes a language learning process at one and the same time.

How far reading itself can be used to teach language is a vexed question. Most children discover what language is and what it does in a face-to-face spoken (or signed) context, before learning to read. The 'round earth' view of reading takes into account what children learn in their active testing out and reinvention of the language system, as they interact with adults in meaningful, purposeful social contexts. To become readers, children apply their hypothesis-forming and rule-using to the reconstruction of meaning in print. It is true that hearing children gain access to information, new vocabulary and language forms, and a medium for reflective, disembedded thinking as they become fluent readers. Children learn to use a range of sophisticated linguistic conventions which are specific to print and which outstrip the capacity of spoken language for handling complex ideas. But the expectation that reading can give deaf children the very first linguistic insights, that objects and actions have symbolic representations negotiated and understood by others, may be ill-founded. The view expressed here is that all children need to discover the power and function of language in interpersonal contexts before, or perhaps in parallel with, their discovery of print.

Teaching usually begins by marking out an area of interest, and the way to achieve the greatest impact is to present a topic through real-life experiences. The teacher of the deaf who began her 'animal' project with a visit to a local working farm where the children fed lambs, muddied their boots and rode on a hay cart was well on the way to creating an impulse in the children to talk and write. Contrast this with the teacher who broaches the topic as an information-processing exercise: 'Today we're going to learn the names of farm animals'. Working with very young deaf children, Söderbergh (1985) describes how written whole-words were introduced as children spoke about, or signed, their everyday experiences. Deaf children in this study had few problems learning to read the names of relevant and meaningful objects, such as 'pyjamas', 'overall', 'sausages', 'ice-cream' and 'granny'. Children having difficulty with words like 'slowly' or 'quickly' played a running and walking game to act out their meaning.

Söderbergh's recipe is to present, as early as possible, words, sentences and stories linked through pictures, spoken words or signs to real situations. A linear approach — rehearsing single words and simple sentences out of context — is rejected. Five-year-old profoundly deaf children in this Swedish study were reading stories written about themselves, with connected discourse and enough clues from pictures, real life, and signed or spoken accompaniment, to enable the children to break into their meaning.

Even for mildly hearing-impaired children, it is important to use reading materials which are written around familiar experiences with language patterns which meet the child's expectations. The adult's role is as facilitator, providing opportunities to interact with relevant print rather than teaching letters, sounds or sight words using rote methods devoid of context or meaning. Words are acquired in both spoken and written form almost as a by-product of an experience shared. This is one reason why deaf children should be encouraged to write their own first 'books', relating a story to the teacher which is then written down and shared with others. The language of print is then bound to reflect the interests and expectations of the child as a language-user.

'Breakthrough' materials also utilise this principle (Mackay, Thompson and Schaub, 1970). The child has a bank of vocabulary: a personal store of printed words relating to family, self and interests, together with action words, such as 'go', and function words, such as 'to'. A special frame holds the cards on which the words are printed and this is used to compose sentences, which are later written down. Plenty of opportunity is given to discuss the topic and any vocabulary that the child may wish to use. A hearing-impaired child who had just acquired a baby brother began a 'baby' book, including details of crying, feeding, changing and first teeth. This was also the basis for much shared writing, as the teacher and parents added comments to the book. Home-made books like this can also be a reading resource for other children to enjoy.

Despite what has been said about the 'round earth' view of learning, whereby reading is integrated with the child's active and wider discovery of language, many teachers still rely on drills and schemes which run counter to this view. The respective merits of 'phonic' versus 'whole-word' methods are still argued hotly and have influenced the form of reading schemes. Traditionally, reading schemes are built around repetition: the rote learning of selected vocabulary, perhaps reinforced by flashcards; or the teaching of letter–sound associations. Sentence structures of the kind 'See Dick, jump Dick, jump up high' or 'Pat a fat rat', which are based on the repetition of key vocabulary or phonic rules, foster the idea that reading is an alien activity, unrelated to everyday language experience.

The principle of expectancy not only covers the language which children expect to find in books, it also extends to other aspects of real books. The worst kind of reading scheme is one which presents unidentifiable characters and lifestyles, sex-stereotyping, and cultural and racial bias, as well as unfamiliar vocabulary and syntax. Hearing children expect stories to have a dramatic plot, emotional involvement, cohesion and resolution. Books in many reading schemes lack these aspects of real literature and it has been said that it makes little difference whether some books are read forwards or backwards in terms of story development.

Is there any justification for teaching hearing-impaired children 'bottom-up' skills, such as phonic decoding? Subskill learning, drill activities, repetition and the rote memorisation of rules are all incongruous with a view of reading as a natural language process rooted in the child's social experience of communication. For a hearing-impaired child, any approach to reading which starts with a phonic approach may be very confusing and draws on the child's weakest point. There are conflicting opinions about whether practising decoding skills helps, or even prefaces, reading. Some researchers feel that there are no true pre-reading skills (Backman, 1983). What you have to do to get better at reading is to read! Having done so may provide the child with insights about letter–sound correspondences, and not the other way round.

Some of the features which characterise the interactive contexts of early spoken language also typify 'shared' or 'paired' reading approaches. Both are concerned with the child's active efforts, in the company of facilitating and familiar adults, to reconstruct the system out of which meaning arises. Both suggest that children learn by experiencing something of the whole process: reading learnt by reading books; speech or sign through dialogue. Both assume purpose and relevance to the lives of the participants. Rules are unearthed and pieced together as the adult guides the child's access to meaning. It has already been mentioned that, when adults are observed reading with deaf children, the occasion is often used to teach the child vocabulary or pronunciation, and to test understanding (Howarth *et al.*, 1981), rather than to enjoy the story.

Books should be selected with care, particularly with older deaf children, whose interests may be more mature than their linguistic sophistication. Some teachers adapt well-illustrated and appealing children's books, which have complex language, by providing an overlay of simplified, natural language for the text. In the early stages, some teachers annotate text with pictures of hand shapes for children learning sign, or provide an overlay which reflects sign structure. For comprehensive reviews of both materials and practical strategies using 'real' books, see Meek (1982) and Moon (1985). Reading sessions need to be short and frequent, say fifteen minutes per day. The focus of sessions is to enjoy books together in a positive, relaxed way, not to work at them reluctantly. The strategies listed in Table 5.5 can be handed on to parents or other reading partners (more able pupils, perhaps), and a record kept of books read, with any comments.

Essentially, shared reading activities should encourage deaf children to use whatever clues they can to discover the meaning of text. This includes an awareness of where to begin, how to move across the page and what help can be obtained from headings, illustrations and the unfolding story structure. To start with, the adult may want to read the story to the child a number of times as the pictures are followed, discussing the story and characters.

Table 5.5 *'Shared' reading for meaning strategies with deaf children*

Reading with the child to begin with, pointing to the text and praising any guesses
  the child makes.
Encouraging child to predict events from experience of other stories or reality.
Using clues in the text to guess words, such as letter shapes and sounds.
If child hesitates, reading onwards using picture clues, guessing from sentence or
  story context.
Supplying a word if the thread of a story is likely to be lost.
Correcting a child's reading error only if the meaning is likely to miscarry.
Praising good guesswork by confirming, rephrasing and expanding on what the
  child has discovered.
Taking turns with child to read portions of the text.
Encouraging child to read to other children and adults.
Aiming to keep meaning flowing with as few interruptions as possible.
Reading little and often, providing opportunities for child to choose books and
  aiming for mutual enjoyment.

Children very quickly want to identify parts of the print which carry meaning, and to work out what happens next. Children are motivated by the experience of enjoying authentic books. They learn what reading is by interacting with good readers around a text, learning the questions to ask of print, but drawing on their own resources and thinking of themselves as sources of information. The adult responds to the child's efforts to make sense of print, rather than correcting failure at the decoding level. What that does is to expect the child to behave as a reader right from the outset.

One of Bruner's (1984) arguments, introduced in Chapter 4, is that the collaborative process of reading enables adults and children to enter other 'possible worlds' through story. We also know from the Bristol studies, referred to in Chapter 2, that growing up in a literate family environment in which reading and writing are daily occurrences, and where stories are frequently read with children, is a factor often associated with later academic success in school. The sharing of meaning in stories is no less important for hearing-impaired children than for hearing children, in helping to give significance to events and to construct models of how the world works, through relating to the experiences of others, both real or imaginary. Discovering the powerful function of stories as a means of representing events, shaping feelings and organising thoughts is felt to be the best preparation for all children, in approaching more formal literacy work in school.

READING TO LEARN

Deaf children's reading founders when there is a large gap between the syntax under the child's control and the grammatical complexity of text. A number of approaches are sometimes used to get around this. One is to highlight different parts of speech through some kind of coding system. One system uses colours: red for nouns, blue for verbs, green for adjectives, and so on. Another system uses shapes to mark parts of grammar. Nouns might be written in a diamond, verbs in a circle, definite articles in a square. The child might be asked to organise a sequence of words with the possibility of seeing the syntax expressed as a series of geometric shapes. The pitfall is that the teaching of sentence structure becomes a pencil and paper exercise, devoid of context. Whilst shapes and colours may help to reinforce a child's sense of grammar in the early stages, it is difficult to know how far this approach can be taken before grammar becomes too difficult to describe visually.

Another approach is to simplify the language of text by deliberately restricting vocabulary, syntax and information content. Unfortunately, modifying reading materials in this way tends to remove cue sources and make text harder, not easier, to read. Perera (1984) gives the example 'The boat was approaching the island', where 'boat' might be substituted on the grounds of simplicity and familiarity for 'canoe' or 'submarine'. Yet the less familiar words enable the reader to predict more of what follows in the story. Ewoldt (1984) has come out strongly against the use of modified or rewritten materials. Her view is that deaf students can read for meaning using predictions about the schema of the story, cause and effect, plot, likely relationships between setting, beginning and ending, and cohesive ties between sentences. That brings us to what might be considered the most fruitful approach to enabling reading in hearing-impaired pupils: modifying the reader.

Earlier it was suggested that poor readers, in general, are slow to develop automatic skills, and that when they ask questions of print they draw on more limited resources of language or experience, interrogating text poorly or not at all. We may have to agree that deaf children will rely more heavily on alternative routes to meaning, using other cue sources in text to offset their limitations in syntax or vocabulary. It makes sense, then, to teach strategies which enable children to become more active enquirers of text. Better use of active guesswork and search-for-meaning strategies have been recommended for all children with reading difficulties (Lunzer and Gardner, 1979; 1984). One of the dangers of teaching and testing reading as a decoding skill, going from print to spoken sounds, is that children may be led to believe that reading entails no more than this. To read for meaning requires a deliberate effort to make sense of text and to relate what is uncovered to what is already known. In other words, children need to be shown how to learn from their reading.

A series of techniques to foster active reading for learning has come to be known as 'DARTs' (Directed Activities Related to Texts). Briefly, the activities are rooted in curriculum areas such as history, geography or biology. Children work in pairs or small discussion groups so that they can test their ideas against one another. They learn how to ask the right questions of text, what to record of the information they derive, and how to check whether they have the right answers. In 'location' tasks, children are asked to locate specific information points in text, such as underlining the words which describe the subject of a story, place or time. They may be asked to set out the sequence of events in a story, to label a diagram by reading a passage, or to complete a table by interrogating a text. The exercises sharpen the child's ability to seek out meaning by highlighting the parts of text which carry relevant information.

In 'deletion' tasks, important words or phrases are deleted from a passage and replaced with a line. The puzzle is to complete the gaps using the passage for clues. There are no absolutely correct answers to deletions, which leaves room for discussion. In another DARTs task, a passage in a relevant topic area is reproduced, cut up into about eight sections and mounted on card. The cards are jumbled and children are asked to restore them to a logical sequence. The puzzle then is to think carefully about the concepts and information in the material, in order to discover the sequence in which the ideas develop. Children's own writing can be used for this, and well-illustrated reading materials will make the task easier and more immediate for some children. (For more information about DARTs see Webster, 1986a, 1988c.)

The principle of reading to learn, as opposed to learning to read, can be applied in a number of ways. Children can be shown how to use reference books more efficiently, how to use chapter summaries, the contents page and index, how to locate a name or topic, and how to read a passage to seek out specific details by skimming and scanning. Children can be helped to find their way about a dictionary, *Yellow Pages*, newspaper, gas bill, holiday brochure, shopping catalogue, train timetable, telephone directory or A to Z map. Practice can be given in summarising content, providing headlines for newspaper cuttings, isolating the sequence of events in a story, predicting outcomes from unfinished stories and judging whether authors are writing particular pieces in order to inform, amuse, sell or persuade.

Reading to learn demands a different level of awareness of the purpose of reading. Good readers acquire an explicit knowledge of the rules involved in reading. In other words, they know and can describe how they go about a task and the strategies they use. This kind of control or awareness of a phenomenon always follows the acquisition of the phenomenon itself. So deaf children will need quite a lot of experience of reading stories, for example, before they can begin to analyse how stories are generally constructed. They will require a lot of experience of writing and reading features such as pronouns, determiners, co-ordinators (and, but) and connectors (then, later), together with other features which help text cohere, before these can be taught explicitly.

The knowledge and control children have over their own thinking and learning ('metacognitive' awareness) can be the focus of teaching, so long as this is tied to the child's existing language repertoire. Teachers can ask deaf children to make judgements about the 'acceptability' of sentence forms but, in order to analyse a sentence, children must be capable of producing sentence units themselves, and be aware that words and sentences exist. Deaf children should become aware of the different forms that writing can take: letters, poems, stories, lists, instructions and textbooks, and how these vary. Metacognition in reading involves the reader becoming aware of how to reread a text to extract and summarise main ideas or arguments, and how these develop. Can children identify errors, confusions, inconsistencies or contradictions in text? Do children know when to speed up in order to skim a piece for a specific point of information, and how to vary strategies when reading for fun or to memorise? Do children know when they have failed to understand text? If so, can they reread, look ahead or back in the text to resolve a comprehension difficulty, or consult another source, such as a dictionary or teacher?

Reflective reading strategies include taking notes, underlining key vocabulary and ideas, self-questioning, compiling questions for others on a text, reassembling information from a text in a flow chart, matching illustrations to parts of text, and drawing captions or cartoons to illustrate each stage of a story. Deaf children can be asked to construct a character grid after reading a story, matching central characters against personality types, such as 'selfish', 'brave' or 'cruel'. Finishing stories, predicting outcomes or choosing between alternative endings encourages reflection. Using adverts, magazines and official forms can lead to discussions about the purpose of reading matter, and its intended audience. All these activities encourage deaf children to ask themselves 'What do I want to find out?', 'How can I find the information I need?' and, having read, 'Did I achieve what I set out to?'

THE CURRICULUM AS LANGUAGE RESOURCE

For children with hearing-impairments it is important to seize all the opportunities presented in school, across the subject boundaries, where children are involved in talking, questioning, listening, reading and writing. Many teachers accept that language is best learnt through using it, as well as being a means to learn other things. This view is sometimes expressed as language being both system *and* resource. In practice, the most effective learning experiences are those which impel the child to use language in situations which are meaningful to themselves and their lives. In science, for example, language enables the child to categorise experience, collect observations, organise findings, explain confusions and weigh evidence in order to reach solutions. This view of language learned indirectly as children 'get things done with words' stands in stark contrast to approaches where language forms themselves are the focus of teaching.

The greatest impact is often achieved by marking out a topic area through real-life or participatory experiences. Actual visits, for example, to farms, shops, airports, factories, breweries, building sites, bus depots and whatever is nearby, produce a lot of momentum. Where teachers want to use more remote subject matter, this can be brought to life with photographs, artefacts, tools or implements, archive materials, recordings, videos, rôle-play, stories, poems and printed evidence, such as news reports. A number of sources (Dowling, 1980; Hutt, 1986; Webster, 1989b) give useful ideas for young children, covering a diversity of topics, both banal and esoteric, from the jobs people do to infant mortality in different historical periods using the evidence of gravestones. An important principle is that it is not only formal teaching contexts which give rise to the most productive language interaction. Some of the richest interchanges arise out of mundane tasks, such as putting toys and materials away, caring for class pets and taking messages, and in situations where deaf children co-operate to learn with peers.

Having introduced the subject stimuli, a topic then has to be mediated by children so that they can make the content their own. Mediation can take many forms, such as discussion, model-making, exhibitions and displays, experimentation, measuring and recording. Outcomes are the means by which children respond to their learning for a specified audience, and include written exercises, worksheets, letters, journals, diagrams, posters, collages and free writing. A topic on canal boats was mediated by one class visiting a local heritage centre, taking photographs, rôle-playing incidents in the barge families' daily lives and retelling stories from different points of view. Outcomes include writing diaries and photo essays, colouring posters, making replicas, drawing flow charts sequencing the haulage of materials from ship to factory, and assembling an exhibition of artefacts. It is in this kind of learning encounter that language and literacy become an integral part of the deaf child's exploration and problem-solving.

A humanities project in one secondary school where hearing-impaired pupils were integrated had the topic of cave painting at its core. Some children constructed a cave set and re-enacted painting by home-made candlelight, using primitive materials. Others drafted a radio script and a TV newsreel story board, relating to the discovery of cave paintings locally. Others gathered photographs, text and other material for a newspaper account. Outcomes included free writing, exhibitions, class presentations and the printing of a news page, together with more formal descriptions of how and what the children had done. For children with special needs there was scope for different levels of response, and for outcomes with varying demands on literacy, rather than a differentiation of curriculum.

In another class project the teacher covered a wall with pictures of faces culled from magazines and newspapers, showing a vast range of ages, emotions and cultures. Children began by discussing what can be learned from faces in terms of feelings, experience and social position. They observed each other's tics and habits, recording instances of hair-twiddling, thumb-sucking and head-scratching. They read poems about individuals, looked at clothes, hair styles and make-up, and acted out situations where particular emotions might be felt. In a balance of outcome activities, children wrote the biographies of chosen faces, reported incidents leading up to the photographs being taken and drew each other's portraits.

Some schools achieve a co-ordinated approach to language and literacy, with links across subject department boundaries. In a secondary school, rural science included bee-keeping, poultry and egg-hatching, together with greenhouse culture. The youngsters were involved in looking after beehives and their colonies, feeding and cleaning out hens, and watering and marketing plants. Opportunities were exploited for linking with mathematics, for example, using topics on costing profit and loss in the sale of produce; whilst in science, plans were drawn for constructing new feeding boxes.

THE EXPERIENCE OF WRITING

Writing, like reading, can be considered an integral part of the language curriculum and should not be taught separately as an isolated skill. A number of curricular examples have been given where a balance of activities can be achieved in listening, talking or signing, reading and writing, as topics are introduced to children, mediated in ways which actively engage the learner, and outcomes negotiated. Writing shares many of the features discussed earlier in relation to spoken (or signed) communication and reading. The social context of written language, the sense of purpose in writing and the rôle of adults in facilitating children's efforts are paramount. What should be noted are the differences between face-to-face communication and the more formal structures of writing, as language increasingly becomes decontextualised, self-contained and abstract. Awareness of these formal differences can both inform teaching practice and enable hearing and hearing-impaired children to write in order to learn.

Just as in spoken language contexts, writing has more relevance when it is the child who takes the initiative and feels an inner pressure to set something in print. Good teachers create situations which demand a genuine urgency to write something down. More typically, teachers tend to decide the topic, the form of writing and its audience, whilst an exercise in writing set for a whole class is unlikely to have a motivating effect. In authentic writing contexts, people write because they have feelings to express, information to give, stories to tell, requests to make or someone to persuade. The purpose of writing is much more apparent when children are recording aspects of 'hands-on' experience, sending letters to people and receiving replies, writing notices, labels, reviews and personal journals, as opposed to filling in workcards and course books associated with commercially available language 'laboratories'. So the starting point for really creative writing must be that the child has something to express.

In Chapter 4 we outlined three distinct stages in writing. At the first stage children may need help to think out what they are going to write about, who the writing is for, what vocabulary and which sentence patterns may be useful, and how to link material together. In writing, deaf and hearing children rarely utilise all that they know, and a 'brain-storming' or 'key-wording' session can draw attention to relevant ideas and information which children already have. Very young children can trace over captions on their personal drawings. They may copy or select simple labels from a word bank, which fixes an interesting or important experience. Early written attempts should be part of an overall learning encounter: seeing, touching, feeling, talking, drawing, making, and then encapsulating the whole in a written message for others to see. The 'Breakthrough' approach, mentioned earlier, is an effective way of relating writing to the deaf child's interests, oral or signed language, and reading.

The classic stumbling block of thinking up something to write about can be overcome by teachers widening the reasons for children writing. These might include labelling personal possessions or writing notes about oneself on a photo, self-portrait or silhouette. Other children can be informed about good books, tapes, films or TV programmes. Instructions can be written on how to look after the computer, class pets or plants. A school magazine, newsletter or guide to the school for new pupils could be produced. Poems or stories can be written for other children to read (for example, older children writing for the nursery), together with comments on other children's work. Children can report on local activities and events, or interview people. Letters can be sent to others in the community: local shops, factories, press, radio, hospitals, football clubs or pensioners' groups. Writing can be directed to congratulating or complaining (local amenities, availability of things in shops, places where children are welcome).

At the second stage of writing, when children actually put pen to paper, the child has to translate ideas into sentence patterns, and this requires a deliberate and conscious analytical effort. It has been argued at several points that, in face-to-face encounters, the language that children use to communicate is transparent in the sense that we focus rarely on the form of language, but on the meaning conveyed. Non-verbal gestures and aspects of spoken language such as rhythm, pitch and intonation, together with the interactive features which arise from the relationships between speaker, audience and social context, all contribute to the meaning which is negotiated.

However, in writing children plan what they wish to say in advance. The audience is more remote. Written communication must be more self-contained and less reliant on social context for interpretation. Because of their permanence, written forms of language are inherently able to handle more complex and abstract data than the fleeting presence of speech or sign will allow. But in order to write, children must acquire the conventions which mark the written mode. To put this another way, children have to be aware explicitly of the written features of language, how the code is put together and how it works. The 'opaque' qualities of language become objects of learning and analysis in their own right.

Joint composition between adult and child is as important to early writing as the active sharing of books is to reading. This is in fact one of the most useful potentials of microcomputers, where a text-editing or story-board program allows adult and child to compose together. Openings and endings can be discussed, as well as aspects of vocabulary, sentence structure and story sequence. If a deaf child sticks to rigid sentence patterns, more flexible ways of presenting material can be tried. The adult can introduce conventions such as connectives (and, because, but, instead, anyway, if, so, although); cohesive ties, such as pronoun substitution ('Lizzie loves sweets and her Mum said she could have some'); and time sequence markers (then, after, later, now, next, last). Joint composition can be an occasion to discuss punctuation, full stops, capital letters and speech marks. Writing partners can take turns at starting or finishing sentences, or developing a story entry by entry.

In Table 5.6 some of the differences between spoken and written language conventions are given. As with other 'metacognitive' skills, explicit awareness of a phenomenon generally follows a richness of experience in simply using the phenomenon functionally, without being able to describe or discuss the strategies themselves. Some common sense is required so that attention is drawn to devices that are within the deaf child's conceptual and linguistic reach.

The third and final stage of any act of writing should involve reappraisal and review. Yet this is rarely asked of hearing or hearing-impaired children. In this last stage, initial drafts are worked over to produce a finished article. Without reviewing, it is difficult to see how a writer can create sentences which relate to one another and make a cohesive whole. In the editing and proof-reading process, many writers reflect on and shape their thoughts, and search for the best expression of their intended meaning in relation to the particular audience. Through drafting and rewriting, children can be helped to discover what they think. Children can help to check over each other's first drafts, and copies of these can be kept in children's folders to show how a piece of writing develops. The word-processor allows correction and redrafting without fuss, before final printing out.

We have said that only in school are deaf and hearing children asked to write as a daily chore, filling in worksheets and course books, or writing news, where no one sees the finished product. The purpose and target audience of children's writing may often be obscure. Authentic writing involves the sending of letters, reportage and commentary to its intended audience. Journal reviews, collections of poetry, signs, instructions, notices and warnings should all be displayed and published. Links can be made with other people's writing and attention drawn to society's print, such as weather charts, TV guides, posters, forms, menus, magazines, birthday cards, logos, signs, lists and directions. Adults can write their own notes and messages in the presence of children. Responses to what people write are also important. Replies to class letters can be discussed and displayed. Opportunities for teaching spelling and handwriting may well arise in the writing process, but these are seen as secondary to fostering the child's impulse to communicate meaningfully in print. (Further suggestions along these lines are given in Raban, 1985; Webster, 1989b.)

Table 5.6 *Some differences between conversation and print*

	Conversation	Written language
Situational	Non-verbal gestures, facial, body and postural clues.	Clues rooted in text: headings, illustrations, contents, index.
	Meaning negotiated in social context with familiar partners.	Remote audience not present when text composed.
	Adult–child adjustments to meet needs of language novice.	Some accounts of audience taken, e.g. in children's books.
	Spontaneous, rarely planned, revised or remembered.	Writer plans, edits, revises.
Functional	Wide range of functions: social contact, fantasy, feelings, enquiry, personal needs.	Record of information, medium for ideas, news, stories, culture.
	Range of formality according to function: 'chat', sports commentary, speeches.	Society's print has a range of formality: signs, logos, adverts, letters, forms, tests.
Structural	Pauses, hesitations, repetitions.	Spelling, punctuation, layout conventions.
	Syntax not analysable.	Grammatical structures.
	High redundancy, large number of words to express meaning.	Low redundancy.
	Turn-taking signals, checks that partner is listening and involved.	Cohesion of text through cross-reference, pronouns, connectives, ellipses.
Physical	44 phonemes.	26 graphemes.
	Speech and sign have fleeting presence requiring ongoing processing.	Permanent visual trace can be reread and worked over.
	Pitch, tone, speed, stress, volume and rhythm convey meaning.	Few means of expressing intonation, volume, speed, regional accent.
	Prosodic features convey emphasis: 'Lizzie likes *Joe's* dog, not Richard's'/'Lizzie likes Joe's *dog*, not his cat'.	Punctuation marks: dots, dashes, question marks, brackets, underlining, exclamation marks, italics, apostrophes.
	Signs are moderated to achieve emphasis: amplitude, speed, direction from body.	Written genres identified by layout: plays, poems, letters, newspapers.

Most authorities agree that spelling is not usually a problem for deaf children, relative to achievements in reading or other areas of language use. Whilst the main aim is to get writing to flow, spelling and punctuation can be developed and improved by helping children to redraft their work. In just the same way as there are many sources of information in reconstructing meaning in reading text, so there are many routes to storing and retrieving the way words are spelt. Drawing on the evidence reported in Chapter 4, it is good practice for deaf children to learn to write words as visual wholes, paying attention to the internal structure of words and using visual analogies (e.g. 'sign'–'signal') as a basis for spelling new words. Rather than the rote learning of isolated lists, children are helped by drawing relevant vocabulary from words they wish to use in their own writing, using a read–cover–write–check strategy.

COMPUTER-ASSISTED LEARNING

Most schools now have access to microcomputers and there is a rapidly expanding range of software available, some of which is specifically designed for deaf children. At first sight, computer-assisted learning appears to have some marked advantages for children with special needs. Material is presented visually; children find microcomputers non-threatening, non-judgemental, stimulating and highly motivating; learning steps can be individually paced and controlled by the child; children can take risks and make mistakes; and there is opportunity for repetition and overlearning for children who have difficulty in retaining ideas and forming concepts, linked with immediate feedback and praise.

For deaf children, programs have been designed to 'teach' the written vocabulary of shapes, animals and body parts, and concepts of difference, order and sequence, together with correct spelling. British Sign Language hand-shapes and movements have been recorded in computer graphics with a variety of tasks involving English glosses. In a second kind of program, the 'revelatory' program, children uncover linked pieces of information, such as unearthing clues to find the way out of a haunted waxworks. A third kind is 'conjectural', where children test out hypotheses within the program. For example, using a picture format children are asked 'if … then' and 'why … because' type questions: 'Why wear a hat and scarf … Because it's sunny/raining/snowing.' A fourth category, the 'emancipatory' program, has a wide range of activities which reinforce the teacher's role, such as a computerised thesaurus which scans a child's written work and suggests alternative vocabulary or phrasing. Some programs animate written commands or concepts, linking language with observed action.

Computer-assisted approaches to language and literacy are not, however, a panacea. There are problems in designing software for young deaf children where the language content to be taught may be far less complex than the task instructions. Many programs foster a respondent, decontextualised style of language behaviour, in which the child is a passive recipient of software prompts and demands. It is, of course, possible to use microcomputers as a means of establishing a social context for learning, where the child and adult interact around the program content. Text-editing software and story boards provide an opportunity for joint composition between peers or between child and adult. 'Interactive video' is an area of development with incredible potential for education. Essentially, software acts as a database where pictures, maps, statistics, programs and simulation games are stored. The materials are then used to foster co-operative learning, problem-solving, research skills, decision-making and creative thinking strategies.

TOWARDS A COGNITIVE CURRICULUM

In its full sense, the curriculum embodies all the learning opportunities within a school. In planning the curriculum, thought should be given to the range and balance of subjects to which a child has access, whilst the nature of informal and non-timetabled experiences should also be considered. The starting point is a clear and full appraisal of a child's educational needs, collecting together professional opinions and the views of parents. In Chapter 1, an important principle of the 1981 Education Act was highlighted: the tailoring of provision as closely as possible to individual profiles of need. Questions for specialist and school staff to address revolve around which areas of the curriculum the child has access to, is withdrawn from or can participate in through adaptation. At the time of writing, the Education Reform Act proposes a national curriculum which will define the core subjects which must be taught for a major portion of time. Whilst it is not yet clear how 'statemented' children will be affected by these reforms, all aspects of the curriculum will continue to require regular planning, monitoring and review.

For very young hearing-impaired children, play opportunities can be structured and planned as sources of social and language interaction. Play involves the child in using symbols at different levels of abstraction, and directly supports the child's receptivity to language. So we incorporate into the curriculum play activities which engender problem-solving and provide opportunities for representational play using life-size objects and materials, together with imaginative play, for example using resources for creating and assembling. (For further discussion of play see Webster and McConnell, 1987.) We can also plan and monitor the social experiences for hearing-impaired children in school, by using strategies such as grouping children for genuine collaborative activities, both in class and more informally in chess or art clubs at lunchtime. Social skills, such as entering conversation at the right point, acceptable forms of address for adults and appropriate behaviour in relation to social circumstances can all be built into the curriculum.

For children who are supported by additional help, or a unit resource, decisions will need to be made about who is to be responsible for the 'core' subjects, such as mathematics, science and English. Many decisions, particularly at the secondary level, will be determined in practice by linguistic demands: the amount of new and technical vocabulary encountered; whether the teacher uses formal methods with a heavy emphasis on listening, reading and recording; and how adaptable a subject teacher may be. Many severely hearing-impaired children are much less confident in joining in mainstream lessons involving a lot of oral discussion, rote learning of facts and work done mainly from textbooks or the blackboard, with little practical content. Non-specialist staff may have anxieties about safety aspects, such as in a laboratory or on a canoeing expedition, where warnings may be difficult to signal. Where it is felt that some areas of the curriculum may be too demanding, the range of options may have to be adjusted as a function of the amount of extra help available.

As we saw in Chapter 4, there are no 'inevitable' barriers to what deaf children can achieve in subjects such as science, mathematics and technology. The attainments of hearing-impaired children are only partly related to degree of hearing loss or type of school placement. They are influenced by the way a subject is taught, how information is given out, recorded, enriched and generalised, and the range, depth and complexity of language involved in instruction. Where subject teachers are able to plan ahead in a degree of detail, if only in topic-based subjects such as geography, history and mathematics, then arrangements for pre- and post-tutoring can be made. One of the points which Bruner stresses, and which we raised in Chapter 2, is that effective learning introduces children to the skills and sense of purpose which underlie a subject. Effective support staff may set out to achieve this by exploring study methods and cross-curricular links in tutorial sessions, rather than by simply checking over information absorbed.

An important assumption in curriculum planning is that teachers will keep relevance to the fore. We live in a world of greater automation, increased leisure and fewer unskilled work opportunities. Communication demands may preclude some job openings. It is essential that hearing-impaired children are prepared for life after school. A life-skills curriculum cuts across many subject boundaries and includes social acceptance and self-esteem; positive attitudes to cultural, ethnic and gender differences; as well as skills which can be extended in leisure time, or with vocational outlets. It is particularly important for deaf children to be familiar with form-filling, job interviews, budgeting, insurance, renting a flat, paying gas and electricity bills, hire purchase, running a vehicle, and so on. No less important are the subtle complexities of social and sexual relationships, and family life and its responsibilities.

Until recently, approaches to children with special needs have tended to focus attention on the limitations of individuals, taking little account of the contexts in which teaching and learning take place. Deaf children, in particular, have suffered from the 'deficit' perspective which assumes that any learning difficulties are inherent and fixed in the child's disability. A new orientation is proposed in this book, emphasising conditions for learning and the quality of adult–child partnerships in enquiry and problem-solving. An optimal learning environment is outlined in Figure 2.2. Aspects of the 'north-west' quadrant include adults thinking forward with children, identifying tasks and enabling children to choose the best routes for tackling them. Having marked out a topic area, children are guided to resources and helped to think out how information will be collected, recorded and presented to an audience. Adults think back with children, reflecting on what was learned and how this can be connected to personal knowledge, or how skills can be applied more widely. The aim is to develop active, self-motivated learners who are able to tackle a wide range of problems in and out of school. A cognitively oriented curriculum is geared to knowing 'how' rather than knowing 'that' — learning how to learn.

How can the curriculum be monitored and evaluated? Ongoing appraisal is essential, in order to know whether the child's needs are met within the provision which has been made. Regular review meetings keep everyone informed about a child's progress. A feature of the 'effective schools' literature described in Chapter 2 is that parents have open access to teachers, with honest and regular feedback. One way to evaluate a child's learning experience is to determine clear objectives on a day-to-day, weekly or termly basis.

These objectives are set in relation to a child's existing skills, and assessment is formative, leading to the setting of new targets. Such an approach has been advocated for hearing-impaired children in some detail in other texts (Webster and Ellwood, 1985; Webster, 1986a). It is time-consuming, but gives a clear idea of what teaching hopes to achieve, and can involve children in evaluation of their own learning. This approach also finds expression in records of achievement and school profiles, which build up a broad picture of children's achievements across the curriculum, using pro-formas or 'comment banks'.

An alternative approach to curriculum-generated evaluation is to adopt a more 'objective', external method of assessment which has been specifically designed to reflect the needs of hearing-impaired students. For example, some schools use the 'Communicative Use of English Scheme' devised by the Royal Society of Arts Examination Board, which avoids many of the pitfalls associated with the use of standardised tests with deaf students. There are grounds for disquiet, given the momentum of the Education Reform Act to assess children against national attainment targets, since any child who is excluded or 'falls short' of age norms will inevitably feel failure. A more telling and challenging form of evaluation is for teachers to assess their own behaviour. How well do teachers behave as active researchers, hypothesis-testers and creative problem-solvers, in much the same ways as have been suggested for hearing-impaired children? For more effective teaching and learning, we need to review how far *all* participants in the curriculum have a footing in the north-west quadrant of Figure 2.2.

NOTE

1. A booklet and tape-recording, *Reaching Our Children Through Song*, is available from Margaret Tait at the Deafness Research Group (see Appendix).

Overview

It is important for any practical guide, whether aimed at parents, teachers or other professionals, to have a firm theoretical grounding. Adults, no less than children, gain a great deal from knowing the underlying intention and function of an activity or experience. In this book we have set out what we hope is a coherent and convincing approach to the development and education of hearing-impaired children, which spans a broad continuum of special needs. Our thinking has been influenced by the views of Piaget, Soviet psychologists, and contemporary scholars such as Bruner. Whilst the emphasis on close interactions between adults and children may be criticised as reflecting Western culture, there is no doubt that this is an important perspective for exploring the impact of deafness on development. Many of these ideas have been put to the test, so that there is now a growing body of research evidence on both hearing and hearing-impaired children, which explores aspects of language, thinking and learning within a framework of social interaction.

Wherever possible we have drawn on recent research, particularly the work of the Deafness Research Group at Nottingham University, in order to substantiate our views. However, there is no attempt to be didactic, and teachers are best placed to judge for themselves whether this book has helped them to reappraise their classroom practice. For those teachers coming new to the field of hearing-impairment, it will be evident that there are a number of controversial issues which continue to be debated. No claims are made on behalf of one method of communication as opposed to another, or in relation to where children are placed educationally. The simple truth is that there are no guarantees attached to any one approach, and that what works with one child may not work with another. Questions should be asked about the efficacy of all kinds of educational intervention: if children appear not to be making progress, there is a professional responsibility to ask why.

The majority of children with sensori-neural deafness, including many youngsters with severe-to-profound hearing losses, spend at least part of their time in mainstream school settings. Within the primary age-range there can be expected to be children in every class group who will suffer some of the consequences of an intermittent conductive hearing loss, at one time or another. The professional development needs of staff who work in all school settings, but particularly where hearing-impaired children participate, must include information about hearing loss and appropriate teaching approaches. There are a number of fixed variables to be aware of in relation to deafness, such as aetiology and degree of hearing loss, and the child's home circumstances, ethnic background, personality and intellectual variables. But the factors which are most powerful in relation to teaching and learning, if only because they are open to change, are the ones we have highlighted here.

A SUMMARY OF PRINCIPLES AND PRACTICE

(1) *The image we hold of children as learners influences how we set about the teaching process*

Infants are oriented from the outset to test out the environment, recognise regularities and make sense of the world, but above all else to maintain social contact with others. We place the child centrally in the learning process, actively using the evidence which language encounters provide to reconstruct the rules of the system.

(2) *Pre-verbal experiences lay the foundations for thinking and language*

Well before first words appear, children are engaged as language partners in social contexts where meaning is inherent in predictable events and familiar routines. Adults expect infants to express meanings, read intentions, take turns and reciprocate in 'conversational' exchanges which serve as a microcosm for later dialogue.

(3) *Responsive adults are contingent*

Contingency is the timing of help given by adults on the basis of the child's moment-to-moment understanding, standing back to allow initiative when the child has grasped the problem, giving prompts when the child veers off course, and structuring the task with the child so that success is experienced at each stage.

(4) *Learning and development arise out of the child's own problem-solving*

Children have been described as 'architects of their own understanding', whereby concepts are generated from the child's own enquiry. Empty learning, which cannot be generalised or used to solve real-life problems, results from passive, rote teaching not tied to direct or relevant experience. Literacy and numeracy are good examples of areas where the child needs to know 'how' and 'why' strategies are used, acquiring the sense of purpose which underlies a subject rather than information contained within it.

(5) Adults help children accomplish more than they could alone

Children are not lone investigators. Through social encounters with siblings, peers, parents and teachers, children are introduced to value systems and more mature ways of organising themselves. Co-operatively achieved success lies at the heart of learning and development. Adults hand on problem-solving strategies as they share activities such as reading. The cognitive curriculum includes opportunities for discussion and planning how to go about learning.

(6) Adults can be facilitators as well as teachers

Adults' best efforts may be directed towards creating conditions for learning. Language is often a by-product of shared experience and learned least effectively through direct teaching, imitation or correction. In conversation the focus should be on reaching understanding, embedded in the social context. Children do not copy: they reconstruct the rules which enable them to join in the 'game' and reciprocate. When adults try to teach language directly, the focus moves from the sharing of meaning to the form of language *per se*.

(7) Conversational styles have an impact

Children's spontaneous language flourishes when adults respond by listening to what the child has to say, agree topics, expand, paraphrase and clarify the child's intended meaning, relate what is said to previous turns, give phatics and personal contributions, and avoid high-control moves, such as enforced repetition and display questions. It is the adult's input which provides the linguistic evidence from which children learn, and which sustains and engages the child as a language partner.

(8) The transition from home to school marks a turning point in the nature and purpose of adult responsiveness

In school, language is used for giving information, questioning, analysing and recording, and to help children think about abstract concepts beyond the here and now. Language is both system *and* resource: the aware teacher seizes opportunities which arise across the curriculum boundaries to learn language through using it. Some teaching styles are directive and managerial, and lead to interactions which are less sustained or wide ranging, and which discourage children from taking the initiative. Some children are expected to take a passive, respondent rôle in school.

(9) Deafness threatens broad features of adult–child interaction

The impact of any degree of deafness affects children in unpredictable and largely unchartered ways. Not all hearing-impaired children have special needs. Obstacles to learning which may arise include a range of interactive, behavioural, social, linguistic, conceptual and psychological factors, as well as reflecting a diversity of individual circumstances. Teachers exert most influence over the framework for learning, and it is to the teaching environment that we look for ways of meeting special needs.

(10) An optimal learning environment can be created

The learning partnership is enhanced when adults negotiate tasks with children and think forward towards the purpose, shape and point of an enquiry, guiding children to resources and helping children to reflect back on what they have learned, within a cycle of plan–do–review. Teachers are asked to set clear objectives with and for children, paying attention to conditions for learning and weighing the effects of their own interventions and styles on children's progress. Both adults and children are invited to take on rôles of active, creative problem-solvers, extending and challenging one another. Parents, particularly, play a crucial rôle and are essential partners in assessment, decision-making and the curriculum. There are no simple solutions for overcoming the learning difficulties associated with deafness. But it is to the process of learning that we look to provide some of the answers.

Appendix: Further information sources

1. National Deaf Children's Society (NDCS),
   45 Hereford Road,
   London W2 5AH
   Aims to promote public interest in and awareness of the needs of deaf children and their families, and to improve welfare and educational support; represents 140 regions and branches; provides information through its education officer, booklets and information sheets on topics such as 'glue' ear and hearing-aids; publishes a quarterly magazine, *Talk*.

2. British Deaf Association (BDA),
   38 Victoria Place,
   Carlisle CA1 1HU
   Represents and campaigns on behalf of the adult deaf community, particularly for recognition of British Sign Language; funds scholarships, holidays, leisure and education services for deaf families; issues information leaflets and a monthly magazine, *British Deaf News*.

3. British Society of Audiology (BSA),
   80 Brighton Road,
   Reading RG6 1PS
   Promotes developments in scientific, educational and research aspects of audiology; is the major UK forum, through conference activities and the quarterly *British Journal of Audiology*, of professional advancements in audiology.

4. British Association of Teachers of the Deaf (BATOD),
   Secretary Ms S. P. Dowe,
   Service for the Hearing-impaired,
   Icknield High School,
   Riddy Lane,
   Luton LU3 2AH
   The professional association for teachers and others involved in the education of hearing-impaired children; holds national and regional courses, conferences and meetings; promotes policy,

research and training issues; publishes a range of technical, practical and theoretical articles in the *Journal of the British Association of Teachers of the Deaf*.

5. Royal National Institute for the Deaf (RNID),
   105 Gower Street,
   London WC1E 6AH
   Provides a wide range of information, scientific, educational and support services to deaf individuals, families and professionals; publishes leaflets, films, tapes, slides, posters, videos, reading lists, journal updates, an information directory and the magazine *Soundbarrier*.

6. Deafness Research Group,
   Department of Psychology, University of Nottingham,
   University Park, Nottingham NG7 2RD
   A group of researchers, teachers and other professionals working on a range of projects with children who experience communication difficulties.

References

Backman, J. (1983) The role of psycholinguistic skills in reading acquisition: a look at early readers. *Reading Research Quarterly* **18** (4), 466–479.

Ballantyne, J. and Martin, J. A. M. (1984) *Deafness* (4th edition). Edinburgh: Churchill Livingstone.

Bamford, J. and Saunders, E. (1985) *Hearing-impairment, Auditory Perception and Language Disability*. London: Edward Arnold.

Bench, J. and Bamford, J. (eds) (1979) *Speech-Hearing Tests and the Spoken Language of Hearing-impaired Children*. London: Academic Press.

Bennett, N., Desforges, C., Cockburn, A. and Wilkinson, B. (1984) *The Quality of Pupil Learning Experiences*. London: Lawrence Erlbaum Associates.

Bishop, J. and Gregory, S. (1983) Going to school. *Talk*, Winter.

Bishop, J. and Gregory, S. (1984) Linking home and school. *Talk*, Spring.

Bissex, G. L. (1980) *Gyns at Wrk: A Child Learns to Read and Write*. Cambridge, Massachusetts: Harvard University Press.

Black, N. (1985) Glue ear: the new dyslexia. *British Medical Journal* **290**, 1963–1965.

Bond, D. E. (1984) Aspects of additional impairment and multiple handicaps. *Journal of the Association of Educational Psychologists* **6** (5), 50–61.

Booth, T. (1983) 'Integrating special education'. In Booth, T. and Potts, P. (eds) *Integrating Special Education*. Oxford: Blackwell.

Bower, T. G. R. (1977) *The Perceptual World of the Child*. London: Open Books, Fontana.

Brennan, M. (1981) 'Grammatical processes in British Sign Language'. In Woll, B., Kyle, J. and Deuchar, M. (eds) *Perspectives on British Sign Language and Deafness*. London: Croom Helm.

British Association of Teachers of the Deaf (1981) Audiological definitions and forms for recording audiometric information. *Journal of the British Association of Teachers of the Deaf* **5** (3), 83–87.

Brown, R. (1977) 'Introduction'. In Snow, C. E. and Ferguson, C. A. (eds) *Talking to Children*. Cambridge: Cambridge University Press.

Bruner, J. S. (1971) *The Relevance of Education*. New York: W. W. Norton & Co.

Bruner, J. S. (1983) *Child's Talk: Learning to Use Language*. Oxford: Oxford University Press.

Bruner, J. S. (1984) 'Language, mind and reading'. In Goelman, H., Oberg, A. and Smith, F. (eds) *Awakening to Literacy*. London: Heinemann.

Bruner, J. S. and Haste, H. (eds) (1987) *Making Sense: The Child's Construction of the World*. London: Methuen.

Bryant, P. and Bradley, L. (1985) *Children's Reading Problems*. Oxford: Blackwell.

Cataldo, S. and Ellis, N. (1988) Interactions in the development of spelling, reading and phonological skills. *Journal of Research in Reading* **11** (2), 86–109.

Clark, M. M. (1976) *Young Fluent Readers*. London: Heinemann.

Clopton, B. M. and Silverman, M. S. (1978) Changes in latency and duration of neural responding following developmental auditory deprivation. *Experimental Brain Research* **32**, 39–47.

Cole, M., Gay, J., Glick, J. A. and Sharp, D. W. (1971) *The Cultural Context of Learning and Thinking*. London: Methuen.

Conrad, R. (1979) *The Deaf School Child*. London: Harper & Row.

Cooper, C. and Arnold, P. (1981) Hearing-impairment and visual-perceptual processes in reading. *British Journal of Disorders of Communication* **16** (1), 43–49.

Dalzell, J. and Owrid, H. L. (1976) Children with conductive deafness: a follow-up study. *British Journal of Audiology* **10**, 87–90.

Davie, R., Butler, N. and Goldstein, H. (1972) *From Birth to Seven*. London: Longman.

DES (1967) *Units for Partially Hearing Children* (Education Survey No. 1). London: HMSO.

DES (1975) *A Language for Life* (The Bullock Report). London: HMSO.

DES (1978a) *Special Educational Needs* (The Warnock Report). London: HMSO.

DES (1978b) *Primary Education in England*. London: HMSO.

de Villiers, J. G. and de Villiers, P. A. (1979) *Early Language*. London: Open Books.

DHSS Advisory Committee on Services for Hearing-impaired People (1981) *Final Report of the Committee Appointed to Consider Services for Hearing-impaired Children*. London: HMSO.

Dodd, B. (1976) The phonological systems of deaf children. *Journal of Speech and Hearing Disorders* **41**, 185–198.

Dodd, B. and Campbell, R. (eds) (1987) *Hearing by Eye: The Psychology of Lip-reading*. London: Lawrence Erlbaum Associates.

Donaldson, M. (1978) *Children's Minds*. London: Fontana.

Donaldson, M., Grieve, R. and Pratt, C. (eds) (1983) *Early Childhood Development and Education*. Oxford: Basil Blackwell.

Dowling, M. (1980) *Early Projects*. London: Longman.

Downs, M. P. (1977) 'The expanding imperatives of early identification'. In Bess, F. (ed.) *Childhood Deafness: Causation, Assessment and Management*. New York: Grune Stratton.

Ewing, I. R. and Ewing, A. W. G. (1944) The ascertainment of deafness in infancy and early childhood. *Journal of Laryngology and Otology* **59**, 309.

Ewoldt, C. K. (1984) Problems with rewritten materials as exemplified by 'To build a fire'. *American Annals of the Deaf* **129** (1), 23–28.

Ferreiro, E. and Teberosky, A. (1982) *Literacy Before Schooling*. Exeter, New Hampshire: Heinemann. Educational.

Fiellau-Nikolajsen, M. (1983) Tympanometric prediction of the magnitude of hearing loss in pre-school children with secretory otitis media. *Scandinavian Audiology*, Supplement 17, 68–72.

Folsom, R. C., Weber, B. A. and Thompson, G. (1983) Auditory brainstem responses in children with early recurrent middle ear disease. *Annals of Otology, Rhinology and Laryngology* **92**, 249–253.

Freeman, B. A. and Parkins, C. (1979) The prevalence of middle ear disease among learning impaired children. *Clinical Pediatrics* **18**, 205–210.

Furth, H. G. (1973) *Deafness and Learning: A Psychosocial Approach*. Belmont, California: Wadsworth Publishing Company.

Galton, M., Simon, B. and Croll, P. (1980) *Inside the Primary Classroom*. London: Routledge & Kegan Paul.

Gleitman, L. R. and Wanner, E. (1982) 'Language acquisition: the state of the state of the art'. In Wanner, E. and Gleitman, L. R. (eds) *Language Acquisition: The State of the Art*. Cambridge: Cambridge University Press.

Gottlieb, M. I., Zinkus, P. W. and Thompson, A. (1980) Chronic middle ear disease and auditory perceptual deficits. *Clinical Pediatrics* **18**, 725–732.

Gregory, S. (1976) *The Deaf Child and his Family*. London: George Allen & Unwin.

Gregory, S. and Mogford, K. (1981) 'Early language development in deaf children'. In Woll, B., Kyle, J. and Deuchar, M. (eds) *Perspectives on British Sign Language and Deafness*. London: Croom Helm.

Halliday, M. A. K. (1975) *Learning How to Mean: Explorations in the Development of Language*. London: Edward Arnold.

Hamilton, P. and Owrid, H. L. (1974) Comparisons of hearing-impairment and socio-cultural disadvantages in relation to verbal deprivation. *British Journal of Audiology* **8**, 27–32.

Hegarty, S. (1987) *Meeting Special Needs in Ordinary Schools*. London: Cassell.

Hohmann, M., Banet, B. and Weikart, D. (1979) *Young Children in Action*. Ypsilanti, Michigan: The High/Scope Press.

Howarth, S. P., Wood, D. J., Griffiths, A. J. and Howarth, C. I. (1981) A comparative study of the reading lessons of deaf and hearing primary-school children. *British Journal of Educational Psychology* **51**, 156–162.

Hutt, E. (1986) *Teaching Language-disordered Children: A Structured Curriculum*. London: Edward Arnold.

Jensema, C. J. and Trybus, R. J. (1978) *Communication Patterns and Educational Achievements of Hearing-impaired Students*, Series T, Number 2. Washington: Gallaudet College, Office of Demographic Studies.

Johnson, D. W. and Johnson, R. T. (1986) Mainstreaming and cooperative learning strategies. *Exceptional Children* **52** (6), 553–561.

Karmiloff-Smith, A. (1978) 'The interplay between syntax, semantics and phonology in language processes'. In Campbell, R. N. and Smith, P. T.

(eds) *Recent Advances in the Psychology of Language*. New York: Plenum Press.

Kuhl, P. K. (1983) 'The perception of speech in early infancy: four phenomena'. In Gerber, S. E. and Mencher, G. T. (eds) *The Development of Auditory Behaviour*. New York: Grune Stratton.

Kyle, J. G. (1980) Reading development of deaf children. *Journal of Research in Reading* 3, pp. 86–97.

Lane, H. (ed.) (1984) *The Deaf Experience: Classics in Language and Education*. Cambridge, Massachusetts: Harvard University Press.

Light, P., Buckingham, N. and Roberts, A. H. (1979) The conversation task as an interactional setting. *British Journal of Educational Psychology* 49, 304–310.

Lunzer, E. and Gardner, K. (eds) (1979) *The Effective Use of Reading*. London: Heinemann, for the Schools Council.

Lunzer, E. and Gardner, K. (1984) *Learning from the Written Word*. Edinburgh: Oliver & Boyd, for the Schools Council.

Luria, A. R. (1961) *Speech and the Regulation of Behaviour*. Oxford: Pergamon.

Luterman, D. (1987) *Deafness in the Family*. Boston, Massachusetts: College-Hill Press.

Lynas, W. (1986) *Integrating the Handicapped into Ordinary Schools: A Study of Hearing-impaired Pupils*. Beckenham, Kent: Croom Helm.

Mackay, D., Thompson, B. and Schaub, P. (1970) *Breakthrough to Literacy*. London: Longman.

Mackay, G. F. (ed.) (1986) *The Named Person*. Glasgow: Jordanhill College.

Martin, J. A. M. (1982) Aetiological factors relating to childhood deafness in the European Community. *Audiology* 21, 149–158.

Masters, L. and Marsh, G. E. (1978) Middle ear pathology as a factor in learning disabilities. *Journal of Learning Disabilities* 11, 54–57.

Meadow, K. P. (1980) *Deafness and Child Development*. London: Edward Arnold.

Meek, M. (1982) *Learning to Read*. London: The Bodley Head.

Moon, C. (ed.) (1985) *Practical Ways to Teach Reading*. London: Ward Lock Educational.

Mortimore, P., Sammons, P., Stoll, L., Lewis, D. and Ecob, R. (1988) *School Matters: The Junior Years*. Wells, Somerset: Open Books.

Murphy, K. P. (1976) 'Communication for hearing-handicapped people in the United Kingdom and the Republic of Ireland'. In H. H. Oyer (ed.) *Communication for the Hearing-handicapped: An International Perspective*. Baltimore: University Park Press.

National Deaf Children's Society (1983) *Discovering Deafness*. London: NDCS.

National Deaf Children's Society (1987) *For All Deaf Children* (Annual Report and Accounts 1986/87). London: NDCS.

Nelson, K. (1973) Structure and strategy in learning to talk. *Monographs of the Society for Research in Child Development*, 38.

Newton, V. E. (1985) Aetiology of bi-lateral sensori-neural hearing loss in young children. *Journal of Laryngology and Otology* 99, Supplement 10.

Northern, J. L. and Downs, M. P. (1978) *Hearing in Childhood*. Baltimore: Williams & Wilkins.

Paradise, J. L. (1981) Otitis media during early life: how hazardous to development? A critical review of the evidence. *Pediatrics* **68**, 868–873.
Payton,. S. (1984) *Developing Awareness of Print: A Young Child's First Steps towards Literacy* (Educational Review, Offset Publication No. 2). Birmingham: University of Birmingham.
Perera, K. (1984) *Children's Writing and Reading: Analysing Classroom Language*. Oxford: Basil Blackwell.

Quigley, S. P. (1978) 'Effects of early hearing-impairment on normal language development'. In Martin, F. N. (ed.) *Pediatric Audiology*. Englewood Cliffs, New Jersey: Prentice-Hall.
Quigley, S. P. and Kretschmer, R. E. (1982) *The Education of Deaf Children: Issues, Theory and Practice*. London: Edward Arnold.
Quigley, S. P. and Paul, P. V. (1984) *Language and Deafness*. London: Croom Helm.
Quigley, S., Wilbur, R., Power, D., Montanelli, D. and Steinkamp, M. (1976) *Syntactic Structures in the Language of Deaf Children*. Urbana, Illinois: Institute for Child Behaviour and Development.

Raban, B. (ed.) (1985) *Practical Ways to Teach Writing*. London: Ward Lock Educational.
Reed, M. (1984) *Educating Hearing-impaired Children*. Milton Keynes: Open University Press.
Reichman, J. and Healey, W. C. (1983) Learning disabilities and conductive hearing loss involving otitis media. *Journal of Learning Disabilities* **16** (5), 272–278.
Ross, M. (1982) *Hard of Hearing Children in Regular Schools*. Englewood Cliffs, New Jersey: Prentice-Hall.
Rutter, M., Maughan, B., Mortimore, P. and Ouston, J. (1979) *Fifteen Thousand Hours: Secondary Schools and Their Effects*. Wells, Somerset: Open Books.

Shah, N. (1981) 'Middle ear effusion — glue ear'. In Beagley, H. A. (ed.) *Audiology and Audiological Medicine*, Volume 2. Oxford: Oxford University Press.
Silva, P. A., Kirkland, C., Simpson, A., Stewart, I. A. and Williams, S. M. (1983) Some developmental and behavioural problems associated with bilateral otitis media with effusion. *Journal of Learning Disabilities* **15**, 417–421.
Smyth, G. D. L. and Hall, S. (1983) Aetiology and treatment of persistent middle-ear effusion. *Journal of Laryngology and Otology* **97**, 1085–1089.
Snow, C. E. and Ferguson, C. A. (eds) (1977) *Talking to Children: Language Input and Acquisition*. Cambridge: Cambridge University Press.
Söderbergh, R. (1985) Early reading with deaf children. *Prospects* **15** (1), 77–85.
Stanovich, K. E. (1986) Matthew effects in reading: some consequences of

individual differences in the acquisition of literacy. *Reading Research Quarterly* **21** (4), 360–406.

Tait, D. M. (1987) Making and monitoring progress in the pre-school years. *Journal of the British Association of Teachers of the Deaf* **11** (5), 143–153.

Tait, D. M. and Wood, D. J. (1987) From communication to speech in deaf children. *Child Language Teaching and Therapy* **3** (1), 1–17.

Teele, D. W., Klein, J. O. and Rosner, B. A. (1984) Otitis media with effusion during the first three years of life and development of speech and language. *Pediatrics* **74** (2), 282–287.

Thomas, G. (1985) Room management in mainstream education. *Educational Research* **27** (3), 186–193.

Thomas, G. (1986) Integrating personnel in order to integrate children. *Support for Learning* **1** (1), 19–26.

Tizard, B. and Hughes, M. (1984) *Young Children Learning: Talking and Thinking at Home and at School*. London: Fontana.

Trevarthen, C. (1979) 'Communication and co-operation in early infancy: a description of primary intersubjectivity'. In Bullowa, M. (ed.) *Before Speech: The Beginnings of Human Communication*. Cambridge: Cambridge University Press.

Tucker, I. and Nolan, M. (1984) *Educational Audiology*. Beckenham, Kent: Croom Helm.

Tumin, W. (1978) Parents' views. *Education Today*, Summer.

Van Uden, A. (1977) *A World of Language for Deaf Children, Part 1: Basic Principles. A Maternal Reflective Method*. The Netherlands: Swets & Zeitlinger.

Vernon, P. E. and Miller, K. M. (1976) *Graded Arithmetic–Mathematics Test*. Sevenoaks: Hodder & Stoughton.

Vygotsky, L. S. (1962) *Thought and Language*. Cambridge, Massachusetts: MIT Press.

Ward, A. (1985) *Scots Law and the Mentally Handicapped*. Glasgow: Scottish Society for the Mentally Handicapped.

Webster, A. (1985) Review of H. Lane (ed.) (1984) *The Deaf Experience*. *History of Education* **14** (3), 244–246.

Webster, A. (1986a) *Deafness, Development and Literacy*. London: Methuen.

Webster, A. (1986b) Update: the implications of conductive hearing loss in childhood. *Association of Child Psychology and Psychiatry Newsletter* **8** (3), 4–14.

Webster, A. (1988a) Conditions: 'glue' ear. *Special Children* **20**, 26–28.

Webster, A. (1988b) Deafness and learning to read 1: theoretical and research issues. *Journal of the British Association of Teachers of the Deaf* **12** (4), 77–83.

Webster, A. (1988c) Deafness and learning to read 2: teaching strategies. *Journal of the British Association of Teachers of the Deaf* **12** (5), 93–101.

Webster, A. (1989a) 'Assessment of children with visual, hearing or physical impairments: hearing-impaired children'. In Beech, J. and Harding, L. (eds) *Educational Assessment of Children*. Windsor: NFER-Nelson.

Webster, A. (1989b) Deafness and learning to read 3: literacy across the curriculum. *Journal of the British Association of Teachers of the Deaf* **13** (3), 82–92.

Webster, A., Bamford, J., Thyer, N. and Ayles, R. (in press) The psychological, educational and auditory sequelae of early, persistent secretory otitis media. *Journal of Child Psychology and Psychiatry*.

Webster, A. and Ellwood, J. (1985) *The Hearing-impaired Child in the Ordinary School*. Beckenham, Kent: Croom Helm.

Webster, A. and McConnell, C. (1987) *Children with Speech and Language Difficulties*. London: Cassell.

Webster, A., Saunders, E. and Bamford, J. (1984) Fluctuating conductive hearing-impairment. *Journal of the Association of Educational Psychologists* **6** (5), 6–19.

Webster, A., Scanlon, P. and Bown, E. (1985) Meeting the needs of hearing-impaired children within a local education authority. *Journal of the Association of Educational Psychologists*, Supplement to **6** (5), 2–10.

Webster, A., Wood, D. J. and Griffiths, A. J. (1981) Reading retardation or linguistic deficit? I: interpreting reading test performances of hearing-impaired adolescents. *Journal of Research in Reading* **4** (2), 136–147.

Webster, D. B. and Webster, A. B. (1979) Effects of neonatal conductive hearing loss on brainstem auditory nuclei. *Annals of Otology* **88**, 684–688.

Wells, G. (1981) *Learning Through Interaction*. Cambridge: Cambridge University Press.

Wells, G. (1985) *Language, Learning and Education*. Windsor: NFER-Nelson.

Wells, G. (1987) *The Meaning Makers: Children Learning Language and Using Language to Learn*. London: Hodder & Stoughton.

Wiles, S. (1981) 'Language issues in the multi-cultural classroom'. In Mercer, N. (ed.) *Language in School and Community*. London: Edward Arnold.

Wood, D. J. (1988) *How Children Think and Learn*. Oxford: Blackwell.

Wood, D. J., Bruner, J. S. and Ross, G. (1976) The role of tutoring in problem solving. *Journal of Child Psychology and Psychiatry* **17** (2), 89–100.

Wood, D. J., Griffiths, A. J. and Webster, A. (1981) Reading retardation or linguistic deficit? II: test-answering strategies in hearing and hearing-impaired school children. *Journal of Research in Reading* **4** (2), 148–157.

Wood, D. J., McMahon, L. and Cranstoun, Y. (1980) *Working with Under Fives*. London: Grant McIntyre.

Wood, D. J., Wood, H. A., Griffiths, A. J. and Howarth, C. I. (1986) *Teaching and Talking with Deaf Children*. Chichester: John Wiley.

Wood, D. J., Wood, H. A. and Howarth, S. P. (1983) Mathematical abilities in deaf school leavers. *British Journal of Developmental Psychology* (1), 67–74.

Wood, H. A. and Wood, D. J. (1984) An experimental evaluation of five styles of teacher conversation on the language of hearing-impaired children. *Journal of Child Psychology and Psychiatry* **25** (1), 45–62.

Zinkus, P. W., Gottlieb, M. I. and Schapiro, M. (1978) Developmental and psychoeducational sequelae of chronic otitis media. *American Journal of Disabilities in Childhood* **132**, 1100–1104.

Name Index

Subject Index